BRESCIA COLLEGE LIBRARY

3 6277 00008228 1

Popular wisdom and many rural centres make the claim that the country is a great place to raise kids. But is it? Kieran Bonner explores this question by examining the epistemological, political, and ethical issues involved in the claim.

Bonner analyses historical contributions to the urban-rural debate by Karl Marx, Ferdinand Tonnies, Max Weber, Georg Simmel, Louis Wirth, and Robert Redfield, as well as contributions by contemporary theorists such as Ray Pahl, Anthony Giddens, and Peter Berger. He shows how both societal developments and scientific assumptions unwittingly shape the debate, making a distinctive rural culture more and more difficult to identify, and suggests that phenomenology can rescue the urban-rural debate from its conceptual predicament.

Through an analysis of statements by parents in both urban and rural settings, Bonner goes on to point out the limitations of a narrowly scientific approach to research, demonstrating how a more radical interpretive approach that combines phenomenological, hermeneutic, and dialectical analytic methods and theories can further our understanding. He argues convincingly that practical/ethical matters and theoretical assumptions are inextricably intertwined.

KIERAN BONNER is vice president, academic dean, and professor of sociology at St Jerome's University, University of Waterloo.

A Great Place to Raise Kids

Interpretation, Science, and the Urban-Rural Debate

KIERAN BONNER

McGill-Queen's University Press
Montreal & Kingston · London · Ithaca

BRESCIA COLLEGE
LIBRARY
68196

© McGill-Queen's University Press 1997
ISBN 0-7735-1613-1 (cloth)
ISBN 0-7735-2026-0 (paper)

Legal deposit second quarter 1997
Bibliothèque nationale du Québec

Printed in Canada on acid-free paper
First paperback edition 1999

This book was first published with the help of a grant
from the Humanities and Social Sciences Federation of
Canada, using funds provided by the Social Sciences
and Humanities Research Council of Canada. Funding
was also received from Augustana University College.

Canadian Cataloguing in Publication Data

Bonner, Kieran Martin, 1951–
    A great place to raise kids : interpretation, science,
and the urban-rural debate
    Includes bibliographical references and index.
    ISBN 0-7735-1613-1 (bound)
    ISBN 0-7735-2026-0 (pbk)
    1. Child rearing – Social aspects. 2. Sociology, Rural.
    I. Title.
    HT453.B64 1997   307.72'085'4   C97-900263-X

Typeset in Palatino 10/12
by Caractéra inc., Quebec City

To Margaret and our children,
Róisín, Maeve, and Devin.

Contents

Acknowledgments

This book has had several lives. Its first life began when Rod Michalko and I collaborated on a research proposal to the Social Sciences and Humanities Research Council (SSHRC) of Canada. The intention then was to collaborate on all stages of the research as we did on the proposal. The actual idea for the project came from Alan Blum, who reminded us of the importance of the relation between lived experience and theorizing. SSHRC approved the project with a small but vital seed grant, thus formally initiating the project. In the meantime, Rod left for Toronto, making the intended collaboration impossible. Within the limits and constraints of finances and geography, he provided important support and encouragement for the completion of the research report. However, the issue of the adequacy of the research, the conceptualization of the literature evaluation, the formal and informal conversations with the people from Prairie Edge, the analysis of the material, and the writing are all my responsibility.

In this regard I want to acknowledge the cooperation of the people of Prairie Edge (my pseudonym for Camrose) in general and the interviewees in particular. From the project's first life through to its last incarnation, their voices ring throughout these pages, lending authenticity and a sense of lived experience to this research. Some may not agree with the conclusions and the direction of the analysis, especially in its later incarnations, but I hope all will recognize my need to think honestly and critically through their talk and the Prairie Edge experience.

Because of the importance of re-reading the discourse on the urban-rural debate, the project turned out to be bigger and more theoretical than initially intended. My colleague Scott Grills and our senior sociology students were very helpful in participating in a Work and Life group where some of the classic readings were discussed.

Two senior students, Melody Stover and Kate Anderson, helped as research assistants, the former in the early exploratory stages and the latter with skills of research, writing, typing, and critical evaluation in the later stage. Paul Harland read through this first version and gave, as always, his honest, useful, and insightful comments. The research report was submitted to sshrc in fulfilment of the seed grant conditions, thus bringing closure to the manuscript's first incarnation.

It was subsequently submitted for scholarly review to the Aid to Scholarly Publications Programme (aspp) where three reviewers gave it mixed reviews because of its theoretic orientation. The reports helped me realize the potential for controversy surrounding a radical interpretive approach to sociology. I proposed to clarify and deepen what is involved in a radical interpretive research project and to show the way it solved certain problems in the urban-rural debate. The aspp agreed to my suggestions and asked me to resubmit it. The book entered its second life.

The opportunity for re-search was created through the sabbatical leave given to me by Augustana University College in Alberta. I secured a visiting fellowship in the Humanities from University College Galway in Ireland and began the comprehensive re-thinking and re-writing. During that sabbatical year I presented several new chapters at Galway University and at Trinity College in Dublin. Lively discussions ensued, reinforcing for me the sense of provocation that radical interpretive sociology creates. I thank all three institutions, but in particular Augustana, for this opportunity.

Almost a year later I re-submitted the work to the aspp, where it was again reviewed and approved for a publication subvention. Don Akenson of McGill-Queen's University Press encouraged and supported me in this project. My colleague Skye Hughes read and commented on the manuscript, giving me an opportunity to again re-engage the text. Her knowledge of phenomenology and her copy-editing experience, the comments by Reader A from the aspp review process, and the reactions of students in my Community class provided the impetus for the incarnation you now see. Given this time of government cutbacks, I want to acknowledge the important role that sshrc and the aspp play in Canada in the support and dissemination of scholarly research.

Throughout all the lives of this research, I have been helped in crucial ways by the extremely competent and helpful support staff at Augustana. Helen Saude dealt with its first life, Janice Lewsaw with its second, and Linda Richardson and Chris Jensen McCloy with its last. All in different ways were patient, good-humoured, flexible, and generous with my chaotic and spontaneous style. As well, Susan Malone and the McGill-Queen's copyeditor, Maureen Garvie, brought their excellent copyediting skills to the manuscript and proof stage of the book.

Needless to add, my family suffered through all three incarnations. For them the different versions blur. Margaret heard my ideas as they were forming and responded with suggestions, listened to rehearsals of the various presentations I did in Canada and Ireland, and read through the final manuscript submitted to McGill-Queen's. Naturally, my relation to our children, Róisín, Maeve, and Devin, has been an important touchstone, helping me to ground the necessary theorizing involved. The desirable integration of theory and practice (or work and life), the importance of which I learned from Alan Blum and Peter McHugh, has always to return to this relation – though the integration does not reside there. Lastly, I would like to acknowledge the enjoyable place my parents and my brothers and sisters (all twelve of them) give me in the extended family in Ireland as well as the help my uncle, Danny McHugh, gave me during my sabbatical in Ireland.

Augustana created the conditions which made this work possible and was my institutional affiliation when the cloth-bound version of the book first came out. Now that my affiliation has moved to St Jerome's, I am all the more appreciative of the fact that this work is the result of the wonderful collegial conversation that happens at Augustana. It is a small miracle that this conversation can still find a home in the modern university.

My experience with the clothbound version of this book has taught me that it addresses readers with different interests. While the narrative is organized around demonstrating the integrity and comprehensiveness of a reflexive research project, each of the four parts can be read independently.

For example, some readers are interested directly in the study of rural parenting and the conclusions which emerge from my Prairie Edge research. I advise these readers to begin with Part Three. Those who are more methodologically interested could begin with Part Two. Those who are interested in the contemporary issues of globalization, consumerism, and postmodernism can begin with Part Four. Obviously, those interested in the sociological discourse on the urban-rural debate and modernity's problem with otherness would begin with Part One. The Epilogue is the most personal part of this book – one that I still find difficult to re-read.

On the other hand, those who are interested in how a strongly reflexive research project can work within the narrative and conventions of scholarly social science research (that is, theory and literature review, methodology, research findings, and analysis) should go through the four parts as they are presently organized.

K.B.

April 1999

A Great Place to Raise Kids

Parenting, the Urban-Rural Debate, and the Logic of Social Inquiry

Rural respondents were asked to compare their community with that of Edmonton, while Edmontonians were asked to compare their city with that of a smaller rural centre. When asked which community was a better place to raise a family, a dramatically [higher] percentage of rural respondents believed that a rural setting was a better place to raise a family (80.9%). In contrast, only 20.4% of urban respondents believed that an urban setting was a better place to raise a family. Urban respondents were more inclined to state that an urban or rural setting would make no difference in raising a family.   Yerxa Research, 1992

The city is not conducive to the traditional type of family life, including the rearing of children and the maintenance of the home as the focus of a whole round of vital activities.   Louis Wirth, 1938

MOTHER: Even the people I worked with at the bank – they had no intentions of moving [from the city]. They had moved away, got married, when they started raising a family, moved back to Prairie Edge. A lot of them. I kept saying, "Why?" Because it's a good place to raise your kids. We know enough people, it's small enough, you can't get lost, you know you can locate your kids within a few minutes, family. They come back to raise their kids.

FATHER: It's better, it's safer, kids have more things to do.

MOTHER: It's easier, speaking more of the safety factor … The [children] are very confident; this is their town and they run all over the place and feel very comfortable, and they know a lot of people by now.

MOTHER: By living in a small place like this you pretty well know who they're with pretty well all the time.

FATHER: I really believe that ... it's better ... It's a lot easier for kids to get into trouble in the city.

MOTHER: The trust, I guess, is not as great in a large city. I think it's not so outstanding, such a revelation. We feel very strongly that it's a lot more comfortable in a town this size.

MOTHER: I feel more comfortable, more relaxed because you would hear what your child was up to.

PARENTING

The idea endures that small town or rural life has a more positive influence on family life and child-rearing than does its urban counterpart. Popular culture, survey research, and traditional sociological literature all appear to present wide support for the validity of the claim that it is "better" to raise children in a more rural setting. The claim is one of the few that a more rural centre can confidently assert in the face of opportunities offered by the city. Simultaneously, it is a claim that many (if not most) city dwellers are willing to concede. The *Globe and Mail* magazine *Toronto* (June 1990, 22–6) cited the results of a poll of the Greater Toronto area in which "58% said it was more difficult to raise a happy, well-balanced child in the city than in a small town, and a surprising half of those surveyed have considered packing up and moving." The idea is so pervasive that it almost has the character of an obvious and unquestionable truth. Yet what is the basis for it?

My own personal, familial experience provides an important background for this study. I was raised in a small town in Ireland and lived in Dublin during my university years. With my wife, I lived for one year in San Francisco, two years in Alaska and then moved to Toronto where our three children were born. We lived in mid-town and downtown Toronto for seven years until we moved in 1987 to a small prairie city/town. As a family we enjoyed Toronto, had many friends and a sense of community there, and were sad to have to leave it. We enjoyed raising our children in Toronto and had no *parental* reason to want to leave the city. When we moved to Prairie Edge, we were constantly assured that the particular virtue of the town for people like us was (and is) that it is good for young kids and "a great place to raise a family." Even people who were not particularly attached to the town, and who, if given the opportunity, would leave, still conceded this claim. There was more argument and debate as to whether the town was good for older teenagers, lacking facilities for them, or for single adults who had no place to go to meet other singles; but for kids and for families the claim was confidently asserted.

Is this claim a myth (in the scientific sense of the term) promulgated by popular culture but without empirical support? For instance, a recent survey done in the United States found that rural children fared worse than non-rural children in terms of being "at-risk" students. (Rural students were more inclined to be involved in the categories of substance abuse, suicide attempt, child abuse, poverty, illiteracy, crime, etc., than their urban counterparts.) The study concluded: "The fact that rural children fared worse than non-rural children in 34 out of 39 statistical comparisons in the study merits concern. The analysis suggests that the social and economic strains facing rural students are every bit as bad, perhaps worse, than those facing inner-city youth. The images of rural children leading wholesome, trouble-free lives compared with youth in more crowded settings may be in need of revision" (Helge 1990, 3).

Does this conclusion mean that the claim for the advantage of a rural setting for child-rearing is an ideology that, as Marx argues, seeks to disguise the vestiges of a hierarchical family system and to prevent the recognition of rural idiocy? On the other hand, when "asked which community was a better place to raise a family, a dramatically [higher] percentage of rural respondents believed that a rural setting was a better place to raise a family" (Yerxa Research 1992, 15). Does the claim therefore have some truth value, in the sense that it is true to the reality of parents' own experience of raising children? If the opinion surveys are to be given any credibility at all, then a sizeable percentage of the population, both rural and urban, subscribes to the truth of the claim.

Even if one concedes the widespread nature of the belief, what is meant by "better"? Does it mean that parenting is easier and less stressful? Does saying that a task is easier automatically make it better? If "easier" leads to being less involved in a child's life, can we say that this is better? Does "better" refer to being easier to assert parental power? Does it mean less anxious parenting? How do we measure and evaluate such claims, since epistemology, politics, and ontology are as much bound up with everyday claims as they are with the sociological literature on the subject? More to the point, how are we to understand what the claim means?[1]

THE URBAN-RURAL DIFFERENCE

Any attempt to tie particular patterns of social relationships to specific geographical milieux is a singularly fruitless exercise.   Ray Pahl, 1969

The disappearance of the word "rural" is a case of urban imperialism ...
If nothing out there is deserving of a name then it becomes a place to
play in, play with, override and destroy at will.   R. Alex Sim, 1988

This issue is bound up with what we see (perspective), what we
know (epistemology) and with the way we live in the world (ontology). The concern of whether the urban or rural setting is better and
what "better" means rests on the issue of the relevance of the urban-
rural distinction in the first place. The British sociologist Ray Pahl
argues that in modern societies much of the population is culturally
if not physically urbanized and so attempting to link "particular patterns of social relationships to specific geographical milieux is a singularly fruitless exercise." Following Gans's (1968) critique of Wirth,
Pahl states that while class, gender, or life cycle can be shown to be
sociologically relevant categories, geographic settlement cannot. Yet
if geographic settlement is not sociologically relevant, does this not
also mean that the claim for the rural advantage has no basis in
reality?

Canadian sociologist Alex Sim argues on the other hand that the
disappearance of the word "rural" is a case of urban imperialism.
Even though, on an everyday level, people have no trouble recognizing the difference, that recognition, it seems, cannot be validated by
scientific sociological research. This inability to validate a recognition, Sim says, has dangerous social consequences not only for rural
life but for society as a whole. Therefore, an investigation into the
popular image described above involves not only testing what parents in more rural settings say but also examining the way sociological theory and methodology have traditionally structured such an
examination. Most of all, we need to know how the rural is being
conceptualized. The research question now becomes: What is the
nature of the perspective that would make the urban-rural distinction a relevant and real one, and what is the nature of the perspective
that would make that distinction unreal and irrelevant?

To investigate the claims made by the parents above, we need to
understand what is meant by urban and rural. The debate concerning the advantages of an urban or a rural setting includes a debate
about *what is* urban/rural. The need to understand this distinction
moves the inquiry into theoretical realms. "The hope of interpreting
'without prejudice and presupposition,'" says Palmer (1969, 136),

ultimately flies in the face of the way understanding operates. What appears
from the "object" is what one allows to appear and what the thematization
of the world at work in his understanding will bring to light. It is naive to
assume that what is "really there" is "self-evident." The very definition of

what is presumed to be self-evident rests on a body of unnoticed presuppositions, which are present in every interpretive construction by the "objective" and "presuppositionless" interpreter.

Science, like all forms of inquiry (including this one), operates on presuppositions that allow certain things about rural life to be noticed and other things to go unnoticed. Another question for study is: What is the importance of the noticed and the unnoticed, and how is *this* importance recognized? Palmer (124–39) argues that the analytic gaze of science is itself responsible for the disappearance of the object to be investigated. Could science, as itself a socially organized mode of producing knowledge, be actively involved in structuring (along very specific cultural, historical, and political lines) the urban-rural discourse? Is the disappearance of the sociological relevance of the urban-rural distinction not only connected with the rise of technological and consumer society but also related to an *intrinsic and concealed interconnection* between the rise of science and the rise of modernity? In other words, what is at stake in this inquiry is not only the claim for the advantage of rural parenting, not only the meaning to everyday members and to sociologists of urban and rural, but also the ethical, political and theoretical implications of doing this (or any) kind of inquiry.

Such epistemological and ontological implications mean that an examination of the claims of parents also requires investigation of the way that such an examination can and should be conducted. The sociology of rural parenting is intertwined with the sociology of knowledge, and both are tied to understanding the way history and community influence understanding. Thus, the particular (rural parenting) and the general (modern western culture) need to be investigated simultaneously. It is the primary task of this study to explore the opportunities and obstacles that various perspectives in sociology offer for the study of the questions outlined above, while simultaneously addressing the substantive issues involved in parenting in a rural setting. Of course, because one inevitably uses a perspective even when one is examining the usefulness of sociological perspectives, this study also seeks to *exemplify* the worth of radical interpretive sociology as it is engaged in the process of examining perspectives. (For a more sustained description of this perspective and of the way it influences the manuscript, see the appendix.)

THE PROCESS OF INQUIRY

This book has gone through several review processes, and the experience has taught me again that radical interpretive sociology is a provocative and controversial perspective. The central principle of the perspective, concerning the inextricable intertwining of theoretical, ethical, and practical matters, flies in the face of the dominant understanding that social inquiry can and should be neutral and factual in a quantitative way. Some see my analysis of positivistic theory and methodology as polemical and ideological. Others see it as a justifiable critique which recognizes the contribution to knowledge that science can make. I have also learned that the ongoing controversy between the interpretive and the positivistic approaches sometimes overshadows the substantive contribution to knowledge made in this study.

Thus, I conclude this introduction by outlining the ways this investigation contributes to our understanding of parenting, to our understanding of the urban-rural difference, and to our understanding of the ways knowledge is created. In the study all of the following are interwoven within the narrative, yet it is useful for the reader to separate them here.

First, I show that the concepts of rural and urban, which have wide application in sociology, are problematic and sometimes contradictory. Through a sustained analysis of the conceptualization of rurality in sociology, I demonstrate that part of the reason for the problematic nature of these concepts lies in the effort of the social sciences to be rigorously scientific and "objective." This aim prevents mainstream sociology from being able to take into account history, culture, and community because it is unable to take these into account in its understanding of itself. Thus, a central contribution of the study is to show that quantitative and typological approaches to social inquiry have real limits (as well as strengths) and that the dialogic approach of radical interpretive sociology has real strengths (as well as limits). This aspect of the study is what many peers in my discipline find controversial. Yet this investigation will show how the radical interpretive perspective can, as one reviewer put it, revitalize and reposition the urban-rural debate.

Second, I show how the phenomenological concepts of life-world and lived experience help break the conceptual log-jam that rural (as well as urban) studies is now in. If, as is widely accepted within the discipline, there is nothing sociologically distinctive about the rural, if the urban and rural are better thought about in terms of the master concepts of class, life cycle, gender, and so on, then the many parents who claim an advantage to rural parenting are mistaken. Or is it the sociologists who are mistaken? Perhaps all are, in different ways. Radical interpretive sociology helps me to show in what ways (and why) the latter is the case.

Third, I track not only the way the concept of rural has changed over time but also what "rural" has come to mean in the context of modern technological society. I show that the neologism "rurban" is a more appropriate concept for describing town life in contemporary society than either urban or rural.

Fourth, by applying the dialogic method argued for in the analysis of the conceptualization of rurality, I show what parents mean when they say "it's a great place to raise your kids." This demonstration involves articulating and highlighting the "high visibility" aspect of town living. I argue that the experience of living in a place where one is aware that one is seeing and being seen is crucial in helping to understand the advantage of rurban parenting.

Along the way I offer an analysis of the dangerous seductiveness of consumerism by addressing the example of what a consumer relation to place looks like. In the process I show how a certain celebration of mobility and certain kinds of phenomenological and postmodern thinking are (unwittingly) implicated in the seductiveness of consumerism. In turn, this analysis requires that I explicate the ethical and the pedagogical implications involved in doing inquiry.

As I have stated, the radical interpretive perspective is used because of its ability to throw light on the inextricable intertwining of theoretical interests, ethical understanding, and practical action. The key unifying thread throughout the narrative is the way the reflexive element of interpretive sociology is productive for inquiry. According to Heidegger (1977, 116), "Reflection is the courage to make the truth of our own presuppositions and the realm of our own goals into the things that most deserve to be called into question."

Courage is not typically understood to be a requirement for social inquiry. Few sociology graduate programs give sustained attention to courage as important for both theory and research. Courage may be seen as needed for the tasks of parenthood, but it is not usually associated with reflection upon them. Yet calling into question the truths of the presuppositions that in a taken-for-granted way are dear to us as social inquirers, as well as calling into question the truth of the goals of our parenting, does require courage. This is true for me both as a radical interpretive sociologist and as a parent.

The interrelatedness of courage and questioning is but one instance of the inextricability of the theoretical and the practical, of the intertwining of the methodology involved in investigating the claim for rural advantage and the practical and ethical issues raised by this investigation for my parenting. For example, this study has taught me of the need to be sensitive to how concern with responsible parenting can seduce one into a consumer relation to place. And is any place "great" if one's relation to it is instrumental?

A number of "deep" questions are touched off by this issue: e.g., How do we/should we relate to our children/the future? What is the contemporary situation/predicament of parenting? What are the possibilities for community in the postmodern age? What are the possibilities for social inquiry in this age? How do/should we relate/understand/act with regard to these concerns? Such questions cannot be avoided even if the response this work represents is, as Geertz (1973, 29) says of the nature of cultural studies, "intrinsically incomplete." As this study is engaged in a socio-cultural analysis, its aim is not to arrive at a final conclusion to these questions but rather to engage in and refine "the debate" (Geertz 1973, 3–30). This debate does not happen in a vacuum; neither is it neutral. Yet this study intends to show that an interested grappling with these deep issues, in the context of a specific case-study, can accomplish the hermeneutic aim of furthering our socio-historical understanding of our contemporary situation. Ultimately, if this work serves the Socratic aim of provoking, even infecting some readers to think about and examine their lives, their social situations, and the interrelation between these, it will have served its purpose.

The whole question of the superiority of a rural setting for parenting rests on the meaning of the rural. What are we thinking of when we say "rural"? In the first three chapters I engage the genesis of the urban-rural debate in sociology, address carefully how the concept of rurality changes as society changes, and trace the way this issue is examined by different sociologists. The debate is about the superiority of one way of life over another, but the meaning of superiority changes depending on the way the rural is conceptualized. I also trace a development in sociology toward positivism. As this development crystallizes, the concept of rurality becomes more and more problematic. I argue therefore that reflexivity has to be included in the process of conceptualization.

While the non-sociological reader may find this examination of the scholarship to be intense, I encourage this reader to see the way the urban-rural debate in everyday life (see part three) is reflected in and clarified by sociological scholarship.

PART ONE

The Urban-Rural Debate in Sociological Literature

The Problem of Otherness in Modernity: Sociology and the Development of the Urban-Rural Debate

A ... disquieting quality of modernism: its taste for appropriating or redeeming otherness, for constituting non-Western arts in its own image, for discovering universal, ahistorical "human" capacities.

James Clifford, 1988

While distinctions between city and country are almost as old as western culture itself (Williams 1973), it is the rise of modernity in general and of the Industrial Revolution in particular that generated the sociological debate about the positive and/or negative consequences of this new development. As Sennett remarks (1969, 3), "Up to the time of the Industrial Revolution, the city was taken by most social thinkers to be the image of society itself, and not some special, unique form of society." The country, whether in its pastoral (Theocritus) or agricultural (Hesiod) representation, was synonymous with nature; the fertility of spring and summer, for example, was contrasted to the barrenness and accident of winter (Williams 1973, 13–34). Rapid changes in society brought on by the Industrial Revolution focused and organized the theorizing and research concerning urban-rural differences. In particular, the drastic shift in population from rural to urban centres meant that many societies that throughout history were demographically rural within the space of one hundred dred years became demographically urban.[1]

This change in turn challenged social theorists to reflect on the meaning and influence of urban and rural social organization. For social theorists who sought to understand the transformation in urban and rural life indicated by the Industrial Revolution, the urban-rural distinction no longer referenced the difference between corruptness of society and the purity of nature (Rousseau) but rather presented social theorists with two different kinds of social organization.

This move in the understanding of "rural" or the countryside from what is "other" to human society/understanding (i.e., nature, beauty, the brutish, the mysterious) to another kind of society (i.e., the traditional, the rural) itself demonstrates what Clifford ironically calls "the healthy capacity of modernist consciousness to question its limits and engage otherness" (1988, 193). Otherness is now understood to represent an alternative way of living. This change in understanding also means that the engagement of otherness raises the issues of choice, evaluation, and change. Modern discourse, by casting other (rural) as an other social organization (rural society), rests on and asserts the claim that any one society represents a particular way of living and that this way of living has to be understood, evaluated, and compared with an other way of living.

As we shall see, the urban-rural debate has its origin in the modern question of what constitutes a better society or a better way of life. The issue of whether rural or urban society is better for parenting reflects the genesis of the urban-rural distinction. The sociological genesis of the distinction is also the genesis of the urban-rural debate. Given this interest in superiority, what needs to be recovered is the meaning of "rural" as a way of life. The term has many connotations and is used in different ways by different people: for some it connotes backwardness, for others community; for some smallness, for others isolation; for some narrowness and for others a traditional way of life based on agriculture. The claim for the superiority of parenting in a rural setting cannot be understood until we know the particular way of life which the concept of rural refers to.

In order to be able to conduct research into this area in a directed and oriented fashion, it is crucial to have a way of deciding what "rural" means. What constitutes a rural setting? Is it any country setting? Is it a small town? Does "rural" refer to a traditional way of life? Does it refer to a certain mental orientation? In other words, without knowing what the concept of rural means, it is difficult, if not impossible, to assess the implications and significances of the various claims and survey results cited in the introduction.

For example, when 58 per cent of Toronto residents say it is easier to raise children in a small town than in a city, what image of small town are they relying on? When 42 per cent disagree, what image are they relying on? What is the meaning of place as rural in the saying "a great place to raise kids?" For this reason it is useful to begin with an examination of the classic and contemporary sociological discourse on this concept, because it is here that we will see one or other aspect of the idea of the rural (as a way of life) being developed. We will also see that it is on the basis of that one aspect that a claim for the superiority of the urban over the rural or *vice versa* can be made.

One of the earliest sociologists to address the differences between city and country was Karl Marx. He and Friedrich Engels (1965, 38) interpreted the rise of capitalism as a simultaneous subjection "of the country to the rule of the town. It has created enormous cities, has greatly increased the urban populations as compared with the rural, and has thus rescued a considerable part of the population from the idiocy of rural life."

Here and in *The German Ideology* (1970, 39–95), Marx argues that rural life nurtures a subservience to nature (68). Because it is a primitive mode of production, he sees this subservience as a primitive form of society. Rural life is not an other to the mode of production of capitalism but rather an early stage in its development. The country involves an exchange between humans and nature, the labour of the farmer for the product of the latter. Humans have not yet grasped the productive possibilities inherent within their own labour because, according to Marx and Engels, "physical activity is as yet not separated from mental activity." "Average human common sense is adequate" in relation to what life demands. "The antagonism between town and country begins with the transition from barbarism to civilization, from tribe to state, from locality to nation, and runs through the whole history of civilization to the present day" (1970, 69).

The very tension between town and country is itself an instance of the rise of civilization as exemplified in the form of the development of nation or state. The existence of the town requires the ability to think independently of the natural task at hand, because exchange and labour as modes of production are liberated from, as against being dominated by, subservience to the land. The town makes human independence recognizable as a possibility and actuality, whereas the country makes domination (of humans by nature, of humans by each other, e.g., landlord/serf) seem natural and necessary.

Marx and Engels argue that the feudal system of ownership prominent in the Middle Ages "started out from the country" (1970, 45). In this feudal system, people were tied to each other in a hierarchical and patriarchal manner that fettered the productive possibilities inherent in human action (1965, 32–48). Thus rural life leads to idiocy, because the nascent productive vitality inherent in all social organization is overwhelmed by the ideology of a deference to tradition which is antithetical to the material and productive possibilities in social organization. According to this formulation, rural life is idiotic because it endlessly and unimaginatively repeats the social patterns of previous generations under the guise of a feudal ideology legitimating patriarchy, hierarchy, and domination of people in general.

From this perspective, the ideology of family, community, and tradition is a mere "sentimental veil" binding the majority of people, particularly women and children, to a subordinate, impoverished life, and encouraging a "slothful indolence." By virtue of its ideological antipathy to the novel possibilities in human action, rural life is therefore antipathetic to the resources that the new – who in any society are the young – can bring to the community. Arendt (1958) says that an openness to the novel (inherent in the condition of natality) is the requirement for developing the possibility of human action; so rural life, and the feudal society it nurtured, have come to stand for a social organization explicitly organized around excluding openness to the possibilities of human action.

Marx interprets the urban-rural difference within a frame that celebrates the development of a society (in this case capitalism but eventually communism) that releases the productive forces (and not merely its economy, as is often erroneously thought) inherent within the relation between humans and the world. This development, in turn, is to enhance the human liberation of all. For Marx the question of the superiority of a way of life is not a mere matter of who prefers what place to live in, as though this issue could be resolved by an opinion poll. Rather, the question is to be answered on the basis of what place best helps us recognize our potential for freedom and the kind of social organization that produces the wealth that, according to Marx,[2] free action requires. Thus what for many city dwellers appears to be the easy-going life of a rural setting is for Marx "a slothful indolence" which is socially constructed by the way rural society excludes the novel (the enterprising, the beginning of something new) in its midst.

In outlining Marx's position I am not suggesting that either feudal or rural life is adequately or completely grasped by this formulation. Yet it raises the question of the adequacy of survey descriptions of rural life as a way of assessing the claim to superiority. Marx provides us with a paradigm that makes problematic accepting the self-understanding of the rural actor as the true or best understanding of the situation. Just because parents in a rural setting claim advantage to rural child-rearing does not make it true. The self-understanding of the rural actor, in this case, would more than likely reflect a false consciousness, as the very possibilities inherent in human action are automatically excluded from a true understanding of the situation. In other words (and to put it crudely), if rural respondents claim their quality of life is better, or that raising a family is easier, is this a knowledge claim grounded in a life of "slothful indolence" or "rural idiocy"? In formulating rural life in this way, Marx simultaneously raises the issue of the criteria we use to measure the "truth value" of the claim and implicitly suggests the limitations built into positivistic science (Blum & McHugh 1984, 13–30).

For our present purpose, the significance of Marx's critique is that what is said to be an easy-going lifestyle rooted in the past may merely be an ideological gloss for the preservation of static social relations (feudal society) that maintain domination of peasants by landlords, of women by men, and children by parents, with the real consequence of slothful indolence.[3] Thus rural life encourages rather than discourages the indisposition to exertion: it does not encourage true human enjoyment but rather the easy pleasure of avoiding the pain of exertion. That someone could be satisfied with such a life would by itself be a sign of a poor upbringing: by this definition, if the ethos of rural life is allowed to dominate (feudal society), children are worse off.

So it seems that with Marx's position we already have a decisive framework to use in deciding the question of superiority. His formulation resonates with the arguments that some parents (a minority in this study) offered for why Prairie Edge is not a great place to raise children. These parents focused on the regressiveness and conservatism of rural life and also firmly argued that such backwardness made for a necessarily inferior upbringing. Yet what presuppositions in the Marxian perspective allow for such a firm and resolute judgment of this issue?

THE RELATION BETWEEN THE MARXIAN PERSPECTIVE AND RADICAL INTERPRETIVE SOCIOLOGY

If we assume, along with those working in the phenomenological, critical theory, and hermeneutic traditions (e.g., Gadamer 1975; Habermas 1988; Palmer 1969), that "knowledge is a transactional product of the knower and the known" (Littlejohn 1989, 9), then what perspective mediates the relation Marx and Engels have to rurality? For Marx and Engels the fully aware experience of rurality is of necessity an experience of deprivation. The countryside is formulated in terms of a lack (of civilization, state, nation); it is known in terms of what humans could have but do not have (freedom, wealth, the power of the general, the abstract, the universal). As not wanting what could be developed is unimaginable (who would not want freedom, not want to develop their human potential, not want to be civilized?), the lack of commitment to social development can only be seen as idiocy: only an idiot would view backwardness as a better way of life. As a consequence, the rural represents an empirical but not an analytic possibility.[4] As an empirical possibility the rural is preferred because it is not fully experienced for what it is (because of, for example, a false consciousness) or it is experienced precisely as a regression (because of the condition of exile, for example). In either case it is not a chooseable alternative.[5] Rurality is not a real other but rather a reminder of what we, as humans committed to development of human potential, *must not be*. Rurality as a way of life, therefore, connotes a blindness or an indifference to individual and collective possibility. It exists only because of imposition (oppression) or ignorance (idiocy). The association of the "rural" with idiocy is, therefore, not mere polemic; it is a genuine conception of rurality, grounded in the Marxian framework.

The perspective of Marx and Engels personifies "the healthy capacity of modernist consciousness to question its limits"; at each stage of societal development the collective (that is, the relevant class) is required to come to terms with, and transcend, the limits inhibiting the mode of production. All other forms of otherness are subsumed under the dominant concern with the mode of production. Otherness is a limit to be overcome as the collective develops a true consciousness of its situation. The polyphony of voices and experiences celebrated by postmodernism (Clifford) are absent in this analysis. In particular, rural or urban experiences, as unique and particular experiences, are not recognized as phenomena in their own right, separate from the development of the productive forces of society (Sennett 1969, 3–19).

This brings us to the criticisms that have been levelled against the position of Marx and Engels, as these pertain to developing an understanding of the superiority of the urban way of life. First, as has been stated, Marx did not seek to understand the rural or urban experience in its own right. For him the significant collective was the one that sought to develop the productive forces of society: the various stages through which society was transformed (ancient, feudal, capitalist, communist) all reflect an analysis of a collective committed to developing its productive forces which, in turn, makes human liberation from the pain of endless labour and poverty possible. The standard by which a society is to be judged is the social organization that has developed its productive forces to their highest realization, which, in turn, maximizes the possibilities of human liberation. Rurality as itself referencing a particular and unique experience has no place in this theoretic scheme.

A second criticism, following from the first, is that the focus on materialism led to a one-sided (Weber 1958) and "nomological" (Habermas 1988) understanding of history and society. Marx's perspective by itself does not make room for the *complexity* of human experience, since it privileges a singular theoretical development over an understanding of the particularity of experience. There is no real need for the Marxian actor to consider the interpretive possibilities in his or her situation, because, analytically speaking, there is no real choice. Rather the actor now has to do what she or he knows needs to be done. As Marx himself says in his *Theses on Feurbach* (1978, 145), change (in the world) rather than interpretation is what is required.[6] For Weber, it is precisely by virtue of the subjective orientation of humans that action is social; this means theory has to make a place for meaning and experience. That is, the understanding of a "great place" needs to make room for the lived experience of place. The Marxian view conceptualizes the rural as backward, providing a theoretic background for the everyday conception of the rural person as a hick or a redneck. And while this conception brings one aspect of the truth of rurality to view, it is essentially an urban perspective; the self-understanding of the rural experience has been theoretically dismissed.

Weber developed the conception of ideal type (1947) as his method to account for social action/organization that preserves self-understanding. In doing this he was influenced by the *gemeinschaft/gesellschaft* conceptions of German sociologist Ferdinand Tonnies, who in turn was influenced by Marx. What connotative aspect of the urban-rural debate does Tonnies's conceptualization initiate and highlight?

FERDINAND TONNIES: THE URBAN-RURAL/*GEMEINSCHAFT-GESELLSCHAFT* DISTINCTION

In 1888 Ferdinand Tonnies published his classic text *Gemeinschaft und Gesellschaft*, coining terms that have now become standard in the discipline of sociology. While Marx addressed the urban-rural difference in terms of a collective committed to actualizing the potential for human liberation, Tonnies (influenced by Nietschze's Appolonian/Dionysiac polarity), through the terms *gemeinschaft* (community) and *gesellschaft* (association), recast the difference in terms of a more fundamental dichotomy and opposition.

With Tonnies we have neither evolutionary (Darwin) nor revolutionary (Marx) development but two sharply opposed social systems based on sharply opposing ways of life. The city, by virtue of the primacy given to commerce, encourages *gesellschaftlich* relations; the country, the village and the town, by virtue of the primacy given to family and history, give rise to *gemeinschaftlich* relations. For Tonnies the town is not an example of the rise of the division of labour (Marx) but an example of a community where the social and the natural are kept in balance.

By *gemeinschaft* Tonnies means a "social order bounded together by a unity of wills. Family and social institutions naturally created cooperation in a *Gemeinschaft* prior to its members' voluntary choice" (Liebersohn 1988, 7). *Gemeinschaft* is prevoluntary but nonetheless cooperative, a community built on a familial orientation. That is, one does not choose one's parents (social background, gender, etc.) but one cooperates with that "givenness": "The basic unit of the traditional community was the house ... Bonds of blood relation, place and friendship tied individuals to one another and drew houses into larger units of clan, ethnic groups and people, of village, country and province. The traditional town, no less than the countryside, was organized on communal lines, its guilds regulating production in harmony with the general needs of collective life" (Liebersohn 1988, 2–9; Tonnies 1960, 62–76).

Although in the literature (e.g., Dasgupta 1988, 3–5) *gemeinschaft* is closely associated with a rural setting, Tonnies does not use the term to describe the influence of place *per se*; rather, *gemeinschaft* references a social order "which – being based on a consensus of wills – rests on harmony and is developed and enabled by pathways, mores, and religion" (Tonnies 1960, 223). Tonnies is ambiguous as to whether the term refers to historical precedent or ideal type (Liebersohn 1988, 7). Using Nietschze's Appolonian/Dionysian polarity (Liebersohn 1988, 23–31), he wants to present the two kinds of social organization in not merely an evolutionary fashion (where one evolves out of the other) but as social organizations rooted in different orientations toward the world and life. His "method was supposed to be hermeneutic, describing each type from its own perspective" (Liebersohn 1988, 30). What this famous distinction actually initiates is the association of rurality with community. It is this image of community that many have in mind when they think of the rural advantage. On the whole, Tonnies (1960, 223–59) sees rural life as sustaining *gemeinschaftlich* relations between people because of its focus on establishing and nurturing common bonds, while the city tends to nurture *gesellschaftlich* relations because of its emphasis on competition and individual advantage.

Tonnies's theory of *gesellschaft* was strongly influenced by his readings of both Marx and Hobbes (Liebersohn 1988, 1–39). It refers as much to modern capitalist society as it does to city life, though, as we already know from Marx, the rise of modernity, capitalism, and urbanization are intertwined. However, perhaps because of Tonnies's own isolated rural town upbringing, he does not celebrate *gesellschaft* as an important step on the way to liberation (communism). Rather, with Tonnies we have the beginning of the recognition of the dark side of modernity – a recognition that Weber was to later name the "iron cage."

Gesellschaft, as a social order, is constituted by commodity exchange and rests "on a union of rational wills." Whereas *gemeinschaft* has "its roots in family life," *gesellschaft* "derives from the conventional order of trade" (Tonnies 1960, 223; Loomis 1960, 3–11). Here the relations between people are regulated by contracts and exchange which, in turn, are governed by the rational means-end attitude, i.e., in terms of an evaluation "of the advantages that people expect to get from others" (Hale 1990, 107). Because of this orientation, people are mobile, both socially and geographically, and competition rather than cooperation is the dominant ethos. On a theme later developed by Weber and Habermas, Tonnies saw that the dominance of the rational will would ultimately lead to undermining a genuine attachment between people and to community. Therefore, the question of the superiority of the rural way of life is to be assessed on this criterion of genuine attachment.

While Tonnies was not directly concerned with the issue of the benefit of rural life for child-rearing (perhaps he would see the very question as reflecting a *gesellschaftlich* mentality, as place is not invested with any sense of sacredness but is implicitly understood in rational-instrumental terms), there are, nonetheless, strong implications in his famous work for an answer to this question. By virtue of this close association between rural life and *gemeinschaft*, and the fact that *gemeinschaftlich* relations are rooted in the family, rural life privileges family relations. What makes rural life superior in this schema is the way the task of raising children is supported by the community at large. Tonnies is not arguing for a romantic notion of the countryside as other (opposite) to social life: rather, rural life is better because the family aim (child-rearing) is simultaneously a communal need. Genuine attachment to others begins in the family and flows into the community.

If family life is rooted in the ethos of mutual cooperation, then the individualistic competitiveness of the city, organized on *gesellschaft* relations, is in direct opposition to the family. Because of this, "in the city … family life is decaying" (Tonnies 1960, 229). The city, by virtue of privileging commerce, appeals to the actor in terms of individual interests (in particular, the individual's self-interest), while the *gemeinschaftlich* attitude of rural life appeals to the actor as a member of a group sharing common bonds and common interests. In this community, parents and children are not seen to be separate actors with individualistic interests but rather are a unity (family) with a shared interest, as this interest has been articulated by the authority figures.[7] For Tonnies, these relations are invested with a sense of sacredness making reason subordinate to the activities of the whole and the common good they are directed toward.

This formulation certainly resonates with a certain conception of the rural and the superiority of the rural way of life. Here rural life is associated with the idea of a close-knit community. Some of the parents I talked with explicitly mentioned the advantage of raising children in a setting surrounded by the extended family. For these parents the family, the extended family, and the community seemed to flow easily into each other. Tonnies's formulation is a rigorous development of this idea, framed, as we shall see, by a concern with scientific exactitude.

Sociologically and historically, and in terms of our narrative, the meaning of the object to which the concept of rural refers has changed from Marx's image of "backwardness," an obstacle to progress that must be overcome, to a competing social organization and way of life. For Tonnies what is significant about rural life is not its landscape nor its comparative primitiveness but the kind of social organization it nurtures. *Gemeinschaftlich* relations receive their highest social expression not on the farm but in the town, the "highest … form of social life" (Tonnies 1960, 227). This means that rural comes to reference a particular way of relating to people rather than a way of relating to nature. Under Tonnies's influence (and despite his explicit critique of capitalism), rural came to reference a community that was an extension of the "natural" source of community, the family (Tonnies 1960, 176–7). "Marriage was organized not around individuals, as in modern society, but around the house whose members received a fixed place within their own house and related to outsiders as members of other houses" (Liebersohn 1988, 32). Sociologically speaking, therefore, the town rather than the countryside is the relevant object for the concept of rural.

As noted, Tonnies's categories were ambiguous as to their status as ideal types or historical experiences. Tonnies's aim was to write in a spirit of scientific objectivity, to show the same dispassion towards society as towards any other object of study (Liebersohn 1988, 27). Thus the fact that the town was destined to be taken over by commercial interests and thus evolve into a *gesellschaft* society was a fated event which Tonnies, the sociologist in pursuit of the objective truth, had to acknowledge, in the way the laws of physics force the physicist to recognize that the earth is not the centre of the universe. Yet, as Liebersohn argues (1988, 30–1), Tonnies was "unable to resist the opportunity to describe *gesellschaft* from the point of view of *gemeinschaft*, as if the communal world of the past, defeated by history, at last had a champion to accuse the modern way of life that had vanquished it ... In the form he presented them, the book's categories were not neutral instruments of empirical analysis. Instead, they embodied a denunciation of one way of life, defence of another."

Tonnies was convinced that

all true morality was rooted in the settled folkways of *gemeinschaft*, [and] he did not restrain his disgust toward the liberties permitted in a *gesellschaft*. Women, delicate creatures of feeling, belonged in the home; a society that let them leave it and diminished the differences between the sexes could only be a decadent society. Intellectuals tended to deny the pious beliefs of their fathers and to replace them with the arbitrary products of their own reason ... The merchant, the most complete embodiment of *gesellschaft*, was an enemy of the people: homeless, a traveller versed in foreign ways without piety toward his own, adept at using any means to achieve his goals, in all these respects the opposite of the farmer and the artisan (Liebersohn 1988, 32–3; Tonnies 1960, 151–69).

This kind of description leaves Tonnies open to the charge of idealism. His formulation of *gemeinschaft* represents the romantic dream of a conflict-free community as much as any empirical community. More importantly, Durkheim (in Giddens 1972, 146–7) accuses Tonnies of psychological reductionism, because *gesellschaft* is no less natural or no more artificial than is *gemeinschaft*, even if it is apparently organized on rational grounds. *Gemeinschaft* and *gesellschaft* are a conceptual opposition, organized more by the opposition between organism and machine (Liebersohn 1988, 136) than an opposition of world views emerging from the basis of different lived experiences. Thus, *from the scientific perspective,* Tonnies's conceptualization does not easily translate into empirical research and does not adequately measure up to standards of neutral objectivity. In Weber's terms, the conceptualization is value-laden rather than value-free. Yet *from the perspective of radical interpretive sociology,* this scientific critique can itself be criticized.

TONNIES AND RADICAL INTERPRETIVE SOCIOLOGY

A significant aspect of the distinction between *gemeinschaftlich* and *gesellschaftlich* relations is the different wills that each social organization strengthens. In the move from *gemeinschaft* to *gesellschaft* (a move Tonnies saw happening with the increasing dominance of modernity) "a complete reversal of intellectual life takes place ... [T]he intellectual attitude of the individual becomes gradually less and less influenced by religion and more and more influenced by science" (Tonnies 1960, 226). This means, according to Tonnies, that usefulness, efficiency, and the learning derived from the impersonal observation of the laws of social life become the dominant way of relating to others and to the world. In *gesellschaft,* reason is not subordinate to but is independent of community spirit. In everyday action, the rational self-interest of the merchant now comes to predominate: in intellectual life, science and impersonal learning predominate. As noted above, Tonnies undertook to do a scientific analysis of the nature of human society; yet, according to Tonnies, scientific thinking predominates in a society where personal human relations have deteriorated.[8]

This brings us to a paradoxical dilemma in Tonnies's analysis. While his conceptualization of *gemeinschaft* and *gesellschaft* failed in its attempt to be an objective and empirically verifiable analysis of the way human society works, he still "aspired to make his book scientific in the strongest nineteenth-century sense of the word" (Liebersohn 1988, 27). The very categories of *gemeinschaft* and *gesellschaft* are generated by an intellectual orientation grounded by the purpose of scientific objectivity, itself a modern orientation. That is, they are the categories of a *gesellschaft* rather than *gemeinschaft* life-world. Thus, if, as Liebersohn says, Tonnies's analysis defended *gemeinschaft* by condemning *gesellschaft,* this is understood to be a failure to realize the aim of scientific objectivity rather than a challenge and critique of scientific objectivity as an aim in the first place.

Tonnies's defence of *gemeinschaft* is that of one who seeks to understand the world from the intellectual orientation of *gesellschaft.* While condemning "modernity" and defending "tradition," he simulta-neously shows, to use Clifford's quotation, the "disquieting quality of modernism: its taste ... for discovering universal, ahistorical 'human' capacities" (e.g., natural will versus rational will). This raises important theoretical and methodological issues, not the least of which is the question of the way one's presuppositions about the nature of adequate inquiry (an ontological as well as an epistemo-logical problem) necessarily influence what we are able to recognize. Scientific objectivity is merely one solution to this problem.

The very categories of *gemeinschaft* and *gesellschaft* are grounded in the *assumption* that an adequate inquiry aims for scientific objectivity – *itself*, according to Tonnies, an assumption of a *gesellschaft* frame of mind. That is, the distinction itself is subject to the very same critique as *gesellschaft*: it is mechanical and impersonal. The question that emerges from this critique is whether the objectivity claimed by the human sciences can adequately understand and analyse the commu-nity that privileges emotions, sees attachments to people as being infused with a sacred character, and is organized on the principle of time rather than space (Tonnies 1960, 232–3) if that objectivity takes modern science as its model. If science is a mode of inquiry that privileges space rather than time, detachment rather than attach-ment, and calculating rationality rather than understanding, is there a mode of inquiry that privileges time in such a way that the social organization based on the principle of time (*gemeinschaft*) can be more adequately taken into account?

Tonnies's analysis of community is flawed by its unquestioning assumption that modern science is the only avenue to knowledge of society. In seeking to describe human society and history as though he were outside of it, Tonnies ends up unquestioningly speaking from *gesellschaft* principles, precisely at the moment he is condemn-ing those self-same principles. In other words, he uses scientific reason to condemn the social organization that allows scientific reason to dominate community spirit.

The issue of theoretical orientation, as we shall see, is of critical decisiveness not only for the way the urban-rural discourse is con-ceptualized but, more fundamentally, for the way much of the very enterprise of sociology is grounded in an understanding of the tradition-modern divide. Tonnies understands from within the parameters of a modernist consciousness (Berger, Berger and Kellner 1973) and simultaneously struggles against the tendencies of that conscious-ness; he condemns the intellectual's tendency to rely on reason alone and proceeds to be rational in a universalist way; he exemplifies the modernist tendency to develop ahistorical concepts and condemns the decadence inherent in that inclination. While Weber is much more consistent in his theoretical orientation, these paradoxes need also to be understood as expressions of the modernist consciousness ("to question its limits and engage otherness"). The otherness of *gemein-schaft* is both oppositional and competitive. It represents the self-condemnation of modernity without acknowledgment of the modern orientation that allows for the condemnation.

At the weakest level of interpretation, Tonnies's work is an early representative of the unreflective self-condemnation of modernity seen in more recent postmodernist studies. A stronger reading of Tonnies also recognizes the inclination, inherent in modernity, to develop a positive relation to resistance. That is, the *gemeinschaft/ gesellschaft* distinction is *a solution to the problem of the need to develop self-resistance*. The rural in this case is the other to modern society. In Tonnies's case, it is the other to be championed as a way of remind-ing the city of its own excess. Might this not be what many city dwellers who perceive a rural setting to be better for raising a family are also doing? Does this championing of the rural represent a gen-uine understanding and embrace of the rural, or does it say more about the urbanites' relation to their own city?

The question of the preference for rural child-rearing is now more complex. Truly to assess this question requires a reflective turn to the taken-for-granted presuppositions that motivate such claims.[9] Is this preference, on the part of urbanites at least, really saying something about the city? About their relation to the city? Are such preferences mere unreflective self-criticism and so lacking in authority? Or do they point to an excess that the city (modernity) might have to resist? In like manner, for the rural residents who believe that a rural setting is a better place to raise a family, is this belief grounded in rational calculation (*gesellschaft*) or in a sense of spirited attachment to family and community (*gemeinschaft*)? To assess the beliefs of either the urbanites or the ruralites on this matter now requires attending not just to their beliefs but to the basis of their beliefs.

GEORG SIMMEL: THE URBAN-RURAL/INDIVIDUAL UNIQUENESS-COMMUNAL SOLIDARITY DIFFERENCE

The tension between spirit (*gemeinschaft*) and reason (*gesellschaft*) was further explored by a contemporary younger colleague of Tonnies, Georg Simmel. Unlike Tonnies, who grew up and spent much of his adult life in a rural town in Germany, Simmel saw Berlin as "an indispensable condition of [his] work" (Liebersohn 1988, 126–58). Berlin was Simmel's birthplace, education place, and workplace, and he himself said "the particular achievements I have produced in these decades is [sic] unquestionably bound to the Berlin milieu" (Simmel, as cited in Liebersohn 1988, 126). His classic essay *The Metropolis and Mental Life* (1971) makes the mentality of the urbanite its primary object. For Simmel the city is "peculiarly central to the destiny of modern man" because it is here that humans have an opportunity to develop their individuality and freedom (Martindale & Neuwirth 1962, 33–7). Not incidentally, developing these traits has involved emphasizing reason and the intellect over spirit and the emotions.

In Simmel's view, "The essentially intellectualistic character of the mental life of the metropolis becomes intelligible as over against that of the small town which rests more on feelings and emotional relationships" (1971, 325). The metropolis "has always been the seat of a money economy." Money along with the intellect has "a purely matter-of-fact attitude in the treatment of persons and things in which a formal justice is often combined with an unrelenting hardness" (328). In a small town personal relationships "rest on their individuality, intellectual relationships deal with persons as with numbers ... of interest only insofar as they offer something objectively perceivable." The metropolis enhances the qualities of "punctuality, calculability and exactness" because of the "complications and extensiveness of metropolitan life" (328):

The mental attitude of the people of the metropolis may be designated formally as reserve. If the unceasing external contact of numbers of persons in the city should be met by the same number of inner reactions as in the small town, in which he knows almost every person and to each of whom he has a positive relationship, one would be completely atomized internally and fall into an unthinkable mental condition ... [This necessary reserve] permits us to appear to small town folk so often as cold and uncongenial. (331)

This reserve can have a positive result not possible in the small town: "It assures the individual of a type and degree of personal freedom to which there is no analogy in other circumstances" (332). In contrast to Tonnies, Simmel views the unity, community, and solidarity of *gemeinschaft* evident in the town and village as having a negative side, for in it the "individual member has only a very slight area for the development of his own qualities and for free activity for which he himself is responsible" (332). "In an intellectualized and refined sense the citizen of the metropolis is *free* in contrast with the trivialities and prejudices which bind the small town person" (336). The price of this freedom may be loneliness (334), indifference (329–30), or impersonality (331), but by virtue of the enlargement of the individual's horizon, the metropolis gives form to the development of the "particularity and incomparability which ultimately every person possesses" (335).

Simmel's recognition of the distinctive virtue of the metropolis relates to his modernism and his conception of sociological purpose as the understanding of the relation between the individual and society, on the basis of the regulative principle of interaction (Simmel 1971, 23–40). The egoism that modern society encourages has its positive side in the opportunity it creates for individuality while yet avoiding the negative consequence of anarchy, by "creating impersonal forms of order, sociologically binding on all members of society. In a complex society even the criminal had to make use of the general forms of law, morality, and communication in order to achieve his ends; and in making use of them he necessarily strengthened them" (Liebersohn 1988, 131–2). This viewpoint shocked Tonnies who, from his rural isolation, said that Simmel's work was solid but limited by its urban centrism (Liebersohn 1988, 131). Tonnies did not see the emancipation from communal constraints as completely wholesome. He acknowledged the increase in sophistication but said that such emancipation also led to the spread of "lack of character" and a decline of a relation to morality based on inner conviction rather than force or convention (Liebersohn 1988, 132).

With Simmel's contribution to this debate, the issue of the relative merit of socialization in an urban or rural setting becomes more complex. We note first of all that for Simmel (as for Tonnies) the urban-rural difference is for the most part a city-town difference. Both refer to different kinds of communities that nurture a different social-psychological orientation in their respective members. Both also acknowledge that the family is a dominant influence on the ethos of the town. For Tonnies, the family, and the community that emerges on the basis of the family, provides for a unity in social life and an "inner" relation to morality (i.e., that the action/life one chooses as good is chosen because one believes that it is good and not merely because this is the way one happens to act [convention] or one is forced to so act because of fear of punishment [force]). Simmel accepts the *gemeinschaftlich* character of the small town but, precisely because of its solidarity, sees it as limiting the freedom to develop individuality of its members. For Simmel (1971), "the smaller the circle which forms our environment and the more limited the relationships which have the possibility of transcending the boundaries, the more anxiously the narrow community watches over the deeds, the conduct of life and the attitudes of the individual and the more will a quantitative and qualitative individuality tend to pass beyond the boundaries of such a community" (333). This very "jealousy of the whole toward the individual" led Simmel to the observation that "the ancient *polis* seems in this regard to have had a character of a small town ... The tremendous agitation and excitement, and the unique colorfulness of Athenian life is perhaps explained by the fact that a people of incomparably individualized personalities were in constant struggle against the incessant inner and external oppression of a de-individualizing small town" (333).

This observation suggests that if the nineteenth-century metropolis allows (individualistic) reason to dominate at the expense of (communal) spirit and the town allows (communal) spirit to dominate at the expense of (individualistic) reason, then the tremendous agitation and unique colourfulness of the ancient *polis* was a consequence of holding reason and spirit in tension with each other. This in turn suggests that both reason and spirit need the resistance that the other offers in order for genuine excitement, agitation, and colourfulness to become cultural possibilities. Here we see the possibility of a relationship between self and other, urban and rural, reason and spirit that is neither appropriative (Marx) nor oppositional (Tonnies). The interest of modern consciousness ("questioning its limits and engaging otherness") has the possibility of developing a positive relation to its limits where unregulated individuality is resisted by a sense of community and, in like manner, the oppressiveness of a de-individualizing community is resisted by the desire to make room for individual uniqueness.

As we shall see, the issues of the tension between collaboration and the need for resistance, between the space the metropolis creates for "individuality" and the "de-individualizing tendency" of the small town, will continue to be relevant in addressing the case of Prairie Edge. In particular, the final chapter examines the potential the modern rural community has to be a *polis* in Simmel's sense. Parenthetically, Simmel's work (despite being limited by an aesthetic conception of individuality/community) shows the possibilities for community and individuality that an interpretive sociology can bring to light.

Simmel's insights raise the issue of a setting that, in supporting a family ethos, makes it difficult to have the freedom to develop individual uniqueness. Apart from the empirical question of whether the city in the late twentieth century actually enhances the possibilities for individual freedom, how does one understand and critically evaluate the different principles that urban and rural now come to represent? If one values the freedom to develop one's individuality, then the small town is not necessarily good for child-rearing. On the other hand, if one values family solidarity and communal ties as an essential principle, then the small town is good for raising children. Simmel's interpretation allows us to recognize the double-edged character of the rural community and, in turn, encourages us to raise the questions of whether (and in what way) the town in late twentieth-century North America in general, and Canada in particular, has communal solidarity or a de-individualizing effect, and what influence either has on child-rearing.

More importantly, Simmel helps us recognize that understanding and evaluating the belief in the superiority of rural over urban involves not only understanding the foundation for the belief but also the value one places on that foundation. An urban resident could say that the city is a better place to raise children and mean that the city offers more opportunity for children to develop their unique personalities. A rural resident could say that the small town is a better place to raise children and mean that family ties and a sense of community are nurtured and developed. Both, according to Simmel, could be right. The urban-rural debate is now more complex because it raises the issue of how different fundamental values are to be understood and evaluated.

Simmel's formulation, in turn, makes this research project more complex. With Marx we recognize that a survey approach to assessing the superiority of the rural over the urban is inadequate. If rural means backwardness, only an idiot would think it superior. However, if, following Tonnies, we take rural to mean a way of life that emphasizes family ties and genuine attachments to others, then these are the practices that have to be investigated. Yet Simmel's position says a rural setting is not superior even when it is better for family and community: because the latter inhibits the free development of individuality, the city is superior. Therefore, a comprehensive research project needs to be able to take into account seemingly different fundamental values. What would such an analysis look like? Is sociology up to this task? Let us now turn to Max Weber, who addressed this very issue of the relation between sociology and value.

MAX WEBER: THE URBAN-RURAL/MODERN-TRADITIONAL DISTINCTION

Like his colleagues and acquaintances Simmel and Tonnies, Max Weber studied the connection between modernity and urbanization.

Like Simmel but unlike Tonnies, he is more influential in urban rather than rural sociology. Like Marx, Tonnies, and Simmel, he was keenly interested and aware of the interconnection between capitalism, urbanization, and modernity. He is credited by Wirth as coming closest to developing a systematic theory of urbanism in his "penetrating essay," *The City* (Wirth 1938, 8). Yet in an early essay *Capitalism and Rural Society in Germany* (Gerth & Mills 1946, 363–85), Weber is the first of the classical sociologists to acknowledge the difference between a European and an American rural society.[10] In relation to this recognition he is also one of the first (though rarely acknowledged as such) to foresee the gradual disappearance of an independent urban community *and* a separate and distinct rural community. In this sense he foreshadows the work of Gans (1968) and Pahl (1968).

The growth of the nation-state, the development of capitalism as an international order, and the bureaucratic rationalization of more and more areas of social life all mean that the distinctiveness of "urban" and "rural" as referencing different communities is gradually disappearing (Martindale and Neuwirth 1958, 56–67). For our purposes, we note Weber's observation that "a rural society, separate from the urban social community does not exist at the present time in a great part of the modern civilized world" (1946, 363). This, he says, is particularly true of the United States because the American farmer is really an "entrepreneur like any other" and not an "agriculturist" who seeks to conserve a tradition.[11] In an analysis foreshadowing the recent dispute over subsidies between the EU and the US, Weber in 1904 argued that "if anything is characteristic of the rural conditions of the great wheat-producing states of America, it is … the absolute economic individualism of the farmer, the quality of the farmer as a mere businessman" (364). This situation is in contrast with Europe in general, and Germany in particular, where the "power of tradition inevitably predominates in agriculture." This tradition rested on an old economic order which, in Weber's terms (1946, 367) took the view, "How can I give, on this piece of land, work and sustenance to the greatest possible number of men? Capitalism asks: From this given piece of land, how can I produce as many crops as possible for the market with as few men as possible?"

Weber knew that the old economic order, even in Europe at that time, was under siege. In this essay he saw rural society as possibly providing an alternative to capitalism because, through the monopolization of the land and hereditary preservation of possession, a nobility (not in form but in fact) would arise. This nobility in turn would provide a political alternative to the professional politician (who must live off politics) by nurturing people able to live for politics and the state. This rural society could bring a more permanent sense of what is valuable (i.e., a sense of value that is not dependent on the shifts of the market) and a sense of authority that respects tradition. Such a rural society could resist, in a practical way, the capitalistic pursuit of "heedless gain."

As would be expected, Weber is more self-consciously sociological when he addresses the urban-rural distinction. What makes the country or the city relevant, sociologically speaking, is neither geography nor demography but rather their capacity to socialize a unique character and community. Thus, even though the industrial cities were where most people had come to live, for Weber this was a decline of the special mark of the city because the people who lived there could not be said to have a special character *as* city people (Sennett 1969, 18). City dwellers are more likely to get their identity from more general social forces like class, occupation, status, even religious conviction (forces which are societal, national, and international), than forces tied to living in a specific city: empirically speaking, what matters to most city dwellers today is not that they are Londoners, Dubliners, or Athenians but that they are women, middle class, young, and so on.

Similarly, for Weber the *sociological* significance of a rural society lies in its ability to sustain an alternative culture to capitalism, which found a home in the city. Thus, the existence of farmers, towns, and villages does not necessarily lead to a distinct way of life that challenges the capitalistic ethos of modern urban life. On this basis, Weber says, "rural society" does not exist in the western United States: there is no meaningful social difference between the farmer and the businessman, or the farm labourer and the proletariat. The disappearance of a "genuine rural society" means the disappearance of a resistance to the dominance of capitalism. If farming is driven by the profit motive, if people identify with their class or occupation rather than a traditional way of living, then there is no sociological relevance to the referent of rural:[12] the rural as an other to the urban no longer exists.

As the reader will recognize, Weber's conceptual development complicates this research project. If the rural as a distinct and separate way of life no longer exists, what is the meaning of the preference for rural child-rearing? Is this difference a mere matter of degree in the way that one has a preference for one neighbourhood over another? Is the preference for the small town similar to the preference for the suburb? If there is no real difference in way of life between the rural and the urban, then the issue is unimportant. It means that modernization has robbed the debate of depth and significance because the choice is similar to the preference for one consumer brand over another. In turn, this formulation means that the deep issue is consumerism. That is, to fully understand the contemporary preference for parenting in a rural setting, one has to understand the way modern consumerism shapes this preference. (Chapter 9 addresses this important contemporary issue.)

Now the research project has become even more complex: not only do different fundamental values have to be addressed but so must the broad socio-historical development of consumerism. In turn, such an examination means that the preference for parenting in a rural setting is not only an issue for parents in Prairie Edge but also concerns contemporary developments in culture. The local and the global, the specific and the general, have to be investigated simultaneously. This is precisely the approach hermeneutics takes to social inquiry (Bonner 1997).

Weber helps us recognize that the urban-rural debate might now need to be understood within the context of modernity. In contemporary Canadian society, rural may no longer reference either backwardness (Marx) or *gemeinschaft* (Tonnies). Rather, what needs to be understood is the modern life-world itself, an underlying phenomenon that embraces and grounds the very way urbanism and ruralism are understood. As I show in chapter 2, phenomenology provides the inquirer with a theoretic orientation that enables a recognition of the way the life-world of modernity "rests on a body of unnoticed presuppositions" (Palmer 1969, 136) which themselves shape the understanding of the urban-rural debate.

Weber's contribution to the discourse raises several questions with both substantive and theoretic import. Substantively, if the difference between the urban and the rural exists only "in the thoughts of dreamers" (Weber 1946, 363), then how do we understand the claim for the benefit of child-rearing in a rural setting? What do we as sociologists do with the claims of parents that the difference between city and town is real? How do we integrate knowledge of the *sociological* irrevelance of the urban-rural difference with the claims many make for the relative advantage of rural child-rearing? In the next chapter I show what some sociologists, who unquestioningly accept the scientific paradigm, would do with such claims. But Weber's prescient interpretations encourage us to recognize the way the stated preference for the rural over the urban or vice versa is bound up with broader socio-cultural questions. For example, what is involved in child-rearing in this technological, consumerized, and globalized age? Is the spirit of consumerism more relevant to understanding the way parents act with their children than whether they happen to live in the city or in the country?

THE CONTEXT OF WEBER'S
SOCIOLOGY

Weber's later work set out to show the tight grip that capitalism had on modern life (*The Protestant Ethic and the Spirit of Capitalism*) and the interconnection between modernity and the calculating rationality of science (*Science As a Vocation*). While he was certainly not happy with these developments, his scientific perspective and commitment demanded that the force of modern life be recognized. The potential of an alternative rural life was no longer seen to be realistic. Yet his initial conception of the term "rural" was motivated by his lifelong interest in coming to terms with the reality ("the iron cage") of the modern socio-economic order and the possibilities of realistic resistance to this force (Liebersohn 1988, 78–125). His work, whether early or late, always had that particular combination of qualities – stating that as scholars and politicians we must "bear the fate of the times" (Weber 1946, 155) while at the same time acknowledging (sometimes sympathetically, sometimes impatiently) the "unrealistic" impulse to resist such a fate (1946, 77–156).

We have noted the inconsistencies in the way Tonnies formulated the problem, using the scientific approach to condemn the kind of social organization (*gesellschaft*) that privileges the scientific mode of inquiry. Weber too recognized the "disenchantment of the world" that accompanies the rise of modern science, but in distinction from Tonnies, he also reflectively acknowledged (1946) that the scientific orientation to the study of social life is part of the same development. As Dreyfus and Rabinow (1982, 165) state:

Weber saw that rationality, in the form of bureaucratization and calculative thinking, was becoming the dominant way of understanding reality in our time, and he set out to give a rational objective account of how this form of thinking had come to dominate our practices and self-understanding. He was led, through this scientific analysis, to see that the "disenchantment of the world" that calculative thinking brings about had enormous costs. He even saw that his own theorizing was part of the same development he deplored, but, as so many commentators have pointed out, there was absolutely no way his scientific method could justify his sense that the cost of rationality was greater than any possible benefit it could bring. Given Weber's starting point, all he could do was point out the paradoxical results of his analysis and the increasing perils to our culture.[13]

With this development (of the acknowledgment of the hegemony of the modern / scientific life-world), we are now beginning to recognize the difficulty modernity may have in preserving a sense of otherness (in this case, rurality) that would truly allow it to question its limits. Modern scientific methods, it seems, are not culturally neutral instruments of social inquiry. As Foucault (1977; Dreyfus & Rabinow 1982) was to show in inescapable detail, the rise of the human sciences is tied to the same modernity they claim to study. The problem is, therefore, that the human sciences by the constitution of their epistemological orientation are so tied to the modern life-world that they are in danger of seeing in the other (*gemeinschaft*/rural/community) a failed version of themselves. Modern consciousness thus may only *appear* to be engaging otherness and questioning its limits; what it ends up actually doing is affirming its own orientation and is thus blind to its limits. In the process a strong sense of *alteritas* is rendered invisible. The urban-rural debate in the sociological tradition can now be understood to be struggling with this very problem of the need for, but difficulty of achieving, a good relation to resistance. At this early stage of our narrative, it seems that the problem animating the discourse is some sense of the potential for self-destructiveness inherent within the modern project. Without "questioning otherness and engaging resistance," it may be that the self-destructive potential of modernity (e.g., as a *gesellschaft*) will go unchecked. At a time when awareness of the problems of nuclear waste, environmental crises, the gap between rich and poor, and so on is more pressing, it is interesting to note the theoretical insights into the potential for self-destructiveness that sociologists in the early part of this century brought to bear on this issue.

If the interest that structures the urban-rural debate in sociology is the evaluation of different kinds of communities with their attendant ways of thinking (Simmel) and ways of living (Tonnies), then, insofar as this is the interest of a modernist consciousness, we need to be aware of the ways this discourse could end up silencing the sense of otherness that could really challenge that interest. For Weber, otherness is acknowledged, but only as an "irrational alternative," the engaging of which requires an "intellectual sacrifice." This otherness cannot challenge modernity itself. There is no rural alternative: all one can do is retreat from modernity (into the arms of the "old churches"). Such a retreat, if it is to have dignity, requires the explicit acknowledgment that one is renouncing intellectual and political involvement in the world. Weber's work forces us to acknowledge that the theoretic problem and the way we recognize the problem in the world are intertwined.

My analysis of the conceptualization of the rural leads to the recognition of the breadth and depth involved in this research question and provides me as well with a sense of direction. The research needs to make a place for reflection. The preferences we have for a good life and the choices we make are intimately intertwined with the taken-for-granted presuppositions we hold dear. These goals and presuppositions are what most deserve to be called into question. This kind of reflection is needed not only for parents who understand a rural setting to be better for their parenting but also for modern social science that understands its way of knowing the world as superior. Both the truth of these goals (parenting) and the truth of these epistemological presuppositions (science) need to be made "into the things that most deserve to be called into question" (Heidegger 1977, 116). The practical and the theoretical are intertwined.

To summarize, if understanding and evaluating the preference for parenting in a rural setting requires some settled notion of what rural means, we now see that this aim is complex and difficult. Marx points to the danger that the belief may be based on a false consciousness. Tonnies points to the danger that the belief may be an expression of self-disgust; he also references the need for the researcher to recover the grounds of the belief. Simmel points to the need to recognize the fundamental value that may (or may not) support the belief and stresses the difficulty of sociologically evaluating that value. Lastly, my analysis of Weber shows that the researcher and the interpretive frame (e.g., science) the researcher uses to understand and evaluate the belief are part of the problem to be investigated. The research project not only has to develop a reasonable conception of the rural but must be reflective about the way such conceptualization influences what is seen as significant. In the meantime, we still do not have a reasonable way of conceptualizing the rural which can ground the assessment of the beliefs about its superiority.

CHAPTER TWO

The Urban-Rural Debate and the Hegemony of the Scientific Paradigm in Sociology

Through mass communication, motion pictures, radio and television, the cognitive and normative definitions of reality invented in the city are rapidly diffused throughout the entire society. To be linked to these media is to be involved in the continuing urbanization of consciousness. Plurality is intrinsic to this process. The individual wherever he may be is bombarded with a multiplicity of information and communication.

Berger, Berger and Kellner, 1973

Western technical achievement has shaped a different civilization from any previous, and we North Americans are the most advanced in that achievement ... [This achievement] moulds us in what we are, not only at the heart of our animality in the propagation and continuation of our species, but in our actions and thoughts and imaginings. Its pursuit has become our dominant activity and that dominance fashions both the public and private realm.

George Grant, 1969

[I]f ways of life do not coincide with settlement types, and if these ways are functions of class and life-cycle stage rather than of the ecological attributes of the settlement, a sociological definition of the city cannot be formulated.

H.J. Gans, 1968

Admittedly, there are theoretical problems in identifying a rural culture. Yet those who come into a rural area to carry on their professions have no difficulty recognising something distinctive about the new countryside.

Alex Sim, 1988

In this chapter we move from a European to a North American setting, and from the eighteenth and (especially) nineteenth centuries to the full flowering of the modernist consciousness in the twentieth

century. As Weber has suggested, the change from a European society still with vestiges of the old order to the New World should lead
to a change in the way the family is understood to relate to the urban-
rural debate. The European conception of the distinction, developed
against the background of changes in nineteenth-century European
society, came to represent the struggle between modernity and tradition. The city was identified with modernity; rural life was an older
and different order. Whether the older order was seen to be regres-
sive (Marx), communal (Tonnies), personal and de-individualizing
(Simmel), or traditional (Weber), all the conceptions of rurality were
attempts to theorize a social order that was other to modernity. As
the New World was a social order more or less explicitly established
within the framework of the modern life-world, we should expect
the conceptualization of the urban-rural distinction to reflect this
context. In this sense we should also expect to be moving to a closer
understanding of what Prairie Edge parents are talking about in
assessing the merit of rural parenting.

As Grant argues in his eloquent essay "In Defence of North America," the interrelation (noted in chapter 1) between the rise of modernity and the rise of the modern sciences is more explicitly and
confidently embraced on a continent whose very societies are
founded on the break with the Old World. The resistance that the
vestige of the Old World offers, embodied in the very architecture
and customs of late nineteenth-century Europe, has less of an effect
in the twentieth century in general, and in North America in particular. In turn, the confidence of the modern sciences, their positivism
(that the world/society *can only be known/ascertained* through the verification procedures of science) influences the way the interest of the
modernist consciousness ("engage otherness and question its limits")
is realized in this socio-historical context.

If, as Grant argues, North America is the apogee of the development of modernity, then the question we must ask is: In what way
does the understanding of the urban-rural debate develop in the
context of a less fettered modernity? We will come to see, as the Sim
quotation illustrates, that as modernity develops, it becomes increasingly difficult to "theoretically identify a rural culture." We will see
as well that this difficulty lies not only with the way modern society
develops (i.e., the enormous increase in the urbanization of society
and consciousness) but also with the way a particular notion of
theory is legitimated. That is, in the twentieth century we are no
longer dealing with the rise of the modern scientific paradigm but
with its hegemony. Using the approach recommended by radical
interpretive sociology, we will try to understand why "a sociological

definition of the city [rural] cannot be formulated" (Gans) even though "those who come into a rural area ... have no difficulty in recognising something distinctive about the new countryside" (Sim).

Resolving this conceptual predicament is crucial if I am adequately to analyse both my own sense of the distinctiveness of parenting in Prairie Edge and the statements that most parents made in the course of this research. The research, or for that matter any sociological research in this area, lacks a conceptual sense of direction if this theoretical problem is not solved, even when solving it means that the research project becomes more complex and difficult. The urban-rural distinction supports a framework that has considerable use in sociology. Without resolution, therefore, not only this research project but the whole urban-rural debate in sociology remain conceptually problematic and highly improbable. In order to resolve this dilemma, I must first examine the formulations of the rural that emerge from the highly influential Chicago School.

THE CHICAGO SCHOOL: THE URBAN-RURAL/ URBANIZATION-FOLK DISTINCTION

The city is not conducive to the traditional type of family life, including the rearing of children and the maintenance of the home as the focus of a whole round of vital activities.   Louis Wirth, 1938

My thesis is that the element of effective-history [i.e., unavoidably being subject to socio-historical influences] is operative in all understanding of tradition, even where the methodology of the modern historical sciences has largely been adopted ...   Hans-Georg Gadamer, 1975

The Chicago School led by Park, Wirth, and Burgess in the 1920s (Stein 1967, 96–154) sought to develop sociological definitions of urban and rural life against the background of the rapid changes Chicago itself was undergoing.[1] At the same time, the group sought to develop a theory that was universal in the empirical sense of that term. These twin aims (understanding the city and developing a scientific theory of it) became more and more intertwined as the sociological literature accumulated in this area. Wirth in particular, in his classic and much-critiqued (see Gans 1968; Pahl 1968) article, "Urbanism As a Way of Life" (1938), advances a theory of the city that aims at being scientific, sociological, and empirically universal. Wirth seeks to "avoid identifying urbanism as a way of life with any specific locally or historically conditioned cultural influences which, while they may significantly affect the character of the community, are not the essential determinants of its character as a city" (7). That is, whether it is New York, Toronto, Dublin, Detroit, Hamilton, or Manchester, what matters is not the particularity of the city but its empirical generality. In this sense the separation of the concepts of urban and rural from a sense of place (particularity) is achieved. If a researcher were to use this framework to analyse what parents in Prairie Edge say, the "place" in "a great place to raise your children" would be obscured if not rendered obsolete. Wirth seeks to establish conceptually what Giddens (1990, 18–19) says is happening empirically.[2]

The radical interpretive perspective, on the other hand, moves in a different conceptual direction. As Gadamer (1975, 6) states, "the aim is not to confirm and expand these general experiences in order to attain knowledge of a law, e.g., how men, peoples and states evolve, but to understand how this man, this people or this state is what it has become." More importantly, Gadamer argues (1975, 192–274) that history and culture are "not simply an impairment" to the objectivity of the human sciences but are on the contrary "something of positive value" (253). Any full understanding of a phenomenon has to include the way community, history, and culture operate in such an understanding, even (and most especially) in the kind of understanding that specifically seeks to exclude these features. Wirth's positivism seeks to exclude history, culture, and particularity from the understanding of urbanism/ruralism. What image of urban-rural difference emerges from such a perspective?

Writing against the background of a city whose population had grown by half a million each decade for three consecutive decades (Stein 1967, 101), Wirth states that the "growth of cities and the urbanization of the world is one of the most impressive facts of modern times" (2). That is, the urbanization of society is increasingly being seen as the outstanding characteristic of modernity. Influenced by Simmel, he argues that since urbanization is what is distinctively modern about western civilization, one can best understand modern society by selecting "those elements of urbanism which mark it as a distinctive mode of human group life" (4). As a sociologist, Wirth recognizes that urbanism (and by implication ruralism) needed to be conceptualized and cannot be adequately characterized on the basis of an arbitrary number.[3] He seeks to develop a "serviceable definition of the city" that denotes "the essential characteristics which all cities – at least those in our culture – have in common" (6). Thus, to understand modern society is to understand urbanization (Martindale and Neuwirth 1962, 41–5), and to understand urbanization necessitates a "sociological definition of the city."

Yet urbanization does not merely denote living in the city. Wirth[4] states, "The influences which cities exert upon the social life of man are greater than the ratio of the urban population would indicate, for the city is not only in ever larger degrees the dwelling place and workshop of modern man, but it is the initiating and controlling centre of economic, political, and cultural life that has drawn the most remote parts of the world into its orbit and woven diverse areas, peoples, and activities into a cosmos" (2).

By virtue of the technological development noted by Berger *et al.* (1973) above but lamented by Grant (1969), modernity is able to solve many problems "that forced the Greeks to settle for small communities" (Minar and Greer 1969, xi). Developments in communication, transportation, and mass media make "a kind of unity" over great spaces possible and transform the way humans relate to each other and to their environment. Wirth is concerned, even anxious, about the nature and quality of this unity as it was expressed in city life of the time.

On the basis of a vast amount of empirical research, he defines the city as a "relatively large, dense, and permanent settlement of heterogeneous individuals" (8). He refers to the city as a "gigantic aggregation" (2) removed "from organic nature" (1). Its influence is far-reaching and spreading. In turn, rurality is defined as the polar ideal-type opposite of the city. Wirth's observations on the difference between urban and rural ways of life, while based on extensive empirical literature, basically flow from this ideal-type polarity. For example, a fewer number of inhabitants increases the possibility of each member of the community knowing most of the others personally. In rural society, one is more likely to make contact with the other as "a full personality" rather than as a segmented role. A smaller population is more conducive to personal, permanent, and complete relations (12). The emancipation of the individual from the personal and emotional controls of intimate groups, which occurs in the city, comes at the price of "the spontaneous self-expression, the morale, and the sense of participation that comes with living in an integrated society" (13). High density of population, according to Wirth (following Durkheim), tends to produce differentiation and specialization in activities and social structure. Physical contacts will be close (crowds) but social contacts (with others as ends in themselves rather than as means to an end) will be distant. The city therefore gives rise to more loneliness than does a town. High density, in turn, increases the heterogeneity of the population: "No single group has the undivided allegiance of the individual" (16). This leads to the weakening of an attachment to the whole, which in turn increases the tendency to be mobile, both socially and geographically. Wirth concludes that "maintaining and promoting intimate and lasting acquaintanceship" between members of organizations and groups becomes difficult (17).[5]

For the purpose of this project, the most relevant aspect of Wirth's theory of urbanism is the claim that "the city is not conducive to the traditional type of family life, including the rearing of children and the maintenance of the home as the focus of a whole round of vital activities" (21). Because of its large size, high density, and heterogeneity of population, the city emancipates the family, as a unit of social life, "from the larger kinship group characteristic of the country and the individual members pursue their own diverging interests in their vocational, education, religious, recreational and political life" (21). For Wirth, as for Tonnies (1960) and Weber (1946), rural life and living in an extended family are closely interconnected. The city frees individuals from the larger kinship group by encouraging members of a group to think of themselves as individuals who can pursue their own interests rather than the interests of the group. Thus, urbanization encourages members of a family to think of themselves as separate individuals with separate individual rights and interests rather than as members of the same group – the family, for example, engaged in a shared project such as home maintenance. In the city, the home is more likely to be a mere place of residence which individuals use as a base to pursue their separate membership in institutions (e.g., school, occupation, politics, recreation) outside that base. The home is transformed into a service station rather than the home centre characteristic of the family embedded in the larger kinship group, and thereby the attachment to the whole family and to others as members of that family is weakened.

Of all the sociologists dealt with so far, Wirth's description seems to cohere most closely with and support the popular image we are examining. He offers the hypothesis that parenting in a rural setting is better because of the smallness of size, low density, and homogeneity of population. These enable the home to become the focus for a whole round of activities, and by so doing, to strengthen the attachment to the group. In this sense rural life facilitates the intimate and lasting relationships reminiscent of the large kinship group. The resulting stability, sense of belonging, and group cohesion are assumed to be good. The superiority of the rural, it seems, needs to be tested by the criteria of stability, sense of belonging, and sense of group cohesion it facilitates.

Second, we can see that for Wirth rurality is equated with premodernity, and the rural family is seen as a "traditional" type of family. At the beginning of his essay, he compares urbanization, symbolized by the metropolis, with a pre-industrial folk society. Yet as he develops his theory of urbanism, he contrasts life in the city with rural life and in the process makes several observations about the character of rural life. As Gans (1968) shows, Wirth's argument is ambiguous about whether rural life or pre-industrial folk society is the relevant ideal-type contrast. If we take his definition at face value, then it would appear that rural life is the contrast; on the other hand, his examples suggest that the pre-modern folk society is the relevant polar contrast. This conceptual confusion undermines his theory (whose fate was to be empirical refutation; Pahl, 1968) and precisely illustrates the danger of taking for granted the modernity that spawned not only the debate but also the science that is now beginning to assert hegemonic control over the parameters of the debate.

As noted, Wirth was attempting both to understand the way modern life was becoming increasingly urbanized and to develop a sociological definition of the city. In another essay, "Rural-Urban Differences" (1969, 165–9), he acknowledges that the "changes in the technology of living ... have made such notions as we have about rural and urban likenesses and differences obsolete. The city has spilled over into the countryside. City ways of life have in some respects taken on a rural cast particularly in the suburbs ... The standardization of ways of living tends to make rural life as we have known it look archaic in many respects" (165–6). All of these developments make understanding the modern era difficult, if modernity and urbanization are intrinsically interrelated. Modernity, particularly in the United States, is everywhere; it is difficult to step outside of it, to conceptualize it, to describe it as a "particular form of human association" (166). Wirth's solution is to construct a polar-type opposite: "Whatever we might discover about the city ... would manifestly have to be checked against what we know or could find out about human settlements which are not cities, i.e., against the country" (166). The ideal-type polar contrast is therefore a solution to an intellectual problem – to know about the city/modernity we have to know what is not city/modernity.

Apart from the question about the usefulness of understanding something in terms of its polar opposite (because this procedure assumes that the form rather than the content of the society is what is significant), Wirth's procedure is compounded by the difficulty that such an opposite no longer exists in much of the industrialized world. The epistemological issue – how to conceptualize the distinctiveness of modernity – is increasingly a factual problem. The otherness to modernity, embodied in the urban-rural discourse, is disappearing from our everyday experience of the world. The very victory of modernity, its hegemony, now "tends to make rural life [otherness] as we have known it look archaic in many respects" (166).

The consequence of this positivistic approach to the creation of knowledge is to reduce a dynamic discourse to a polar-type opposition; the *gemeinschaft* which was the opposition challenging the *gesellschaftlich* way of life has been reduced to a mere intellectual contrast. Urbanism and ruralism are understood in terms of what in hermeneutics is called the intellectual gaze (Palmer 1969, 130–2). What is concealed by this gaze (and the categorization it generates) is the *experience of the meaning* of rurality/urbanism, as this is constituted by the reality definitions of a particular life-world. The dichotomy, because of its attempt to be empirically universal, renders invisible the particular assumptions of the modern life-world and, by so doing, suppresses the analytic focus of the urban-rural discourse. The implicit issue of evaluation and choice of community *and* of ways of understanding, an issue present in the discourse from Marx to Weber, is silenced by the dichotomous approach, thus theoretically compounding the factual concern with the disappearance of otherness, of rurality, from modern life.

This attempt to create unitary concepts repressed and negated differences within both urban and rural life: "The differences *between* entities ... are shown to be based on a repression of differences *within* entities, ways in which an entity differs from itself" (Barbara Johnson as quoted by Scott 1990, 137). Thus, empirically, the nature of intimate relations within the city and of alienated or fragmented relations in a rural setting, and analytically, the issues of otherness and resistance, are negated by Wirth's conception.[6] The analytic issues are condemned to leave their trace in his style.[7] The attempt to develop unitary concepts makes his work vulnerable both empirically and theoretically. Thus, this polar-type opposition cannot be relied upon to provide a conceptual framework for interpreting what Prairie Edgers say. Though Wirth's essay is considered to be one of the more influential essays in sociology, there is a seductive danger in relying on the apparent clarity of the polar-type opposition for research of this nature.

ROBERT REDFIELD: THE FOLK SOCIETY

Robert Redfield (1897–1958), an anthropologist strongly influenced by the Chicago School and the works of the classical sociologists Tonnies, Durkheim, and Maine, developed an ideal type, intended to be the polar opposite of Wirth's urban society, which he called the "folk society" (1947). Redfield based this model on extensive field-work in the Yucatan, Guatemala, and Mexico. He "comparatively studied contrasting cultures in Central America, ranging from rela-tively isolated small tribal villages to a large metropolitan city. The typology developed characterized the folk society as small, isolated, non-literate, and homogeneous and one that had a strong sense of solidarity and intimate communication and stressed the importance of familial relationships and stressed the sacredness of sanctions and institutions" (Hutter 1988, 41).

While Redfield's model was intended as the polar opposite of urban life, it is sometimes mistakenly taken to refer to rural society in its most extreme form (e.g., Hale 1990; Hutter 1988, 41; Dasgupta 1988, 9–11). Again, such an interpretation glosses over the difference between the urban-rural distinction of modern industrial societies and that of pre-industrialized societies. The urban-folk continuum endeavoured to develop a typology along which any actual society could be placed (a rural society in contemporary Canada, for exam-ple, would be more at the urban than the folk end of the continuum). Just as Wirth sought to develop a theory of the city that avoided "specific local or historically conditioned cultural influences," so Redfield sought to develop for the folk society an ideal-typical con-ception that would uncover what all folk societies, whether in Aus-tralia, Africa, North America, or Central America, have in common – "a type which contrasts with the society of the modern city" (293). Again, the particularity of place is irrelevant. In Redfield's time, a folk society in North America was not ordinarily a rural town or village but was more closely approximated by North American Indian societies; thus the key characteristic of Redfield's folk society is its isolation in time (non-literate, homogeneous) and in space (smallness of population). It is the polar opposite not just to the city but, as Redfield says, to the phenomenon of modernity itself.

On the basis of his research Redfield (1947, 193) concludes: "The personal and intimate life of the child in the family is extended, in the folk society, into the social world of the adult and even too into inanimate objects ... The individual finds himself fixed within a constellation of familial relationships ... All relations are personal ... originating in genealogical connection, extended outward into all relationships whatever. In this sense, the folk society is a familial society."

In the folk society, through genealogical connection (mothers, grandfathers, and ancestors who fuse into the myths of the group), the family becomes the way members come to know each other.

Identity, life purpose, occupation, education, and religious affiliation are all interrelated and integrated by virtue of the fact that the family organizes the horizon of possibilities for the members of this society. According to Redfield's conceptualization, this is a society that has no sense of what is other than family, and so folk and familial are intertwined.

While Redfield's folk society has many features similar to Tonnies's *gemeinschaft*, it differs as a sociological conception: it is primarily characterized by its isolation as an empirical other. (When the concepts of folk society and rural society are indiscriminately associated, then rural takes on the dominant meaning of isolation.) By virtue of this isolation, the question of whether a folk society is better or worse for child-rearing activities cannot make sense. From within the self-understanding of the folk society, family is all there is, and there is no alternative that is better or worse. The question of whether rural life is more conducive to child-rearing is a question that *only* makes sense to one who is aware of an alternative, that is, who can grasp the sense of otherness built into the urban-rural dichotomy. For the folk society, the sense of otherness is located in the fusion of nature with religion, and therefore it is not seen as an alternative and competing way of life. The latter sense of otherness is more specifically modern, in the sense that it is plausible to a modernized consciousness.[8]

FEAR, IRONY, AND
THE PROBLEM OF ENGAGING
OTHERNESS: A RADICAL
INTERPRETIVE PERSPECTIVE

As our narrative develops, it is becoming increasingly clear that understanding the concept of rural requires understanding modernity, which in turn requires understanding the structural changes that happen in society (capitalism, industrialization, urbanization) and the changes in the transformation in *consciousness* (Berger *et al.* 1973). The modern scientific perspective on the world is embedded in the urban-rural discourse in a way that shows the discourse to be in the grip of the very historical and cultural influences it seeks to make irrelevant. The discourse is historical and culturally specific, and it rests on an understanding of a dichotomy (or continuum), which even in the attempt to be empirically universal displays a culturally conditioned (i.e., scientific) and historically specific (modern western society) self-understanding. As the postmodern critique of modernist ethnography has argued, the use of a controlled social scientific discourse sought to make the culture of the other – the exotic – intelligible to an imperialistically inclined and culturally specific audience (the academy in the West). The authority of the ethnographer "involved an unquestioned claim to appear as the purveyor of truth in the text" (Clifford as cited in De Vries & McNab-De Vries 1991, 492) and, ironically, the hegemony of the scientific orientation to inquiry allowed such authority to go unquestioned.[9] Recognizing this cultural/historical dimension enables us to highlight ambiguities and tensions developing in this urban/rural discourse.

To understand folk societies Redfield uses scientific categories that make sense to a modern, urbanized, scientific constituency. As Giddens implies (1990, 19), this kind of thinking furthers the very modernity ("the emptying of space") such concepts sought merely to describe.[10] The actual ethnographies are only physically possible because the ethnographer comes from a heterogeneous, literate, large society. Unlike Redfield's account of the folk society, this society has an interest in what is other to itself (i.e., folk society) and can provide the means (i.e., transportation, communication, and most importantly, *the appropriate consciousness*) to collect data and information on that society. Thus, the very construction of the continuum has been described as ethnocentrically western (Hauser 1965, 195). That is, the kind of society that makes the generation of this conception of the folk society intelligible and reasonable in the first place is a modern, urbanized, and technological society, and thus what sociology needs in order to adequately take into account its own ground is a procedure that includes reflexivity. I argue that the phenomenological concept of life-world makes this inclusion possible.

The empirical and literal version of the interest in otherness demonstrates "the restless desire and power of the modern West to collect the world" (Clifford 1988, 196). It is therefore highly ironic that in the attempt to construct an image of what is other to a modern western society, this instance of the discourse constructs an image of folk society that is formulated as having *no* conception of the other. The irony lies in the recognition that such an image is the mirror opposite to itself: the theoretic distinctiveness of the conception of the folk society is precisely its indifference or its inability to engage otherness and question its limits. It is all the more ironic that this conception is constructed on the basis of extensive empirical field studies in other cultures. The other that is now engaged through this literal scientific description appears as a self who is indifferent to engaging the other. Is this not the danger modernist consciousness most fears? Gadamer's point (1975, 324) concerning the attempt of the human sciences to base knowledge on the objectivity of scientific procedures, and the further attempt to deny that this knowledge is influenced by historical circumstances, in reality demonstrates the power of the way the prejudices of culture and history "unconsciously" dominate the formulation. Instead of avoiding the influence of its own history, culture, and community, this scientific formulation can now be understood as ending up with an image of what it most fears about itself; the repressed has returned.

This analysis of the polar-type opposition approach to the urban-rural debate makes the research project not only complex and difficult but also intricate. While the polar types of urbanism-folk society are conceptually clear, there is a danger in relying on them for the analysis of this contemporary debate. As we will see in the next chapter, contemporary urbanism does not mirror Wirth's thesis, and contemporary rurality is far from being a folk society. Also, the debate about the superiority of one over the other is repressed by this form of conceptualization. Most of all, it is now clear how the concepts a researcher uses to analyse a situation can unwittingly end up being part of the situation they sought to describe. This recognition reminds us of the necessity as well as the importance of having "the courage to make the truth of our own presuppositions and the realm of our own goals into things that most deserve to be called into question" (Heidegger 1977, 116).

In terms of offering a conceptual base for assessing the claims of Prairie Edgers, or those of Torontonians considering moving to a small town, the folk society thesis is not applicable. Prairie Edge, like any town in North America or western Europe, is not an isolated culture. The preference for the small town is not a preference for a totally different and isolated setting, and the Torontonians who consider a rural move would not consider moving to a folk society. This tells us that the preference for rural child-rearing is not a preference for what is dramatically other to an urban way of living. It is a preference that has its place in a modernized consciousness. And while it is still possible for those who move from an urban to a rural setting (or vice versa) to experience some "culture shock," its effect is not like that of Carlos Casteneda meeting Don Juan but rather to extend the modern consciousness. Of course, this analysis of the folk society thesis means that the conceptual searching for a sociological meaning for the term "rural" must continue.

CHAPTER THREE

The Conceptual Predicament of the Urban-Rural Debate in Sociology

The urban-rural dichotomy and/or continuum has generated much debate within the social science tradition (Gans 1968; Pahl 1968). As a dichotomy it has been criticized as empirically irrelevant because no "two communities show as sharp a discontinuity as a 'rural' and an 'urban' community as implied by these typologies" (Dasgupta 1988, 8). As a continuum it has been seen as more of an obstacle than a help in research because it involves accepting "a false continuity" (Pahl 1968, 293) which in turn makes it difficult to recognize important and sharp discontinuities between communities.[1] Lastly, from a radical interpretive perspective, the whole notion of causal determinism, whether environmental, occupational, or otherwise, is suspect because the possibility of differential and unpredictable response to social conditions is largely excluded from focus. The "conditions of human existence ... can never 'explain' what we are or answer the question of who we are for the simple reason that they never condition us absolutely" (Arendt 1958, 11). The subjectively meaningful character of all social action (Weber 1947; Schutz 1962; Blum & McHugh 1984) requires that the sociologist not make the mistake of giving primacy to a deterministic external reality and so assume the human agent to be a passive puppet (Blumer 1969). The hermeneutic capacity inherent in the understanding of society recognizes *a priori* that a similar external condition allows for a variety of human responses and actions. For example, a dense living situation can lead to close-knit working-class communities (Young & Wilmott 1963) or to a "spirit of competition, aggrandizement and mutual exploitation" (Wirth 1938, 15). Density, of and by itself, does not and can not automatically determine any one particular social arrangement. Empirically discrediting Wirth's thesis merely confirms what the radical interpretive sociologist would have to assume on entering the field of study.

SOCIETAL DEVELOPMENTS,
EMPIRICAL RESEARCH,
AND THE INCREASING
IRRELEVANCE OF
THE DISTINCTION

Much empirical research has been done to test the conclusions drawn from Wirth's and Redfield's views of urban and rural life. This research has been reviewed in Canada by Sylvia Hale (1990) and in the United States by Mark Hutter (1988, 28–116). Drawing on work by S. Clark, P. Garigue, and P. MacGahan (amongst others), Hale (135) concludes, "the folk-urban thesis popularized by the Chicago School has largely been discredited. Rural communities are not uniformly or even generally characterized by the close-knit, integrated social life envisioned in the notion of the folk society. Neither do urban communities fit the image of shallow and detached associations between strangers. The three key factors [Wirth] of size, density, and heterogeneity do not turn out to be good predictors of the quality of community life."

That is, vital communities and strong family ties are both possible and actual in urban areas (MacGahan 1982); weak extended family ties and anomic social relations can and do exist in parts of rural Canada (Clark 1978). The urban-rural distinction, either as a continuum or a dichotomy has, therefore, not been particularly useful as a paradigm to use to "empirically predict" the quality of life of family or community. Hale (106–36) goes on to argue that the political-economy perspective of Marx and Tonnies and the feminist perspective of Smith (1987) in sociology both provide better theoretical frameworks to understand the quality of community life in contemporary Canada. By virtue of the influence of phenomenology, the methodology of the latter overlaps with that of radical interpretive sociology.[2] Hale also points to differences between Canadian and American cities. The former are more organized, better governed, less violent, and in general "more liveable" than their American counterparts. Canadian literature does not promote the glorification of the frontier and rejection of settled, "civilized" society that is a theme of American literature.[3] Rather, the city or town is seen as the site of safety in contrast to a dark and unpredictable nature.[4]

Hutter (1988) provides an historical account of the development of comparative family analysis as it relates to historical developments in western societies. For him the Wirth/Redfield typologies rest on "an essentially negative view of the city and urban life, particularly in regard to the family. This anti-urban bias tends to depict rural life as basically good, clean, and pure as opposed to the city, which is associated with social disorganization, decay, and filth" (Hutter 1988, 41). The comparison of urban industrial societies with rural agricultural societies on the basis of ideal types was (86) a "direct outgrowth of the anti-urban bias of sociologists in the nineteenth and early twentieth centuries. Their ideological biases were coupled with a strong distaste for emerging urban family forms." These included emphasis on individualism and freedom, the emergence of the nuclear family cut off from the claims of the wider kinship group, the decline of traditional hierarchy, and the rise of egalitarianism between the sexes, and marriage and family sustained by emotional attachments rather than community spirit or economic ties, and so on.

The urban-rural distinction was conceptualized in ideological rather than scientific terms and so distorted the very phenomenon (i.e., the family) it sought to investigate. As ideal types, urban and rural, despite (or perhaps because of) the attempt to be empirically universal, were conceptualized on the basis of fears of the consequences of the rapid growth and change the city was undergoing rather than a true understanding of those changes. That is, these urban-rural typologies can be understood in terms of fearful reactions to the historical changes society as a whole was undergoing, and so the Wirth/Redfield typologies become an *expression of* a societal change rather than a comprehension of those changes.

As Hale has done in Canada, Hutter (1988, 91–102) cites many studies of family relations in a variety of US cities that show that urban families are not isolated. Extended kin networks provided services and aid in a reciprocal exchange system. Sussman (1959, 340) concludes: "While these kin by no means replicate the 1890 model, the 1959 neolocal nuclear family is not completely atomistic but closely integrated within a network of mutual assistance and activity which can be described as an interdependent kin family system." Hutter, following Litwak (1960) and Sussman, contends that sociologists like Wirth failed to see the viability of urban kinship relationships because of the oversimplification of the ideal urban-rural typology.[5] Also, this typology makes invisible the way traditional (extended kin) families acted not as a resistance to modernization but, through adaptation, as agents of modernization (Hareven 1975). Differences in class and ethnicity were also ignored, which means that the ideal typology of the urban family is in actuality more a reflection of the middle-class values of privacy and individualism than a valid universal description of urban family life. In other words, the urban-rural typology ignored differences within the categories, and the opposition built into the typology became increasingly irrelevant with technological developments.

Hutter, like Hale in Canada, would appear to agree with Gans who argues that the urban-rural distinction, as dichotomy or continuum, is sociologically irrelevant. He might even go as far as Weber (1946, 363) in saying that a rural society no longer exists in western culture. Mass communication and mass transportation make this claim more plausible to the rural resident. Meyrowitz (1985, 146) notes that the "millions who watched the funeral of John F. Kennedy, the resignation of Richard Nixon, or the assassination of Anwar Sadat were in a 'place' that is no place at all ... More and more people are living in a national (or international) information system rather than a local town or city." At the time of this writing (1996), Prairie Edge residents have access to forty-four television channels, including a community channel, several pay-per-view channels, and channels from Detroit, Los Angeles, Boston, Vancouver, Spokane, New York, and, of course, Edmonton. Given this exposure, in what way is the urban-rural difference meaningful anymore?

Giddens further articulates this theme:

Even the smallest of neighborhood stores, for example, probably obtains its goods from all over the world. The local community is not a saturated environment of familiar, taken-for-granted meanings, but in some large part a locally-situated expression of distanciated relations. And everyone living in the different locales of modern societies is aware of this. Whatever security individuals experience as a result of the familiarity of place rests as much on stable forms of disembedded relations as upon the particularities of location (1990, 109).

Several examples particular to Prairie Edge illustrate this contemporary intertwining of the local and the global. Because of its location in Alberta, many local farmers and tradespeople developed expertise in the oil business. This often took them to work in places like Scotland, Japan, and Saudia Arabia. On the other hand, Prairie Edge has also been a centre for settling immigrant refugees from conflict-torn rural areas in other parts of the world. During the most active years of the program, in the late 1980s and early 1990s, a small number of refugees from Southeast Asia (Vietnam, Thailand, Cambodia) and Central America (Nicaragua, Guatemala, El Salvador) were settled in Prairie Edge. Thus, the community has locals who regularly work abroad and immigrant families from abroad who are now locals. A university also brings in newcomers.

Given these developments, what kind of distinctiveness can such a "rural" setting offer? Is it meaningful to use rural as a concept at all, given its connotations of isolation, homogeneity, tight-knit community, regressiveness, and so on? Perhaps the idea of the rural as "a great place to raise kids" is misleading and irrelevant. If so, then the so-called rural advantage does not exist at all, and this research project, as it has been initially conceived, is not just difficult and complex: it appears to be impossible.

This is precisely Ray Pahl's position. He (1969, 84–5) describes Britain as a society "where the majority of the population is *culturally* if not physically urbanized. Hence the *size* of settlement may not be a significant variable when people listen to the same radio and television programmes, read the same newspapers and consume the same amount of goods, no matter where they live." This is not to say that the distinction is demographically, administratively, or geographically irrelevant. Rather, sociologically and theoretically speaking, we return to a situation – ironically similar to the pre-modern theorizing – where the claim is made that "the city *is* society" (Westergaard, as quoted in Pahl 1968, 278). Pahl (1969, 293) thus concludes: "Any attempt to tie particular patterns of social relationships to specific geographical milieux is a singularly fruitless exercise."

Modernity, it seems, has through urbanization effectively silenced the challenge that the rural was understood to represent in the urban-rural discourse. Modernity also, it seems, refutes the perception of the rural as different and better. As I will show in chapter 5, scientific sociology is able to demonstrate that *in some ways* the perception of a rural advantage is mistaken. Yet I will show that *in some ways* the claim of scientific sociology regarding the irrelevance of the distinction also is mistaken.

The implications of the conclusions of Pahl and Gans for this project are clear. The preference for parenting in a rural setting is either "the product of an anti-urban ideology which is unfounded on empirical fact" (Pahl 1969, 85), or it may be a reflection of class and occupation and not the size of a settlement. That is,

business and professional people ... may value a small settlement or "rural society" since they think their wives and families may be able to feel members of a "community" more easily ... [But] this mobility through the countryside can be seen as an urban pattern – for the essence of the city, to a true urbanite, is choice. The true citizen is the one who can and does exercise choice, and only the middle and upper-class minority has the means and opportunity to choose: thus when the middle class extends itself from the city into the region then, in this respect, the city has extended itself into the metropolitan region (Pahl 1968, 271–3).

So according to Pahl, the parents I talked with who moved to Prairie Edge and who were either upper or lower middle-class are really extensions of the city, and the claims they make about their parenting in a rural setting are to be treated as "urban." Therefore, by defini-tion/theoretical orientation, whatever these people say about the rural setting is to "be seen as an urban pattern."

Because the city is being defined as "choice," choosing a rural set-ting has to be seen, according to Pahl, as essentially an urban phe-nomenon. Rurality and "rural" culture as an object that these people claim to be choosing cannot, by definition, exist. The idea that there could be an other that challenges/opposes/tempts the urbanized (modern) mind is not to be treated as real; rather, it is urbanism extend-ing itself. Pahl's description of "cosmopolitans" as "self-appointed guardians of tradition and rusticity *as they define it*" (1968, 274, my emphasis) shows that what matters is not the "rural" situation as such but rather the cosmopolitans' *definition* of it. That is, through their actions, the cosmopolitans show that they are not so much engaging an other as expressing themselves. Is this not a good example of the phenomenon of solipsism? Is such solipsism the fate of moder-nity (Bonner, 1994)? Is Pahl's claim that rural as a sociological desig-nation is "fruitless" – a claim bolstered by a science committed to verification – a neutral, "objective" description? Or is it, as Gadamer says of the process of understanding itself, a claim that, despite its scientific status, is influenced by history, culture, and community? If the latter is true, then who is mistaken about the question of rurality: the middle-class ex-urbanites who in choosing to live in a rural set-ting are merely expressing an urban pattern, or Pahl himself, because of his reliance on a univocal and essentialist conception of rurality?

Pahl offers a conceptual solution to the problem of deciding on the particular distinctiveness of parenting in a rural setting: in modern society, it has no distinctiveness, and in this conclusion Pahl has the support of empirical sociology. Accepting this solution (and there is a truth to it) means that the perceived difference between parenting in a rural and an urban setting is not real. Recall the Yerxa Research survey (1992, 15) cited in the opening pages of this book: "When asked which community was a better place to raise a family, a dra-matically [higher] percentage of rural respondents believed that a rural setting is a better place to raise a family (80.0%) … Urban respondents were more inclined to state that an urban or a rural setting would make no difference to raising a family." Given the difference in perception here, it seems (according to Pahl) that the urbanites are right: there is no difference between the urban and the rural in terms of raising a family. Yet the parents I talked with, including people like myself who had moved from a large urban setting, perceived a difference and perceived it to be positive. Is this perception a mirage?

The decisive question would now be: Why do rural residents conclude that the rural is better when there is really no difference? Accepting this solution by Pahl means that the direction of the research moves decisively away from evaluating the superiority of either the urban or rural setting for child-rearing towards trying to understand how a difference could be claimed in the first place, given the facts of the case. This research strategy will be pursued, addressed, and examined in chapter 5.

IDEOLOGY, SOCIOLOGY, AND THE CREATION OF KNOWLEDGE

Sim, the co-author of the classic study of suburbia, *Crestwood Heights*, in a passionate and prophetic report of the changes that have taken place in rural Canada (*Land and Community: Crisis in Canada's Countryside*, 1988), says (59):

I cannot accept the hypothesis of "no rural culture" ... Nor is it good enough to say life in the countryside is watered down urban life or some kind of unsatisfactory extension of the city. Even if this premise were acceptable, one would have to place it beside the well-recognized sub-cultures of the city: the inner city, suburbia, and the gentrified rebuilt sections ... Even if what I choose to call "rural" is an urban sub-culture, there are differences that need a label. "Rurban" has been suggested but seldom used. Urban life and rural life are still urban and rural despite their respective changes.

Sim levels the charge that the disappearance of the word "rural" deprives a large and important element of the country of a name (22). Though "fewer than four percent of Canadians live on farms ... about one-third of all Canadians live in the open country and in towns under 10,000 in population" (21–2). Statistics Canada uses the "absurd cut-off point of 1000 or a density of 400 persons per square kilometre. Thus, about one out of three Canadians are non-farm, non-metropolitan residents!" (22). Because "having a name is so important," Sim (22–3) continues, the disappearance of the word "rural" is a case of urban imperialism ... If nothing out there is deserving of a name then it becomes a place to play in, play with, override and destroy at will. This imperial view provides silent justification for the imposition of regional government on small communities, as well as the closing of rural schools, churches and hospitals ... Meanwhile the city, despite all of its attributes of high culture, despite the richness of resources, has not a counterbalancing influence to restrain its own destructive and colonizing force.

The relevance of Sim's polemic is reinforced by a look at the definition the Commission of European Communities gives to the countryside as "a buffer area and refuge for recreation ... vital to the general ecological equilibrium and ... assuming an increasingly important role as the most popular location for relaxation and leisure" (1988, 2, as quoted by Tovey 1992, 111). The rural is now merely a place for urbanites to have some recreation and relaxation; here, as a concept, the rural is no more than a theme park for urbanites "to play in, play with, override and destroy at will."

Sim's eloquent statement points to the dangerous political implications of Pahl's (1968) and Hutter's (1988) descriptions above. The charge of ideological bias (urban imperialism) is now turned on those who argue for the irrelevance of the urban-rural typology because of *its* ideological bias (anti-urban). The empirical literature describing the disappearance of a rural culture is seen not as a neutral description but rather an expression of urban imperialism. It seems that even the most rigorous empirical descriptions cannot escape the charge that history, culture, and community influence the way a phenomenon is recognized. The problem is that this influence is not understood to have the positive value it needs to have if, as Gadamer (1975) argues, it is to be productive for knowledge. Sim (1988) admits that there are theoretical problems in identifying a rural culture because Canada itself (like the United States, Britain, and most of western Europe) in its urban and rural settlements is a modernized society. "Yet," he says "those who come into a rural area to carry on their professions have no difficulty recognizing something distinctive about the new countryside" (60). In what way can the radical interpretive perspective introduce some light rather than heat into this argument?

Sim (1988) points to, but does not formulate, the problem that exists between the theoretical difficulty "in identifying a rural culture," and "those who ... have no difficulty recognizing something distinctive about the new countryside." As we have been arguing here, the theoretical problems are not technical ones of developing better survey techniques but rather epistemological and ontological. The interest of modern consciousness in engaging the other and in questioning its limits, which is the informing interest of the urban-rural discourse in sociology, *has become* theoretically difficult. But this is only so because of the dominance of a particular social science perspective and its own unacknowledged (i.e., unreflective) relation to the modern life-world. That is, the ontological and epistemological *limits* of the social sciences and their connection to the modern life-world, ironically, *have not been questioned*. This inability (indifference) on the part of the conventional social sciences to question their epistemological limits has led in turn to a blindness to even see, never mind engage, the other.

The rise of modernity and the rise of the (social) sciences are inextricably intertwined.[6] Far from being an "objective" perspective on historical and social developments, the sciences actually further a particular way of seeing, acting, and being in the world. This is not to say, as we shall see, that they have no relation to the truth. Rather, they uncover one aspect of the truth of an object, an aspect that is often taken to be the whole truth. Like all understanding, knowledge that the sciences create is part of the social and historical developments they purport to be "merely observing."

Wirth's attempt to "avoid identifying urbanism as a way of life with any specific locally or historically conditioned cultural influences" ends up being critically evaluated as an understanding based on an "anti-urban bias" which "tends to depict rural life as basically good, clean and pure as opposed to the city, which is associated with social organization, decay, and filth" (Hutter 1988, 41). The empirical conclusion of Pahl and Gans, that a "sociological definition of settlement cannot be formulated" generates the counter-charge from Sim of "urban imperialism." Despite the rigorous attempt to imitate the methodology of the natural sciences, it seems that Gadamer's claim "that the element of effective history is operative in all understanding" is demonstrated in this case. Recognizing the "truth" of the interrelation between understanding and culture therefore requires going beyond "the bounds of a science based on verification to ... a hermeneutic science [where] ... a certain measure of insight is indispensable" (Taylor 1977, 125–6). Of course, as Taylor remarks, this will be seen as a "scandalous" result for those with a particular conception of social science inquiry.[7]

What do the above developments mean for this project? It means that, as a sociologist, I cannot investigate the question of the preference of rural parenting in Prairie Edge without also recovering for examination the historical and cultural assumptions that structure our understanding of the question in the first place. One cannot recognize or inquire into the issue of the preference for "rural parenting" without letting the way this issue is already pre-structured by history and culture become manifest. What needs to be addressed is a more fundamental notion of the whole, which includes "the universe of what can be made objective by science" (Gadamer 1975, 218). That is, rather than privileging the epistemo-logical orientation of logical empiricism, and using that as the sole basis to evaluate the "truth" of everyday understandings, we need a notion of the world that allows both scientific and everyday understandings to emerge. Husserl calls this phenomenological concept of the world "'the life-world', i.e., the world in which we are immersed in the natural attitude that never becomes for us an object as such, but constitutes the pre-given basis of all experience. The world horizon is a pre-supposition of all science as well and is, therefore, more fundamental" (Gadamer 1975, 218). This concept of life-world enables the inquirer to more effectively preserve and develop the interest of the urban-rural discourse, question limits, and engage otherness.[8]

What the historical and conceptual analysis engaged in so far shows is that investigating the issue of the preference of a rural set-ting for parenting in any one case also requires a rigorous conceptual analysis. Otherwise, the researcher is in the difficult position of assuming a conception of the rural that is problematic, arbitrary, or even irrelevant. It is not that the various conceptions developed in the sociological discourse – elements of regressiveness (Marx), com-munity (Tonnies), narrowness (Simmel), tradition (Weber), integra-tion and smallness (Wirth), isolation (Redfield) and so on – are wrong. All of them belong to the notion and experience of the rural. There is also truth to the claim by Pahl and by urban residents that an urban or a rural setting would make no difference in raising a family. But privileging any one element over the other as the mean-ing of rurality has mystifying implications for the direction of this research project and the significance of the findings.

To give up on conceptual analysis is to give up on being able to set *any* direction for the project. One either takes the path of least resistance and goes along with the dominant research paradigm, or one declares oneself a conceptual agnostic. In either case, the surren-der of the ability to direct research in oriented ways is what the researcher who avoids this difficult groundwork of conceptual anal-ysis must sacrifice. On the other hand, engaging in this groundwork now requires that we use phenomenology to address a more funda-mental notion of the whole that allows for both everyday and scien-tific understandings.

PHENOMENOLOGY,
THE CONCEPT OF LIFE-WORLD,
AND THE PARTICULARITY OF
THE MODERN LIFE-WORLD

Phenomenology provides a way for my research to get past the charge and counter-charge of ideological bias; it enables this by first of all describing what is specific to modernity, to the idea of the rural in modernity, and to the *modern* family. Reflexivity (phenomenology) rather than the polar type opposition of Wirth is the procedure necessary if one is to get a sense of the historical and cultural forces surrounding us, and a sense of the influences pervading the meaning and use of the term "rural." Phenomenology allows the inquirer to bring into the open through language the modern assumptions that remain hidden and unseen within the modern scientific paradigm and modern everyday understandings.[9]

Modernization itself both brings with it and is made possible by a different way of experiencing self and other in the world. Whether in the form of capitalism, *gesellschaft*, the metropolis, or urbanization, this transformation in the relation between self and other has been an underlying concern and focus of the urban-rural discourse. What has been at issue all along is the modern life-world itself. Ironically, in order to engage otherness and question limits, a rigorous reflexive inquiry is needed.

In western society, modernization and the transformation of consciousness are simultaneous occurrences. We cannot understand the modern family and its relation to work and community without first of all recovering the particular understanding of the world that modernization both requires and nurtures. As this understanding is built into the very texture of the way we think and act with regard to conceptions like parents and children or urban and rural, understanding the relative merit of raising children in a rural setting now involves recovering *the presuppositions* that we as moderns bring to the meaning of family, and to the meaning of rural, which themselves are structured by the horizon of the modern life-world. We must now allow the issue of the nature of the modern life-world to come into our horizon and, in turn, seek to recover the way the very concern about the advantages of rural parenting reveals a modern interest.

What is the nature of the consciousness that conceptualizes both parenting and rural in these terms? When we addressed Redfield (1947), we discovered that the question of relative merit for parenting would be inconceivable to parents in a putative folk society; the parents would be unable (find it nonsensical) to evaluate themselves and their place in such a detached, self-interested, driven, and rational (i.e., means-end) way. By virtue of the way the folk members' pre-understanding (horizon) is organized, the issue of rural socialization would be seen as drastically implausible (Berger *et al.* 1973, 16), perhaps in much the same way a modern would respond to the claim that children should maintain active contact with their deceased ancestors.

Modern consciousness is based on an organization of knowledge (Berger *et al.* 1973, 3–41) that renders implausible the question of whether one should maintain contact with one's ancestors. Such a question would not be considered worthy of serious, rational investigation. Imagine, for instance, how moderns would respond to the claim that many dead great-grandfathers have communicated through dreams that children should be raised in a rural village. As moderns (whether scientists or common-sense members), we would have difficulty with the strangeness of the claim. The life-world pre-structures what is understood as intelligible and in this way influences the phenomena considered worthy of research in the first place. If in no other way, such pre-structuring shows the unavoidable influence of history and culture on social science research.

The obviousness of the meaning or, to use Garfinkel's (1967) terminology, the uninteresting and unremarkable intelligibility of the rural merit question is now a phenomenon for investigation in its own right. It reveals cultural (western) and historical (modernization) pre-understandings that control what we as researchers are able to recognize. Researchers in Canada are beginning to recognize (Hansen and Muszynski 1990, 4–5) that the sociological question of rural merit cannot be divorced from an examination of ontology. "Ontology draws our attention toward what binds together in a common situation researcher and researched alike" (Hansen and Muszynski 1990, 4).[10] In this case, the common situation of the researcher and the researched lies in the shared pre-understandings that ground the overwhelming obviousness hidden in the issue of rural merit.

Berger, Berger and Kellner (1973) in *The Homeless Mind: Modernization and Consciousness* show the way phenomenology helps bring these shared pre-understandings to light.[11] While I will have occasion to be critical of the limitations of their version of phenomenology, they do provide a clear description of the necessity to understand the concept of the *social life-world*. As phenomenology is not widely known in mainstream sociology, an extended quotation (63) about the meaning and importance of this concept is warranted:

To be human means to live in a world – that is, to live in a reality that is ordered and that gives sense to the business of living. It is this fundamental characteristic of human existence that the term "life-world" is intended to convey. This life-world is social in its origins and in its ongoing maintenance: the meaningful order it provides has been established collectively and is kept going by collective consent ... In order to understand fully the everyday reality of any human group, it is not enough to understand the particular symbols or interaction patterns of individual situations. One must also understand the overall structure of meaning within which these particular patterns and symbols are located and from which they derive their collectively shared significance. In other words an understanding of the social life-world is very important for the sociological analysis of concrete situations.

Berger and associates argue that "to understand fully the everyday reality" of any group, it is not enough to understand the "interaction patterns" and "particular symbols" of individual situations (e.g., locals, cosmopolitans, parents in a modern rural setting, etc.): "One must also understand *the overall structure of meaning* ... from which [symbols and interaction] derive their *collectively shared significance*" (my emphasis). This overall structure of meaning is called the social life-world. "It is this *Lebenswelt*, as Husserl calls it, within which, according to him, all scientific and even logical concepts exist" (Schutz 1977, 232):[12]

Any particular social life-world is constructed by the meanings of those who "inhabit" it. We call these meanings *reality definitions*. Whatever people experience as real in a given situation is the result of such definitions. They are of different types (some, for instance, are cognitive and refer to what *is*; others are normative and refer to what *ought to be*) and have different degrees of theoretical elaboration (as between the consciousness of the man in the street and that of the esteemed philosopher). What they all have in common, insofar as they are relevant to the sociology of knowledge, is that they are collectively adhered to.

The social life-world rests on meanings that constitute the reality of any given situation. These meanings are made up of definitions or assumptions, which give reality its particular character insofar as they are collectively adhered to. These constitutive assumptions found a community insofar as they embody shared ways of looking at and shared ways of being in the world. At this level of analysis the *ought* and the *is*, self and other, are intertwined. Berger *et al.* (1973, 12–13) give a particularly vivid example of how these definitions/assumptions structure the way meaning is constructed in any one interactional situation:

For example, there are meanings attached to bodily experiences. In many traditional societies such experiences are defined as resulting from the intervention of supernatural beings; in a modern society they are generally defined in terms of biological, chemical or sometimes psychological causes. Very different realities result from these definitions. For three successive nights, say, an individual has a nightmare involving his deceased grandfather, who forces him to eat large quantities of a revolting dish. The individual in a modern society might decide that he should desist from his new habit of eating heavy food for supper; alternatively, he might call his psychiatrist for an early appointment. The individual in a traditional society is more likely to wonder just what his grandfather is trying to tell him. The two realities differ cognitively, one includes the possibility of grandfathers coming back in this way, the other excludes it. They also differ normatively. One norm is, "You ought to live healthily"; the other, "you ought to stay in touch with your ancestors." Reality definitions are part of the consciousness of ordinary, barely educated or even illiterate people. They can also, however, be elaborated in very complicated theories, such as a biochemical theory of digestion, a psychoanalytical theory of dreams, and a cosmology in which the living and the dead continue to interact.

A life-world is decisive about what kinds of things are to count as real. The modern life-world, for example, excludes the possibility of grandfathers coming back from the dead and the living and the dead "in reality" continuing to interact. Recognizing these limits simultaneously requires recognizing the way the urbanism-folk society continuum is limited as a conceptual tool. In attempting to categorize all possible societies, it conceals the way *this conception* is grounded in particular reality definitions. In the process the otherness of a "traditional society" is lost by reducing its difference from modernity to one of degree. Because the "reality definitions/pre-understandings" of the modern life-world are unwittingly applied, the radical sense of otherness embodied in a different life-world is repressed. In this way it becomes understandable that the folk society construct ends up being the mirror image of modern social science. The other is quantitatively but not qualitatively different. The folk/rural/traditional is merely simpler/more primitive/more humane/more easygoing, etc., than modernity. It is not so different that our very way of understanding ourselves (and other) is challenged.

On the other hand, engaging the challenge of otherness is precisely the value of life-world analysis. By requiring that we be more "subjective" (i.e., recover through rigorous reflexivity the pre-understandings that structure what we moderns will even consider as real), it actually makes us more "objective" in our attempts to engage otherness. The task therefore is to recover the particular "reality definitions/pre-understandings" that are an essential limit (in the sense that it makes recognition of reality possible and structures that recognition along particular lines) of the social life-world of modernity.

According to Berger *et al.* (1973), what is specific to the experience of living in modern society is the *plurality of life-worlds.*[13] This is to say, the nature of the social life-world of modern western society involves experiencing the pluralization of life-worlds. Unlike premodern or folk societies, modern life is segmented not only in terms of observable social conduct but also in terms of level of consciousness. This pluralization of life-worlds, as constitutive of the life-world of modernity, means taking for granted that in our everyday experience we live in vastly different worlds of meaning. "A fundamental aspect of this pluralization is the dichotomy of the private and public spheres" (63)[14]: that is, the most important segmentation in modern life is between public and private life, the world of work and the world of family. The very question of the relative merit of rural child-rearing takes this dichotomy for granted. The claim is not for life as a whole but for that part of life having to do with child-rearing. Of necessity, the claim assumes that life can be divided into different parts (worlds).

Imagine the following responses, which would challenge the constitutive assumptions that structure the question about the merit of a rural setting for child-rearing[15]: "I can't answer that question because how can I separate what is good for child-rearing from an understanding of what is good as a whole?" "The question does not make sense because how can we ever know what is good for family? Nobody knows what is good for anybody because knowledge of the good is impossible." "Doesn't this question assume a freedom or a choice that fate or the gods do not allow?" "This interest in the question of a good place to raise children itself betrays a lack of loyalty to place and/or community." Imagine someone saying, "Your question is nonsense because the rural does not exist." All of these possible responses make the obvious intelligibility of the question a little more strange. They resist the tendency, nurtured by the modern life-world, to rush to find the answer and encourage a focus on the way the question already pre-structures the answer along certain lines.

We know from Simmel (1971) and Weber (1946) that pluralization is endemic to the experience of urban life. Berger *et al.* (1973) build on their work to link the "urbanization of consciousness" with the sociological understanding of mass communication. They argue (67) that it is the "city that has created the style of life (including styles of thinking, feeling, and generally experiencing reality) that is now the standard for the society at large. In this sense it is possible to be 'urbanized' while continuing to live in a small town or in a farm." Earlier Berger (1963, 17) argued that the "urbanization of consciousness" facilitates the development of a sociological consciousness. The inclination to step outside society's taken-for-granted routines, he says, "is more likely to take place in urban rather than rural cultures." Yet by virtue of the changes in communication that have taken place in the second half of the twentieth century, the thinking and feeling associated with urban cultures "is now standard for society at large."

For example, social and geographic mobility is "a background of knowledge" that the people in Prairie Edge bring to the issue of rural merit.[16] This horizon means that the claims made for the relative value of rural socialization have to be understood against the background of this social life-world (typically the life-world of readers of this document), that accepts that reality is pluralized. The claim for the advantage of rural child-rearing and the examination of the claim take place in a social life-world that at its very foundation assumes the plausibility of pluralized life-worlds. Instead of uncritically taking on this modern assumption, we need a perspective enabling us to recognize the way the assumption works to structure the discourse. I elaborate further on the nature of this "structuring" when I directly address the field material.

Phenomenologically speaking, the urban-rural difference is no longer "unspeakable" in a sociological sense. Rather, "rural" now becomes a way of referring to the experience of a life-world in the broader context of the pluralization of life-worlds. Determinism, whether of class, life-cycle, or settlement type, is not at issue here. Rather, parenting in a rural setting, against the background knowledge of other possible life-worlds, is the phenomenon we seek to understand. We will come to see that the decisive life-world that, in our case, structures how settlement is understood is the parental life-world; the urban-rural distinction is a relevant and "speakable" one within the context of the parental life-world. The modern parental life-world supplies the pre-understandings that allow the differences between urban and rural living to be recognized as real. Themes like spirit and reason, family and community, and *gesellschaft* and *gemeinschaft* will now be clarified, elaborated, and examined as these are relevant for the life-world of parenting, *recognizing that this life-world is established in explicit and implicit relation to the experience of a plurality of life-worlds.*

With the development of the concept of social life-world I now have a way of assessing both the claims made by Torontonians who consider it easier to raise children in a small town, and by parents in Prairie Edge who believe that a rural setting is better for raising a family. In a manner similar to grounded theory and overlapping considerably with feminist methodology (Smith 1987; Lentin 1993), the meaning of rural is developed through recovering the lived experience of ruralness in the context of the life-world of parenting. The concept of the social life-world allows the idea of place in "a great place to raise your kids" to be relevant for analysis because the standpoint that allows for the creation of knowledge is recovered. Humans are always in a place when they create knowledge, and understanding that place helps the researcher to get a perspective on the knowledge created.

As I show, from within the parental life-world, rural means safety, convenience, less anxiety, and appreciating the benefits of high visibility. How this meaning plays out in the relation between parenting and rurality remains to be established. But what is most important at this stage is that I now have a way of engaging the "data" about the merit of rural parenting in an oriented way. The connotations of rurality developed by Marx, Tonnies, Simmel, Weber, Wirth, Redfield, Hale, Hutter, and Pahl amongst others will continue to be relevant as this or that aspect of rurality is referred to. All of these meanings belong to the notion of rurality, though not all are equally useful for analysing the data. Rather, they become relevant when they promise to further the analysis of parenting and rurality within the master frame of the modern life-world. Thus, the analysis of Tonnies will help further the understanding of the parents who are parenting in the context of being close to an extended family (chapter 9); the analysis of Simmel will help further the understanding of the possibilities for community in the new rural community (chapter 10); Sim's description will aid in the development of the concept of the "new rurality" (chapter 6); and Wirth will help in the understanding of the relation between rurality and smallness (chapter 10). Marx's conceptualization will become relevant when I address the minority who did not agree with the claim, and Pahl's idea of urbanism and choice will be developed when the practice of consumerism is developed (chapter 9).

In other words, life-world analysis enables the researcher to recognize what taken-for-granted theoretic frame people are using when they claim to be perceiving real differences between an urban and a rural setting. Recovering this frame is the task of the researcher, and through such analysis he or she is now able to assess whether the other conceptions of the rural developed above are relevant and useful.

Conceptualizing (and analysing conceptualizations of) the rural has been important in three respects. First, it has demonstrated the danger of excluding reflexivity from sociological research. The urban-rural distinction as an oppositional dichotomy most clearly shows the conceptual dead end where sociology can find itself when reflexivity is rigorously excluded. Second, as a researcher I now have a way of engaging and assessing the claims of parents from Prairie Edge and from Toronto. The rural difference can become real when we recognize and recover the life-world that grounds the perception of difference. In this case, the concept of the rural is recovered from the data itself rather than artificially posited in advance. I talked with many parents who were ex-urbanites, and for them the rural setting made a real difference to raising a family. As will be developed, the relevant life-world grounding this recognition is the parental life-world. Third, with this life-world frame in perspective, the researcher now has a method for re-integrating the various conceptions of rurality examined in the first three chapters as appropriate to the analysis. My work of conceptualization has not only led to the solution of life-world analysis: it also enables me, when relevant, to carry forward and re-engage the conceptualizations of rurality by classic and contemporary sociologists. A directed and oriented research project is not only possible now: it has already begun.

The concept of the modern life-world allows the research and analysis to move to a different level. Later, we will come to see that the specific understanding of modernity displayed by Berger and associates reveals a particular relation to history and culture *that it has not itself grasped*. This is because the "phenomenological approach remains within the limits of the analysis of consciousness ... Language has not yet been understood as the web to whose threads subjects cling and through which they develop into subjects in the first place" (Habermas 1988, 116–17). That is, the interrelation of life-world analysis and language has yet to be explicitly developed (Blum and McHugh 1984, 31–59; Gadamer 1975, 345–449). As I will show, the recognition that "what we know about the world is possible only because we can think and speak meaningfully about the world" (Blum and McHugh 1984, 32) means that the pluralization of life-worlds is not absolute. We are not locked within separate and mutually exclusive life-worlds because language is the "web to whose threads" these life-worlds cling. Thus I will argue that, in order to understand more fully the question of the benefit of parenting in a rural setting, the analysis needs to take a hermeneutic and dialectical analytic turn.

Phenomenology, hermeneutics, and dialectical analysis draw on an epistemology very different from mainstream social science. I will be using concepts and frameworks from these traditions to help understand and assess the claims of parents concerning the advantage of a rural tradition. Just what this assessment looks like is the task of the next two chapters. For heuristic purposes I will contrast the radical interpretive approach to understanding and assessment with the more dominant social science methodology in order to make clear the specific kinds of insights that the former can bring about. Thus, I will take one aspect of the claims of parents – the importance of safety – and show the different ways science and the radical interpretive perspective test and assess this claim. In this case, the dominant conception of the rural is as "a safe place," and my interest is in understanding just what that claim means.

There are two consequences to my taking this approach. First, issues concerning our ways of seeing (perspective), ways of knowing (epistemology) and ways of being in the world (ontology) are at stake. This means that the argument is often compact, intricate, and intense. Fundamental and significant issues are at risk even in assessing a relatively mundane claim, and in the next section I demonstrate why this is the case. Second, because my own method is dialogic, the to-and-fro movement of the argument will at times seem to emphasize artificially the differences in approach between mainstream methodology and radical interpretive methodology. Yet the shared fundamental commitment to the creation of knowledge and the shared interest in having all claims tested and evaluated is also addressed.

Life-world analysis and the idea of the pluralization of life-worlds help advance my analysis to another level; we are now in a position to explicate the relation between science as itself a life-world and the everyday life-world of parenting in a rural setting. In turn, I will show what happens to the claims of both Prairie Edge parents and Toronto parents when they are tested and evaluated from within the perspective of a rigorous social science methodology. Up to now the perspective I have used to conceptualize rurality has been treated more as a resource than a topic. Now I begin to address the way radical interpretive sociology allows for the conclusions and insights developed in analysing the urban-rural debate in scholarship, and for insights into the claims of parents which a science constricted by the requirements of verification cannot by itself provide.

PART TWO

The Experience of Parents Regarding Safety: An Evaluation of Scientific and Interpretive Methodology

"It's Better Because It's Safer": Knowledge by Discovery and Knowledge by Interpretation

KNOWLEDGE BY DISCOVERY   The discovery mode is so prevalent in the natural and social sciences that it is often assumed to be the only appropriate route to knowledge, not just one possible avenue. This approach assumes that the world is outside the mind of the observer and lies in wait of discovery. Knowledge, in the discovery game, is something you "get" by "observing." The known is thus revealed to, or received by, the knower, leading to the label "the received view." The standard of good knowledge in the discovery mode is objective and accurate observation, making validity the primary criterion of adequacy.

KNOWLEDGE BY INTERPRETATION   For the interpretive scholar, knowledge cannot be discovered intact because reality is not independent of the human mind. Although a set of knowable events are assumed to exist, those events can be conceptualized in a variety of useful ways and can never be ascertained purely without the imposition of a set of concepts by the knower. Thus knowledge is a transactional product of the knower and the known. Different observers will see different things in the stream of events because they assign different meanings to those events and conceptualize them in different ways. What mediates between knower and known, then, is a perspective, and knowledge is always colored by that perspective. Objectivity as defined in the classical sciences, therefore, is not a very useful construct for the interpretivist.   Stephen Littlejohn, 1989

THE "SUBJECTIVE" APPROACH

Littlejohn summarizes Brian Fay's (1975) discussion of two different views on the creation of knowledge. With the benefit of part 1 behind us, we can see that these two approaches to the creation of knowledge (called here discovery and interpretation), themselves instance the "pluralization of life-worlds" constitutive of modernity. Mind, world, knowledge, and truth all have different meanings for the practitioners who take different "routes to knowledge" and are understood in different ways. Thus, the issue of how one tests claims to truth also interrelates with the informing interest of the urban-rural discourse; engaging otherness and questioning one's limits is no longer a matter of looking to a past now gone (Tonnies/Weber), or a future yet to come (Marx), or looking at a concrete pre-modern folk society without questioning the modern concepts we use to study such a society (Wirth/Redfield). In a real sense the investigators who, in Littlejohn's words, take different routes or avenues to knowledge could also be living in different worlds. Questions of theory and methodology are not divorced from questions of substance. That is, grounding the perspective taken in this investigation will be taken as an opportunity to engage the issue of the life-world of science, the everyday world of parenting in a rural setting, and the relation between these and the radical interpretive perspective.

This research was undertaken against the background of an experience of moving with my wife and children from a large urban centre to a more "rural" setting. The process of uprooting is stressful, and we as a family were ambivalent about the move. My wife and I enjoyed living and raising our children in Toronto, but we moved because of my work. As if to console us about the loss this kind of move represents, those who lived in this rural setting made persistent claims for the benefit it would offer to our parenting. Many people said, with confidence, "this is a good place to raise children." As a parent and as a sociologist who theorizes about parenting, I could not help but reflect on this claim while we went about adjusting to our new living circumstances.

The shock of the uprooting was of course greatest during the first year. With the help of my colleague Rod Michalko, it was decided to make the claim subject to a sociological investigation. Apart from drawing on the lived experience of the investigator/theorist, participation in the community being investigated and that "most sociological of sociological methods," the interview, were selected as the appropriate procedures. These are standard methodologies shared by the different strands within interpretive sociology.

Over the course of five years and in the process of going about my life as a parent, teacher, husband, social theorist, and member of the community, I informally and spontaneously discussed the claim with many people in this setting. This participation, and the perspective that emerged from it, provided the foundation for the more formal and artificial aspect of interpretive methodology – the recorded conversation. By the time I interviewed a selected group of parents, I had lived in Prairie Edge with my family for over three years. This enabled me to put my questions and their answers in perspective. The experience of participation in the community enabled me to be self-conscious about what Garfinkel calls the "irremedial" *ad hocing* that is part of any and all practical sociological inquiry. While from the *knowledge by discovery* paradigm (outlined by Littlejohn above) such *ad hoc* procedures are seen as flawed ways of doing social research, Garfinkel (1967, 18–24) shows that rigorous attempts to suppress such considerations, even in the most scientific type of social research (e.g., following a set of coding instructions), produces not objective findings but bewilderment on the part of the researcher (21). "*Ad hocing* is required if the researcher is to grasp the relevance of the instructions to the particular and actual situation they are intended to analyze" (22). Being a "socially competent member of the arrangement he seeks to assemble an account of" is a necessary resource of all social research (22).

Yet the prevalence of the knowledge by discovery paradigm is such that questions were raised by everyday members and professional colleagues about my procedures. How could one draw a more universal truth about this claim on the basis of my formal and informal conversations with members of this community? How were the parents to be selected? How was I going to control for the effects of class and life-cycle? From a statistical point of view, thirteen recorded conversations would be too small to yield reliable results. From a quantitative sociological perspective, the open-ended nature of the interviews and the informal nature of my contacts with others would make it impossible to quantify the results and thus risk making the conclusions seem impressionistic.

My own personal involvement in the question (I was, after all, a parent in a similar circumstance to many I talked with) seemed to make the whole investigation very subjective. One psychologist colleague, when he read of my procedure in a local newspaper, jokingly said that I should just interview myself – implying that the selection criteria and open-ended interview are mere elaborations of subjective experiences rather than a method for the evaluation of the truth of the claim. Another colleague, in physics, thought that there are so many variables to control for that it is virtually impossible to do a "real" "objective" study of this kind of issue. How was I going to control for both the researchers' and the participants' conscious and unconscious biases?

All of these types of questions take the authority of the knowledge by discovery paradigm for granted. As argued in the last chapter, modern science, despite its attempts to be neutral and detached, is tied culturally and historically to the modern society it seeks to understand. The discovery orientation therefore is a dominant theoretical paradigm that coheres well with the modern attitude of suspicion and scepticism displayed by ordinary members in this community. The paradigm is so prevalent that its authority is often assumed rather than demonstrated. Yet such questions point to fundamental issues about the nature of knowledge and truth. What are the grounds for a claim to universality? What is the authority that compels, forces, or otherwise persuades with regards to *any* knowledge generated by research and inquiry?

Littlejohn's summary of "knowledge by discovery" neatly, if a little simplistically, captures the epistemological assumptions grounding the approach that is "so prevalent in the natural and social sciences that it is often assumed to be the *only* appropriate route to knowledge, not just one possible avenue" (emphasis mine). His summary of "knowledge by interpretation" again neatly, if not simplistically (and, as stated at the end of the last chapter, with the *significant absence* of the acknowledgment of the interrelation of language and knowledge), condenses the recent complex and reflective developments in phenomenology, hermeneutics, and dialectical analysis – the configuration of which is here collected under the title of radical interpretive sociology.

We can see both from Littlejohn's summary of the knowledge by discovery orientation and the reaction of my colleagues that the choice of the radical interpretive perspective is contestable. The material and project could be (and most often is) approached from the discovery mode. Therefore, in the next two chapters I address and examine alternative ways of investigating, examining, and evaluating the rural advantage claim as my way of demonstrating the worth of the theoretical and methodological decisions made throughout the study. The issue here is the authority grounding the various perspectives that seek to discover the "truth value" in the rural claim. The sense of suspicion, scepticism, wonder, and irony that, in different ways underlie the various traditions in social inquiry will be addressed as they relate to the examination of this claim. Later, reference will be made to current conceptions of postmodernism, poststructuralism, and feminism as these promise to help or hinder the process of inquiry.

Littlejohn's summary of the knowledge by interpretation perspective makes explicit some of the theoretical assumptions already put to work in the conceptualization of rurality. In part 1, I made no attempt to distil from the writings of classical and contemporary sociologists an intact definition of the meaning of rurality. The multiple meanings the term conveys were not erased in order to develop an essentialist or unitary meaning of rurality but rather were articulated from the perspectives of different sociologists, and these perspectives, in turn, reflected (on) changes in societies. We saw that rurality was bound up with meanings of regressiveness, community, de-individualization, tradition, smallness, isolation, and, in the end, with the idea of a folk society, even as the way of life distinctive to a rural settlement in modern society was disappearing.

The urban-rural distinction, as typology or continuum, derives its shared significance from the "overall structure of meaning" that posits and actualizes the plurality of life-worlds. Phenomenologically speaking, the urban-rural difference does not fundamentally denote the influence of settlement on behaviour but rather is one example of the plurality of life-worlds in modernity. In this social life-world, it is reasonable to recognize everyday life as composed of different sectors with "vastly different and often severely discrepant worlds of meaning and experience" (Berger, Berger and Kellner 1973, 64). The whole discourse from Tonnies to Pahl is grounded on the assumption of the plurality of life-worlds: phenomenology merely helps us see this ground.

Similarly, when I come in part 3 to address and analyse the material (informal conversations, interviews, notes, personal reflections) that emerged from participation in one rural settlement, I will demonstrate that the question being investigated could only be adequately understood through a recovery of the "pre-understandings" built into the way the modern life-world is organized. Thus, I will show that understanding the claim for the advantage of a rural centre for child-rearing requires understanding the knower (i.e., the modern parent) who is in the grip of a modern "discourse." This knowledge does not exist independently of the knower, who, as he or she lives, comes to recognize what in particular makes the town advantageous for child-rearing.

In particular, and by virtue of the acceptance of the constitutive assumption that reality *is* pluralized, we recognize that *the parental life-world* is the specific mediating perspective between the knower and the known. For example, we will talk about a mother who, within the space of two years, changed her opinion about the town (i.e., from the opinion that it is bad for raising children to the opinion that it is good for raising children), and we will show that this change itself demonstrates the process of knowledge by interpretation. The experience of parenting a young child made it possible for her to recognize advantages such as safety, convenience, reduced parental anxiety, and high visibility that before were not "real" to her. Thus, in accord with recent developments in feminist ways of knowing (Stanley 1990), we will see that these issues of knowledge, truth-claims, and evaluation are not just concerns of the academy (i.e., of specialists) but are also bound up with everyday ways of being in the world (ontology).

TESTING THE CLAIM OF THE SAFETY FACTOR: KNOWLEDGE AND DEMONSTRATION

It's easier, speaking more of the safety factor … The [children] are very confident; this is their town and they run all over the place and feel very comfortable, and they know a lot of people by now.

So one way that the rural place is better than the city is because you feel safer. You feel that there's less harm that can happen to your children – we'll use the example of drugs.

So, I would say for that, we feel our children – I feel that our children had the opportunity to go to the public library from the time they were six by themselves, with a little bit of guidance, initially, from us. But we could let them go, and we just felt from the time that they left from our house, point A, 'till they got to the library, point B, there was a number of people that they would know along the way. Whether that makes them safer or not, I don't know, but for us, that's what we felt. So, we're much more low key.

Yeah, we wouldn't send them that distance in Vancouver.

They can be left alone without having to be watched constantly.

And I think it's harder here because you know more people and there would be more chances of your parents finding out the trouble you're in. Because in the city, I think you're more anonymous than you are here. My kids have a wild party, the neighbour's going to tell me, whereas in the city, the neighbours might not even notice, or care.

There's just, it's just a more secure feeling. And if they're out and it's starting to get dark, I'd be less fearful of them in Prairie Edge, much as I still want them home at dark.

I think that just might be a feeling, whether or not in fact it's true, too. And I think maybe sometimes in a smaller setting, we're lulled into a false sense of security. It can't happen here, so you don't take the necessary precautions, until it does happen and then you say, "How could it happen here?" But I don't know. More opportunity in the city because there's more people.

These statements are examples of a type of reason parents used to support their belief that raising children in a town in western Canada is better than doing so in the city: concern with safety and security. As we know from the Yerxa survey (1992), this belief is widely held. In that study, 81 per cent of small city/town residents "believed that a rural setting was better to raise a family" (15). "Moreover, there was a much stronger perception of personal safety in smaller communities than there was in Edmonton. On this facet of social living, rural people are more satisfied with their communities than are urban people" (24). Again, as we know already, it is also a popular image in the city: the *Globe and Mail* magazine *Toronto* (June 1990, 22–6) cited a poll of the Greater Toronto Area that concluded that "58% said that is was more difficult to raise a happy, well-balanced child in the city than in a small town" (23). In this same article many of those of those interviewed cited safety as an important reason for holding on to the belief. Thus, a rural setting is a great place to raise kids because it is a safe place to raise kids. Safety is one of the contemporary meanings that is emerging for rurality, and like all the other conceptualizations examined in the first three chapters, it stands in contrast to the meaning of the city (as dangerous). But is this association of rurality with safety true? Is it true that rural places are safer and that a rural centre is better *because* it is safer?

In asking these questions I am raising the issue of belief and knowledge and how to go about mediating between them. There are some, a minority according to the surveys cited here, who believe that the city is a better place to parent. These beliefs oppose each other. Which is true? Both? Neither? What is involved in testing the truth value of each?

The different paradigms described above have different ways of testing or evaluating the claim. For the radical interpreter, what counts as knowledge depends on the perspective that mediates between the knower and the known. In this case, we would ask how it is possible for the parents to say what they say. On the other hand, for the empirical knower, the statements of the parents are perceptions about an external reality. The issue here, therefore, is whether these statements are accurate. Is the small town safer than the city?

"The basic premise of most, and perhaps all, work conducted from this [discovery] perspective is that there is an *external reality*, and that science proceeds by discovering ever more accurately what this external reality is like. This is basically the 'correspondence theory of the truth' and it holds simply that something is true to the extent that it can be shown to correspond to what is otherwise known to be real." (Goldenberg 1992, 179–80, author's emphasis.) The discovery mode directly opposes the interpretive approach by its assumption of a unitary and external reality. It therefore cannot see itself as one avenue to knowledge amongst others. From the scientific perspective, the claim for rural advantage on the basis of the "safety factor" is either accurate or inaccurate: it corresponds to the external reality or it does not.

Between discovery and interpretation are affinities and sharp differences. Both share a deep commitment to establishing knowledge of the true and the real. Yet both have sharply different assumptions about the nature of reality and, in turn, different methods for establishing knowledge about reality. On what basis does one choose between these? Empirical procedures are so prevalent that choosing this research mode would generate the least amount of disagreement in the majority of scientific journals. But the mere prevalence of the belief in the advantage for rural child-rearing does not make that belief true. Both paradigms resist the idea that saying something makes it so; both make an essential place for the work of the theorist/inquirer in establishing the truth of a claim: this is the fundamental ground that both paradigms share. Knowledge of what is true is not arrived at arbitrarily or idiosyncratically. Both paradigms agree that claims to knowledge must be tested if they are to be accepted as knowledge. Both also agree that the testing involves some kind of procedure that is shared among a community of scholars.

Where they differ, in significant ways, is in the meaning and nature of the work of establishing knowledge and what this work means for the relation between belief, knowledge, and truth. How is this difference to be mediated? Given the marked epistemological differences in the assumptions of the paradigms about the nature of reality and truth, we cannot rely on the hope that one paradigm will be "objectively" proven to be correct. That is a hope which rests on, rather than questions, the discovery paradigm.

To restate: both perspectives subscribe to the idea that the truth of something has to be tested or demonstrated rather than asserted. Both agree that impression, guesswork, and speculation by themselves are not enough: there has to be some kind of "proof." Thus, despite the decisive differences in approach, it is important to remember this fundamental agreement. Truth is that which needs to be worked out, needs to be established. The difference between a belief and knowledge is that knowledge needs the work of the inquirer to bring it into being, just as the different conceptions of rurality needed the work of different theorists such as Marx, Weber, Simmel, Tonnies, and so on. *Where they divide is on what counts as demonstration.* For the discovery mode, a belief is rejected when, using strict criteria, it is demonstrated that it does not correspond to some kind of verifiable external reality. Thus what parents say about the safety factor of the rural setting is either accurate or inaccurate.

In order to assess their accuracy, members' claims have to be translated into quantifiable and measurable data. Results of such investigations can and for the most part are presented in mathematical or percentage terms. On the other hand, for the radical interpretive sociologist, the members who make such claims are themselves treated as inquirers. The voice of the member is therefore retained. In the above quotations, while there is a motif of safety, members express themselves differently, in a way that reflects their particularity. The issues for radical interpretive inquiry are: What are the parents saying when they make the above claims? What are the grounds parents use to make claims about safety? Are these grounds worth holding on to? Developing a response to these questions requires working with the recognition that the researcher and what is being researched share a world. Parenthetically, this is another important overlap between feminist methodology and radical interpretive methodology.

The critiques of positivism from symbolic interactionism (Blumer 1969), phenomenology (Garfinkel 1967; Schutz 1962), ordinary language philosophy (Winch 1977), critical theory (Habermas 1988), hermeneutics (Gadamer 1975; Taylor 1977), dialectical analysis (McHugh 1971; Blum 1971; Blum & McHugh 1984) and the feminism of Smith (1987) and Stanley (1990) are well established. I have already demonstrated the arguments against positivism, and it is unnecessary to rehearse these in any detailed way. Summarily, they run as follows:

1 The understanding of meaning is central to the task of social inquiry (Weber 1947).
2 Members of society are agents as well as subjects; thus meaning is made as well as received (Blumer 1969).
3 Social understanding involves "grasping the point or meaning of what is being said or done and thus an effort far removed from the world of statistics and causal laws and closer to the realm of discourse" (Winch, as cited in Dallmayr & McCarthy 1977, 8).
4 Meaning cannot be articulated without recourse to language or to a shared pool of signification. Even empirical reality cannot be observed without recourse to an adequate conceptual and linguistic framework (Dallmayr & McCarthy 1977, 7).
5 The notion of life-world shows there is a foundation that the external reality of the discovery paradigm rests on but does not explicate (Schutz 1977; Berger et al. 1973).

6 Understanding is not one human characteristic among many but is
  rather a constituent element of being in the world. It is influenced
  by history, culture, and community even, and most especially,
  when claiming to be outside and above history and community.
  What appears as real, therefore, is what is allowed to appear by
  virtue of the epistemological and ontological assumptions one
  makes. This is as true of the discovery or scientific paradigm as it
  is of the interpretive paradigm (Gadamer 1975; Palmer 1969).

While I will address the important differences within the interpretive tradition, all of the above arguments bring us to the recognition
that the so-called "external reality" is itself a transactional product of
a particular kind of knower. The discovery mode, as an epistemology, is therefore flawed *on its own terms because it cannot adequately
account for its own relation to establishing knowledge.* At the very least
this means that the assumption that it is "the only appropriate route
to knowledge" is seriously undermined. Thus, one way to choose
between the modes is to take seriously the criticisms that empiricism
does not and cannot do what it says it is doing (observe an external
reality) because it is itself an interpretation. The claim that the findings correspond to an external reality and the procedures used to
generate these claims are necessarily and integrally related to each
other, because scientific knowledge is a transactional product of a
knower/known relation.

At this point the social inquirer would have satisfied for himself
or herself the reason for choosing the interpretive perspective: it has
more coherence in that what it says about the world (i.e., it is not
independent of our consciousness), and its own method (doing
interpretation) and what it actually does (interpretation) do not con-
tradict each other. The task would then be to get on with the investigation, while being explicit about the procedures used to establish
the conclusions. This is essentially what ethnomethodologists do,
and they justify this because, in the words of Sharrock and Anderson (1986, 17), "to carry on with established procedures even though
one recognised they were inadequate by their own standards, would
be an example of bad faith because it would be rejection of scholarly
standards."

As McHugh (1971, 332–3) summarized, "nothing – no object, event
or circumstance – determines its own status as truth, either to the
scientist or to science. No sign automatically attaches a referent, no
fact speaks for itself, no proposition for its value ... Truth is completely and deeply a procedural affair, and that is the way claims to
truth are conceded." As a consequence of this recognition, theory

and method are unable to stand apart because a theory about reality as external is itself a claim to truth (rather than "the" truth) that has been asserted/established according to specific procedures.[1] Recognizing the criticisms outlined above means that it "will be no longer possible to carry on with sociological investigations and theorizing in the same way. To do so, to close one's eyes and ignore the problem would be an act of bad faith. We would have sacrificed the scholarly standards of the discipline in favor of an easy life" (Sharrock and Anderson, 13).

Does this mean that the discovery mode is inaccurate? To say this is surely to accept the "scientific" assumption that knowledge is intact and validity the primary criterion of adequacy. The fact that its theory and its methods do not cohere well does not prevent the discovery mode from being productive: rather, it needs to be examined as a powerful and persuasive perspective. To dismiss it as epistemologically inadequate would be to ignore the multidimensional character of reality and language and thus ignore the contribution discovery procedures provide to our understanding of one dimension of reality. To this extent there is a deception built into Littlejohn's outline of the different paradigms: the way they have been presented fosters an impression that the paradigms are mutually exclusive. Yet to pursue the interpretive paradigm to its logical conclusion or, to put it another way, to include the idea that "language is the medium in which consciousness and the world are joined" (Gadamer 1986, 3), means that the *discovery paradigm is one way of conceptualizing and assigning meanings to events*. It is a disciplined, if dominant, subset of the interpretive paradigm.

In turn, this "subset" status means that as a perspective it has to be evaluated in relation to what it enables us to understand and what it prevents us from understanding. This is the basis on which any and all perspectives need to be evaluated. Rather than doing ideological rejection or critique, one needs to evaluate a perspective on the basis of its ability to move us (inquirers/readers) closer to a shareable understanding of the truth. While the "discovery mode seeks to eliminate 'incorrect' versions of reality, interpretive scholarship seeks to identify the powers and limits of various interpretations" (Littlejohn 1989, 9).

The discovery mode, *as itself an interpretation*, should enable us to understand, recognize, and "see" one aspect of the truth of the claim that rural parenting is better for reasons of safety. For example, is it accurate to say that small towns are safer? It would certainly be useful to know whether this claim is correct, but it also follows that strict positivistic procedures will be blind to other aspects of the truth of this claim. For example, it would be useful to know just what parents mean when they mention safety – and this requires interpretation. Therefore, my questions are: What are the powers and limits of the mode of inquiry oriented by the discovery paradigm? What aspects of the truth of the parental claim does the discovery mode bring to light? In what way in particular does radical interpretive sociology bring us to the recognition of other aspects of the truth of the claim? In other words, if the discovery mode is the interlocutor for knowledge by interpretation, the latter is required to engage this otherness in a way that allows the researcher to question and understand limits.

In the next chapter I apply both paradigms to the association of rurality with safety and in the process show what the different ways of knowing mean for practical research and for being in the world.

CHAPTER FIVE

Hope, Fear, and Safety: A Problem for Parents and a Problem for Understanding

SMALLER COMMUNITIES ARE NOT NECESSARILY SAFER PLACES

We will not be far off if we see sociological thought as part of what
Nietzsche called "the art of mistrust" ... [W]ith the beginning of the
modern era in the West, this form of consciousness intensifies, becomes
concentrated and systematized ... [it] marks the thought of an increasing
number of perceptive men   Peter Berger, 1963

What are the powers and limitations of the perspective that would
treat the claim for rural advantage on the basis of safety as an observation of an independent reality? That is, what are the strengths and
limitations of treating the parents' statement about the safety factor
of the small town as itself a perception or observation? In this case,
the parents would be understood to be making an objective statement about the reality of safety in small towns, and the issue is
whether such a statement corresponds with the reality of small
towns. To be accepted, such a statement should hold true regardless
of who the speaker is.

In the positivistic tradition, if the observation is true (read accurate), then it should be possible for anybody to make the same observation. The standard of true speech for science is *anybody* (Garfinkel
1967, 262–83; McHugh *et al.* 1974) and the parents' observations are
successfully accepted as representing a claim to truth if they are seen
to adequately represent anybody, i.e., if their observations "can be
agreed upon by others, regardless of differences in their backgrounds" (Goldenberg 1992, 26). Of course, as these parents (like
everybody) are particular (male / female, parent, ex-urbanite, middle-

class, etc.), science needs complex procedures to establish the validity (accuracy) and reliability (repeatability) of the claim (Goldenberg 1992, 92–114). If one speaks analytically, these are procedures for transforming what *somebody* says into something that *anybody* could say. What the parents from Toronto or from Prairie Edge say about safety should be true for anybody – thus the enormous effort that goes into ensuring that the conclusion drawn from such research is the only possible one, that there is no possible alternative.

From the perspective of the discovery mode, the reality of the safety of the rural setting is understood to exist independently of what is observed, and the issue is then whether these parents have observed accurately. Complex procedures exist to establish the accuracy of the observation because of the problem of bias, favouritism, and prejudice. That is, our senses alone without an adequate procedure might mislead us. For instance, it could be claimed that all those interviewed are suspect observers because they have a stake in the statement: they are themselves raising children in a rural setting and thus have a self-interest in seeing their own parenting practices affirmed. After all, if they observed otherwise, i.e., a rural setting is bad for child-rearing, then it would mean acknowledging failure or at least difficulty in their own parenting practices. Feelings of local pride could also be unconsciously influencing what they say.

In my own experience, local pride was not an issue, yet I had a sense that parenting was easier in Prairie Edge than in Toronto. I did not really know why, and I didn't know if "easier" was "better" – thus one of the reasons for this study. But without the rigorous application of verification procedures, might not my own sense bias and corrupt the whole study? Should I not be suspicious of this influence? Prairie Edge parents and I could be rationalizing rather than observing. The discovery mode therefore requires that disciplined researchers treat any and all claims to truth with suspicion.

This is the "art of mistrust" to which Berger refers, and, as he states, it is an art not only symptomatic of science but of modernity itself. Science is the mode of knowing that most coheres with the modern temper. Both science and the modern way of being in the world intensify, concentrate, and systematize the art of mistrust, or what has now come to be called the hermeneutics of suspicion. What we need to understand is the ground for privileging the art of mistrust. As a way of investigating and recovering this ground, I will use as a case study the approach Patricia Davies in the *Globe and Mail* article referred to earlier takes to the claims of Torontonians that the city is bad (not safe) for child-rearing.

Davies (June 1990, 22–6) cites the results of a poll of the Greater Toronto area where "58% said it was more difficult to raise a happy, well-balanced child in the city than in a small town, and a surprising half of those surveyed have considered packing up and moving." Rather than take what these Torontonians say at face value, Davies evaluates (24) what they say against statistical indicators that purport to measure safety. She finds that the majority of Torontonians are mistaken: "In fact, Torontonians are less likely to be victims of crime than people in many smaller cities and towns. Our kids are taking fewer drugs and staying in school longer."

In stating these facts about the relative safety of Toronto, Davies is agreeing with conclusions drawn by other sociologists. For example, the sociologist Sylvia Hale (1990, 120) notes, "Smaller communities are not necessarily safer places than big cities. The per capita incidence of crime may actually be higher in small towns than in cities … In the same vein, a report of the Advisory Council on the Status of Women indicates that the incidence of wife battery is as high in rural areas as it is in cities." Again, in a study cited in the introduction, rural youth in the United States were found to be more inclined to be involved in categories such as substance abuse, suicide attempt, child abuse, poverty, illiteracy, and involvement with crime than their urban counterparts (Helge 1990). Helge too says (3), "the images of rural children leading wholesome, trouble-free lives compared with youth in more crowded settings may be in need of revision."

The discovery paradigm has a method for distinguishing between a rationalization and an observation. Through its rigorous measuring procedures, the claims of parents for the virtue of rural safety are measured against observations that "can be agreed upon by others regardless of differences in their backgrounds" (Goldenberg 1992, 26). In this case, what such testing procedures produce is knowledge that does not confirm the claims about rural safety. That is, *anybody* who looks at the urban-rural difference (in terms of the incidence of crime) objectively will find there is no real difference. In fact, the "per capita incidence of crime may actually be higher in small towns than in cities" (Hale 1990, 120).

Because the objective facts of the situation are observations that could be made by anybody, the rhetoric of science is always the rhetoric of anonymous facts ("studies show that …" "research shows that …"). It is the rhetoric of what anybody could say. The complex procedures of science are therefore methods for transforming what is a truth for somebody (particularity) into a truth for anybody (generalization). Thus, anybody should be able to assert the facts about safety in Toronto because the methods by which these facts are generated are oriented toward meeting the requirement of what anybody could say.

While the above studies are generalizations and therefore not true of every single rural centre,[1] Davies argues that those Torontonians who generally believe small communities to be safer than large cities are not doing so from accurate observation. They are misperceiving rather than perceiving the "external reality." As she says, "there appears to be a perceptual problem," because these city residents are unable to observe the truth of the relative safety of their own environment. "Why do so many parents worry that city life is a threat to their family's mental and physical health when the indicators suggest that Toronto is not a bad place at all" (26), she asks. Davies wants to go beyond merely correcting the parents who have perceptual problems to understand the source or cause of the perceptual problem, because not everyone, herself included, misperceives the "external reality." "I have to admit flat out I'm part of the [42] per cent that isn't feeling … paranoia about the city. I rather like raising my kids here" (24), she writes. That is, she, like a minority of other parents, observes more accurately the reality of city life. Because there is only one truth, one reality, and some accurately observe this reality while others do not, Davies wants to understand why it is that so many (58 per cent) are unable to perceive properly. Where would one go for such an explanation but to another scientific expert, a psychiatrist? Davies consults Saul Levine, head of psychiatry at Sunnybrook Hospital in Toronto. He says: "Parents want to believe so badly that there is a better, simpler way of life … The gut level reaction is to think that smaller is better, that in small towns you can recreate a perceived golden age of old-time values" (24). Davies goes on to note that "Levine has been counselling adolescents for 20 years, and finds no evidence from any study done anywhere in the world to support the idea that rolling rural fields mean happy children" (20).

With Levine's contribution it seems we have solid reasons to be suspicious of claims that parents, as members of society, make for the benefit of rural child-rearing. Not only are these Torontonians mistaken about the relative safety of their own city but they are drawing on "a perceived golden age of old-time values," a perception that is not true to the past or to contemporary rural life. (Hale [1990], in her review of the research on the difference in quality of life between urban and rural settings in Canada, comes to the same conclusion.) Confirming Davies's findings on the relative safety of Toronto, Levine adds decisively that he knows of "no research done anywhere in the world to support the idea that rolling rural fields mean happy children." Apart from the way the concern with safety has been displaced with a concern for happy children and the way rural is equated with rolling fields, we have here a clear example of the way knowledge is established by science. It would appear that the "art of mistrust" that scientific research requires is justified. The claim to rural advantage is, after all, a myth; it reflects a prejudice rather than accurate observation or clear thinking. As Levine says, the claim is based on "a gut level" reaction, on a bias toward the image (hope) that "smaller is better." In the epilogue, the reader will find a description of a shooting incident involving our youngest child that on the surface seems ironically to underline this conclusion.

All of this would now seem to warrant a similar suspicion and doubt towards the claim of Prairie Edge parents. Like the misperceiving Torontonians, they may be justifying or rationalizing their choice to live in the country. The discovery mode, which privileges suspicion, doubt, and mistrust, now seems to be the best way of assessing truth claims, unlike the radical interpretive perspective that privileges the art of thinking and dialogue developed through the method of question and answer. My decision to use the latter rather than the former approach could now be seen as, at the least, calling into question the conclusions and interpretations based on the claims parents make about their own parenting situation.

The suspicion that leads to this kind of testing is part of the admirable rigour of empiricism. When I present aspects of this study in my classes, or to various volunteer organizations in the local community, these kind of findings tend to be appropriately startling. Rural residents as a rule cannot believe that, in general, there is no real difference in the crime rate between urban and rural centres. When these factual conclusions are put to them, they are surprised to the point of shock, and they wonder then about their own ability to make sense of their environment. As one student said, "Does this mean that we are all stupid?" I have found the conclusions established through discovery procedures to be very useful in getting people to start questioning their taken-for-granted assumptions.

Let me, however, remind the reader of the irony involved in the procedure I am using here. If the radical interpretive perspective privileges the art of thinking developed in the "to and fro" of dialectical conversation, then this "to and fro" is the way the discovery mode must itself be engaged by the radical interpretive researcher. That is to say, I am now in the process of uncovering the powers (and limitations) of the discovery perspective. While the strength of the scientific approach is now beginning to emerge, we are still in the middle of the "to and fro" of dialectic. We now see that the art (mistrust) that science privileges by its method is not arbitrary but a solution to a problem. The problem is that people arrive at conclusions about (for instance) the benefit of rural child-rearing because of a desire or hope for a particular truth. The Torontonian parents arrived at the conclusion that a rural setting is better because that is what they hope is true. Similarly it could be said that the Prairie Edge parents want to believe that parenting is better in Prairie Edge, because that is what they want to believe. Some parents are aware of this possibility, as the final quotation at the beginning of chapter 4 shows. This parent says, "Maybe sometimes in a smaller setting, we're lulled into a false sense of security." She is aware that the sense of security "might just be a feeling," that it might not "in fact" be "true."

While Levine's account for the failure of people to perceive reality accurately is colloquial, it is in essence similar to Francis Bacon's famous critique of the prejudices. In particular, it points to elements in human experience "that are not related teleologically to the goal of science, as for example, when among the *idola tribus*, Bacon speaks of the tendency of the human mind always to remember what is positive and forget all negative instances" (Gadamer 1975, 313). That is, what we are dealing with here is the suspicion that the senses of the body and the faculties of the mind do not automatically lead us to the truth. A desire for a better life led parents to think that smaller is better – in Bacon's terms, to forget what is negative about smaller communities and to "recreate a perceived golden age of old time values." Science provides a procedure that seeks to prevent, as much as possible, this tendency of the human mind.

The method of science makes use of the idea that in everyday life "we generalize on the basis of chance encounters and, if we encounter no contrary instance, we pronounce it valid" (Gadamer 1975, 312). The mind, by virtue of hopes, tends to soar, to develop conclusions that are over-hasty. In the case of the misperceiving Torontonians, the frenetic pace of city life in the 1990s tempts them to generalize that small town life is better, because it is simpler. The hope for a better (i.e., simpler) life is projected onto the image of the small town, not because that image reflects the true reality of small-town life but rather because the image reflects what the Torontonians hope for.

A similar process may be happening with parents in rural settings. The centres of mass media are concentrated in large metropolitan settings; these media give a lot of attention to crime, especially when it involves murder or kidnapping of young children. And where a metropolitan resident may know the area where the crime was committed and not be especially surprised, a rural resident who sees the same news on television may not know the difference between urban areas and associate the crime with the city in general. Rural residents therefore conclude that a rural setting must be comparatively safer – a conclusion more reflective of a fear of what may be happening in the city than reflective of true or accurate observation. Thus, as my earlier analysis of the urban-rural discourse shows, sometimes our generalizations about an object (e.g., *gemeinschaft*) say more about our own hopes and fears than they do about the object of analysis. What applies to the formulation of Tonnies and Wirth is now also true for the everyday member.

The scientific method is therefore a solution to the problem of preventing our hopes and fears from interfering with the understanding of the truth. While the experiment, technically speaking, is done to isolate conditions in order to make them capable of measurement, it is essentially a way of directing the mind in order to prevent it from "indulging in overhasty generalizations, consciously confronting it with the most remote ... instances, so that it may learn in a gradual and continuous way" (Gadamer 1975, 312). Scientific method is therefore a solution to the problem that our observations and generalizations can often be based on hopes and fears rather than perceptions. Scientific procedure is an oriented response to the fear that knowledge about what is true is not knowledge at all but mere prejudice based on a tendency to draw too-hasty conclusions. This tendency, which is built into the very way the human mind works, justifies the attitude of suspicion and mistrust toward all common-sense claims.

Something fundamental concerning the movement of how humans experience the truth begins to emerge: that is, recognizing the truth of reality requires *a willingness to be open to the resistance that the truth offers*. If in part 1 we came to recognize the modern interest in engaging otherness and questioning limits as the interest that structures the urban-rural discourse, we can now also recognize that such an interest is required for the pursuit of the truth. The human experience of truth is itself an engagement of resistance in relation to hopes and fears. Being open to the truth involves us in the discipline of self-formation (Gadamer 1975, 10–19) as we engage the resistance to our hopes and fears. The seeker of the truth about social life needs, as a condition of this project of seeking, to develop ways to be open to the "turning around," the shock or *aporia* that an understanding of the truth of the real requires. It is for this reason that I have found the scientific perspective and the knowledge that this perspective creates to be pedagogically useful in disturbing taken-for-granted thinking. The student who asks, "Does this mean we [rural residents] are all stupid?" can now be understood as perplexed or shocked. With the benefit of such research, I can now show that there has to be more to the claims about safety than one would first assume. Truth-seeking is not about confirming or denying sense impressions but about nurturing the desire for truth-seeking in the first place. The conclusions generated by the discovery perspective help here.

The scientific method can be appreciated not merely as a procedure for developing a substantive body of knowledge about any particular phenomenon but as illustrating a fundamental step involved in the human experience of truth-seeking. The method of science represents a commitment to accepting what the method establishes as true despite the hopes and fears that we as humans necessarily harbour concerning the truth. Science requires that the researcher be committed to the scientific procedure as its way of forcing the truth-seekers to resist being beguiled by hopes and fears. The scientific truth-seeker therefore agrees to accept only what the scientific method allows. Davies and Levine can confidently assert the truth of the relative safety and benefit of city child-rearing because this is the truth that emerges through the application of scientific procedures.

However, there is more to the truth here than these procedures allow. Before recovering that more, I will describe and analyse the life-world of science to show why modern science is able to throw light on only one aspect of the truth of this matter. This requires that I deal with some intense theoretic material.

SUBJECTISM AND SCIENCE'S WAY OF BEING IN THE WORLD

This understanding of the purpose of the scientific method brings us to an ironic insight about the relation between science and truth. For Arendt (1958, 273–86), the simultaneous development of science and modernity, both collected by the emphasis on mistrust and scepticism, gave rise to a consequential alienation from the world. Neither the human mind (thinking) nor the senses (observation) could by themselves be trusted to arrive at a shareable understanding of the truth. Just as our eyes deceive us about the sun going around the earth, so does our mind tend to arrive at conclusions based on our hopes and fears. Where before the rise of modern science "truth had resided in the kind of 'theory' [that] meant the contemplative glance of the beholder who was concerned with, and received, the reality opening up before him, the question of success took over and the test of theory became a 'practical' one – whether or not it will work. Theory became hypothesis, and the standard of the hypothesis became truth" (Arendt 1958, 278).

With the rise of modernity (science), the trust that truth could reveal itself to the thinker, and that human faculties were capable of receiving the truth, was shattered. Truth and the human capacity to be open to the resistance that truth can offer could no longer be relied upon. What now had to be relied upon were human procedures for producing and, through confirmation, reproducing the truth. Thus, another irony in this study: the much-acclaimed procedures for establishing objectivity are in reality a subjectivization of the being of truth, what Heidegger calls "subjectism" (Palmer 1969, 142–6).[2]

Subjectism is a broader term than subjectivity, for it means that the world is regarded as basically measured by man. In this view, the world has meaning only with respect to man, whose task is to master the world. The consequences of subjectism are many. First the sciences take preeminence, for they serve man's will to master. Yet since in subjectism man recognizes no goal or meaning that is not grounded in his own rational certainty, he is locked in the circle of his own projected world.

This concept of subjectism and Palmer's formulation of the danger of this way of knowing the world help to explain how the urban-rural discourse could end up in the kind of solipsism described in chapter 3. Recall my examination of both Redfield's and Pahl's formulations and how their understanding of the rural seemed to eliminate the very other they were seeking to engage: aren't they outstanding examples of a mode of inquiry that, despite the rigours of empirical procedures, is "locked in the circle of [its] own projected world"? Pahl saw the middle-class ex-urbanites who claimed that rural living was different and superior as merely extensions of the city. Redfield, in his formulation of a folk society as other to the city, described a society that has no conception of the other. It is therefore not an accident that the distinctiveness of rurality cannot be seen from within this mode of knowing: "In subjectism" the researcher is unable to recognize a "goal or meaning that is not grounded" in the "rational certainty" of its own procedures.

What are the consequences of subjectism for the case of parents who, according to Davies, are misperceiving reality? Let us recall what happened to the experiences of the Torontonians. The subjective and historical aspect of their conclusions that the city is not safe was treated as a bias. Thus, it was measured against objective indicators (which themselves are socially constructed). In the process, what the Torontonians said was measured against a conclusion that anybody could say.

Davies takes on an assumption of the scientific temper of our age by assuming that when many Torontonians say that the small town is better for raising children because it is safer, they are interested in and claiming to do accurate observation. The statement is therefore interpreted as an empirical claim, which allows the scientist, in turn, to isolate it from the context in which it emerged (their parenting practices in the city) and from which it derives its sense of meaning ("rushed occupations," "rushed city," "reports of gangs," "Toronto's floating population of 5,000 street kids" – the child prostitutes, the drug users – "who are living the worst parental nightmares of city life run amok" [Davies 1990, 22–4]).

The Torontonians' observations represent a subjective experience, yet positivism seeks to objectify it so that no kind of subjective or historical moment clings to it any longer. The everyday member is then *assumed to have the same interest and epistemology of the scientist* – i.e., accurate observation – as if he or she were attempting to make an independently verifiable statement. The object (the experience of raising children in the city) is taken out of its socio-historical context and restructured to suit a form of asocial (anybody) knowing. The inaccuracy or misperception on the part of members is recognized only because scientific rationalities are "treated as a methodological principle for interpreting activity" (Garfinkel 1967, 282). Yet as ethnomethodology shows, "actions governed by the attitude of daily life are marked by the specific absence of these rationalities either as stable properties or as sanctionable ideals" (270).

The claims that emerge from the daily life of parenting are interpreted and evaluated from within the life-world of scientific rationality. These actions and interpretations are oriented to another order, and interpreting the claims from within the framework of scientific rationality is to focus on only one side of the truth of the matter. The openness to the resistance which the truth can offer to the life-world of science, ironically, is methodically constrained. Again, recognizing that science not only discovers but also projects a world amplifies my discussion in the first three chapters about the predicament of the urban-rural discourse.

In the Davies article, the interpretation of everyday claims from within the life-world of science takes a comic and ironic turn. Because some, Davies included, have perceived accurately (Toronto is a relatively healthy place to raise children), the issue then becomes a matter of explaining the failure of many Torontonians to be accurate observers. At this point we get a theory by the head of psychiatry at a major metropolitan hospital to explain the perceptual problem of these Torontonians. The comic implications of his explanation reverberate when we remember the nature of his claim: it is a *speculation* by a respected psychiatrist about why we do not need to pay attention to the claims of these Torontonians. Why? Because these people pathologically think with their gut and thus misperceive the external reality.

This conclusion is ironic because the claim to objective and accurate observation of an independent reality is itself a claim stipulated and enforced by a positivistic epistemology. By only applying the art of mistrust to this subjective experience, the researcher is robbed of the opportunity of further exploring and seeking out the hidden truth for which the belief is but the surface expression. Human experience is isolated from its subjective and historical aspects, the very characteristics that define human experience as experience. This is the argument of phenomenology in general, and ethnomethodology in particular, which demonstrates that we cannot really understand any so-called empirical fact without understanding the analytic process by which that fact came to be produced and seen as a truth (Garfinkel 1967).

To summarize, the danger of the discovery mode, in its positivistic expression, is that its very epistemology requires that claims be interpreted using the properties of a scientific rationality. It presumes the very phenomenon (i.e., what is it that the parents are saying when they make these claims?) that itself should be subject to investigation. It does so by presuming a unitary and external reality and by presuming that truth *is* correspondence with this reality. The knower who is in the best position to discover the truth is the one who is most detached from the influence of human experience – the very life-world that made possible the interest in (hope for) truth in the first place.

This mode of creating knowledge fits with the temper of the modern age. Both emphasize the art of mistrust, and as such both see the detachment of "objectivity" rather than the involvement of dialectic as the superior mode of being for the researcher. The wariness of many of my colleagues and many people in Prairie Edge about my research procedure is now understandable. They could plainly see that I was far from detached from the research question; I was (and still am) a parent in the same setting being investigated.

What the discovery mode enables the researcher to know is that the claim for rural advantage on the basis of safety is, in a general sense, not empirically accurate. Yet this conclusion does not have to mean that the parents who say this are wrong or, as one student said, stupid. Rather, it means there is more to uncover, because the truth is more complex than either that which the everyday member assumes or the verification methodology proves. What now needs to be done is to build on the initial insight about the human experience of truth as a process of perplexity made possible by a willingness to have one's hopes and expectations resisted. At the same time, the researcher needs to resist transforming that insight into a formulaic methodology that closes itself off to further development in relation to a shareable understanding of the truth (through the encounter with perplexity). That is, if the claim about the interrelation between rurality and safety *is not reflected* in the crime statistics (as the discovery mode proves), then what can the parents who were quoted in the last chapter mean?

The discovery mode helps the journey of truth-seeking but only when the truth of the pre-understandings of this mode of knowing is called into question. In the next section I digress from the analysis of the question at hand in order to elaborate on the focus and principle of radical interpretive research. The following section then applies this perspective to the claims parents make about the association of the rural with safety. Readers who are more interested in the latter can move directly to that section.

A DIGRESSION: SCIENCE,
SYMBOLIC INTERACTIONISM,
AND HERMENEUTICS

Dialectic, as the art of asking questions, proves itself only because the person who knows how to ask questions is able to persist in questioning, which involves being able to preserve his orientation toward openness. The art of questioning is that of being able to go on asking questions, i.e., the art of thinking. It is called "dialectic," for it is the art of conducting a real conversation.

To understand what a person says is, as we saw, to agree about the object, not to get inside another person, and relive his experience.

All understanding is interpretation, and all interpretation takes place in the medium of a language which would allow the object to come into words and yet is, at the same time, the interpreter's own language.

Hans-Georg Gadamer, 1975

Interpretive sociology recognizes that we can only understand what any claim (e.g., "a small town is better for child-rearing") means by engaging the context that makes it possible. The claim therefore cannot just be seen as a description: it also expresses a social relationship. Phenomenology helps us show that all claims, whether by everyday members or by scientists, are expressions of a relationship, that knowledge is a transaction between the knower and the known. Thus, for example, we understand what the discovery mode is trying to do by recovering its relation to the social life-world (knowledge and the problem of hopes and fears) that initiates *its* orientation. Similarly, if one is to make a serious attempt to understand what is involved in claiming that small-city and town life is better for child-rearing, one needs to place the claim in the context of the social experience from which it emerged. This means that my own experience of living and parenting in the same setting where the study is being conducted does not prejudge the outcome. Rather, the subjective element, the meaning of the claim for human action, is precisely what has to be developed, examined, and transformed rather than eliminated.

While ethnomethodology (Turner 1974) has formulated the flaws of positivism more rigorously, the symbolic interactionism of Blumer (1969) and Mead (1934) has generated a tradition of methods that sought to overcome the methodological limits of quantitative sociology. Following the Weberian legacy (Wallace & Wolf 1991, 236–89), symbolic interactionism recognizes that any understanding of social life requires preserving the meaning-making process of the individual actor. Interviewing and participant observation are then seen as offering ways of recovering the subjective element in experience.

W.I. Thomas's concept of the *definition of the situation* (i.e., if a situation is defined as real, it is real in its consequences) is an attempt, within a more generous scientific framework, to acknowledge minimally that human interpretation of reality is itself intertwined with that reality. Though this concept is still scientific because it posits a reality independent of human knowing, it allows some recognition for the importance of human knowing (real in its consequences). Thus, if parents in a town define their situation as safe, perhaps unaware of the indicators that make it no more so than large cities, then that definition is real in its consequences. Parents may allow kids to play in the streets, travel alone at night, and deal with neighbours and shopkeepers, oblivious to statistics that show the town to be no safer than the city. The parent who worries about her sense of security being false is implicitly aware of this gap between her definition of the safety of rural setting and its actual or factual safety.

The same holds true for Toronto parents. Though Toronto is a relatively safe place in terms of the official indicators of crime, parents who define it as unsafe are especially vigilant with their children, keeping a close tether on them, never letting them out of their sight, and so on. The definition of the city as dangerous has real consequences for the way the parents act, despite the fact that it does not correspond with an accurate perception of reality.

The researcher who introduces this concept into the research is suspending "the facts of the case" in order to try to understand the consequences of the misinterpretation of those facts. That is, the sociologist recognizes that there is a disjunction between truth and social reality and that the latter is a more complex phenomenon than the former. But might not the truth of the claim to advantage on the basis of safety also be more complex and in need of further research?

While Thomas's concept moves us closer to recognizing the complexity of the safety issue, it is limited in the way that it still privileges a world that is independent of human knowing. The consequence of this assumption is that variation in reality comes about only because of the variation in the "incorrect" ways people know this reality. Truth is still understood in a unitary and independent fashion, but because people misperceive their situation, the truth of the relative danger of rural life is not seen. That is, reality is complex only because the everyday member is treated as a "judgmental dope." Thus, if the Torontonians only knew that their city is as safe as most small towns, they would not act in so paranoid a fashion, or, conversely, if the rural parents only knew that the small town is not much safer than its city counterpart, they in turn would not be so complacent. The implication here is that if the everyday member were educated, if parents were to know the truth in the way the social scientist does, then truth and reality could come into a closer correspondence with each other. But is the real issue perhaps not that the parents misperceive the truth of their own situation but that knowledge of the truth of the relation between rurality and safety still needs to be understood?

Ultimately, the limit of the usefulness of Thomas's concept of the definition of the situation is that the independent Cartesian ego (*I think therefore I am*) is still the privileged knower, and thus the process of uncovering knowledge is a process of uncovering what this kind of knower knows – of, in Gadamer's terms, getting inside or reliving this kind of knower's experience. From a radical interpretive perspective, the process of establishing knowledge is not a process of using the interview to get inside the heads of the interviewees but rather engaging in conversation to come to an understanding about an object.

While many useful studies have been done within the symbolic interactionist tradition to describe the point of view of the member or group being studied, the hermeneutic element of radical interpretive sociology aims rather at an understanding of the object of the experience (i.e., the safety and security of the smaller setting) rather than the member's point of view (Bonner 1994). This approach is a process of coming to a shareable understanding of the object which, through language, the parents are trying to articulate. Thus, the researcher does not necessarily assume that he or she automatically knows the object or the "what is it" that parents are referring to. What do the parents mean when they say that rural is better because it is safer, and how does the researcher get at this?

The lived experience is the usage or material with which the inquirer has to work (theorize) in order to try to understand the claim it makes on him or her. The researcher can no longer automatically restructure the claim to suit quantitative methods under the assumption that the claim means to be an independent description of an objective reality. Neither can the researcher assume that parents' claims are the consequential but ultimately flawed attempts to define or understand an external reality (Thomas). Both assumptions presume too much about what is meant by these claims in the first place. This is not to say that the member "knows" and the task of the inquirer is to report on and reproduce the member's knowledge. Rather the meaning has to be developed through the process of questioning and dialogical examination; the researcher has to ask the question: What is the nature of the hidden truth for which the association of rurality with safety is a surface expression? In Gadamer's terms (1975, 349) what is the object that their claims point to, which the researcher now needs "to bring into words"?

Participation in the community, informal conversations with members of the community, and open-ended conversations all provide a good opportunity to search for this hidden truth because they privilege the knower whose understanding of the truth of his/her situation is based upon reflections on lived experience. That is, they enable rather than prevent a real conversation, and it is through conversation, according to Gadamer (1975, 325–41), that understanding of the truth of the object develops. Conversation involves opening oneself up to the truth or rightness of the claim that the other raises. This kind of testing is a seeking that requires not suspicion and mistrust but goodwill and the art of questioning. As Gadamer says (1975, 330), "the art of questioning is that of being able to go on asking questions, i.e., the art of thinking. It is called 'dialectic', for it is the art of conducting a real conversation."[3]

Goodwill presupposes a different relation to knowledge and truth. Knowledge is not something that is acquired as a possession, but rather it is what emerges through participation in a social process. The inquirer has to allow him/herself to be guided by the nature of the object being understood (Palmer 1969, 165) and to be directed, even possessed, by the process. While any one actual conversation or even a whole range of conversations might or might not allow this process to take hold (because of contingencies of personality, mood, setting, wariness, etc.), the interpretation of the material must involve a commitment on the part of the researcher to give him/herself over to the conversation. It is through the dialogical approach that the identity of what the rural parents are talking about will emerge. Thus, the art of interpretation is involved at every stage of the research from the conceptualization of the research project to the lived experience of the researcher to the methodology, the interviewing, the analysis of the field material, and so on.

As should by now be clear, the dialogical process also informs the organization of this narrative. It is not the detachment of mistrust but the involvement of dialectic that draws the reader and writer into a conversational engagement with a text.[4] The relation of the researcher to the question being investigated and the relation of the reader to the text being engaged are analogous in terms of the process of developing understanding. Understanding develops when the claims of the other are strengthened by referring to the object at stake. The reader does this work with a text and the researcher does it with the claims being investigated. Understanding the association of rurality with safety is developed by referring to the particular character of rurality. As Gadamer (1975, 331) describes it, dialectic "consists not in trying to discover the weakness of what is said but in bringing out its real strength. It is not the art of arguing that is able to make a strong case out of a weak one, but the art of thinking that is able to strengthen what is said by referring to the object." My research task now, therefore, is to try to strengthen what the parents say about rurality and safety by referring it to the object of their talk.

INTERPRETATION AND THE PRAIRIE EDGE CASE

What is the object about which the parents talked and on which they agreed? Let us return to the claims made by the parents of Prairie Edge to see whether we can tease out the meaning behind the claim for safety.

We could let them go and we just felt from the time that they left from our house, point A, 'till they got to the library, point B, there was a number of people that they would know along the way.

You know more people and there would be more chances of your parents finding out the trouble you're in … because in the city, I think you're more anonymous than you are here. My kids have a wild party, the neighbour's going to tell me.

Prairie Edge feels more comfortable, relaxed, because you would hear what your child was up to.

In a number of cases where children's misbehaviour was involved, slight misdeeds, of not coming home when they were supposed to be home … the smallness of the town has worked as an information system for us.

The sense of safety these parents talk about is not a logical argument bolstered by statistical indicators; rather, it is a lived experience. If, as Dilthey says, lived experience is an awareness that is not yet aware of itself (Van Manen 1990, 35), then reflection rather than empirical observation is needed to make that awareness into a social object. From the above statements we can begin to recognize the basis of the sense of security. One parent talks about feeling more secure because when the children were out, "there was a number of people that they would know on the way." The children are out on the town, away from the gaze of the parent, yet the parent feels more "low key" because of the sense of trust of knowing people who know your children; the parent feels in touch with what the child is doing because "you would hear it." Another parent talks about the way the neighbour would inform on the children's activities: "the chances are that you would hear what your kids were up to." Elsewhere, parents referred to the smallness of the town as working like a kind of "information system"; others said "the town talks" about the actions of its members. That is, you can be involved in and informed about what your child is up to without having to put a rigid set of controls in place. You can know what your children are up to without having to be with them, precisely because of the so-called "gossipy" characteristic of the small town. As another father said, "The bad part of being in a town is that you are continually a subject of gossip. The good part about it is that you hear eventually what people say about you."

The sense of safety emerges out of what for Simmel (see chapter 1) is the defining characteristic of small town community, i.e., the way it "watches over the deeds, the conduct of life and the attitudes of the individual" (1971, 333). While this "jealousy of the whole toward the individual," this watching eye of the community, is felt to be oppressive in terms of personal freedom of expression, parents experience it as a positive factor. The high visibility within the small town enables parents to give greater freedom to their children without feeling they are abandoning parental responsibility. What is typically thought of as the disadvantage or problem of the small town (i.e., the absence of anonymity, no escape from the watchful eye of a narrow community) is thought of as a positive feature from the life-world of parenting. Recall a quotation from a mother cited at the beginning of the introduction: "They had moved away, got married, when they started raising a family, moved back to Prairie Edge. A lot of them. I kept saying 'Why?' Because it's a good place to raise your kids. We know enough people, it's small enough, you can't get lost." Precisely the feature that is often frustrating and even oppressive for adults who want relief from the narrowness and watchful eye of a rural community is what gives the parent a sense of security. If the adult can't get lost, neither can the child. The feeling that your child can't get lost is a very comforting one. This sense of security comes not because the crime rate is lower or the problem of drug abuse or violence is less; rather, it is based on the sense of familiarity and mutuality that emerges from the lived experience of the town setting.

The object that these speakers are "bringing into words" is the mutuality of the small town. The sense of safety and security is itself a reflexive experience in that it is based not on correspondence with a (constructed) external reality. Instead, the essentially social basis of the sense of safety is uncovered as mutuality. The object is mutuality, and what we now need to do is bring out "the real strength" of what is said by referring to the object.

Remembering the reflexivity built into the nature of understanding itself (Dallmayr 1988, 1–15), the radical interpretive orientation encourages the researcher not to try to observe whether someone is observing accurately but to try to understand how whatever is being observed comes to be observed as that. In other words, the researcher does not study just the object but also the rationalities employed that enable the object to appear in this way. The sense of security that Prairie Edge parents feel appears as safety because the experience of mutuality grounds the appearance. The high visibility characteristic of the small town is experienced in a lived way as mutuality and, it is this ground that makes the association of rurality with safety rational. Mutuality works for parents because the town is engaged in the supervision of their children. While true, this formulation needs to be strengthened further in order to arrive at a deeper understanding of the matter. The formulation that the sense of familiarity creates a sense of security is still too passive, even if it is a formulation with which many rural parents would be satisfied. It suggests that the process of interpretation is passive and reactive, merely reacting to this structural feature of the town rather than itself an attempt to come to terms with the social object (mutuality) in a strong way.

What the parents in this case are oriented to is the town as a community where, by virtue of its smallness, members are aware in a taken-for-granted way of the watchful eye of the small town. That is, we have the awareness of the intersubjectivity (Schutz 1972) of social life where neighbours, friends, or acquaintances are not just oriented to the behaviour of the child but *are oriented to the child as an instance of a parent's responsibility.* That is, the parents feel in a pre-reflective way that other people in the town are not just oriented and reactive to their child's behaviour but are oriented to the parents' orientation to the child, i.e., the anxiety, worry, fear for the child's well-being. The high visibility and corresponding enhancement of the faculty of surveyability (to be developed in parts 3 and 4), when placed in the context of the dialectic of social life, mean that *parents are able to take into account the way their neighbours take their own interest in parenting into account.*

We are now in a position to formulate what the relation between the small city/town and a safe upbringing really is. The advantage of rural child-rearing is not based on the idea that kids who grow up in the town are better off or that "rolling rural fields mean happy children." Rather, this is a surface expression for *the deeper truth that the town more successfully addresses the anxieties and fears of the modern parent.* Thus, the real object is not whether the town is "really" safer than the city. It is not a question of which children have a greater probability of being at risk. Rather, the statements about rural safety are a response to the way the mutuality of the town can address and reduce parental anxiety. *What is at issue here is not children per se but parental anxiety and fear about children.* The high visibility of the town successfully addresses those fears. Thus if, as Davies says, responding to the channels of mass communication in the city "can become an exercise in panic control" (26), the mutuality that comes from the high visibility minimizes the need for that kind of exercise.

In chapter 3 I introduced the concept of the parental life-world, suggesting that this interpretive frame promises to be productive for research into the urban-rural difference. The way this concept contributes to research is now clearer. The association of rurality with safety is a reasonable concept to develop when we recognize the particular lived experience that structures the interpretation. This lived experience refers to the anxieties and challenges associated with modern parenting (Bonner 1997). The research project now has an oriented way of understanding the data that emerges from participation in Prairie Edge material. This data needs to be analysed and understood in relation to the anxiety and challenge associated with modern parenting. Proceeding in this way should help the research project resist the danger of being "locked in the circle of [its] own projected world" (Palmer 1969, 144).

THE ANXIETY OF THE MODERN PARENTAL LIFE-WORLD AND THE SMALLER SETTING

Radical interpretive sociology contributes to knowledge concerning the meaning of the claims for the rural advantage because reflexivity is included in the research procedure (Van Manen, 1990). Research can now be directed and oriented in a way that is true to the life-world grounding the understandings that emerge from both science and everyday life. In the case under consideration, examination of the conceptualization of rurality demonstrated that it is modernity and the way life-worlds are pluralized by modernity that structures the discourse. In particular, it is the parental life-world, and the challenge inherent in this practice in the late twentieth century, that provide the rationalities to enable the researcher to understand the claims.

The description, interpretation, and analysis of the Prairie Edge material is oriented to developing an understanding of how smallness of place influences parenting activity as a way of engaging the broader issues – of relation to community, to the extended family, to place, and most importantly, the modern concern with engaging otherness and questioning limits. The materials (inquirer's experience, notes, recorded interviews) are addressed not in order to give a "thick description" of the life history of parents in Prairie Edge but to engage the life-world of modern parenting as this is reflected by the issue of the benefit of a smaller setting for parenting. It is not, and does not aim to be, a standard ethnography of parenting in Prairie Edge, as the last three chapters demonstrate.

It should be apparent by now that there is no interest in, nor claim being made for, establishing empirical generalizability as the unquestioned standard by which this study is to be judged. As should also be clear, this lack of interest is principled, not happenstance. Empiricism objectifies experience in such a way "that no kind of historical moment clings to it. Through rigorous methodical arrangement," a scientific methodology takes the object (e.g., claims about the benefit of parenting in a rural setting) out of its social, historical, and cultural moment and "restructures it to suit its method ... Insofar as this spirit prevails, only what is verifiable is real: no place is left for the non-objectifiable and historical side of experience" (Palmer 1969, 194).

The critique of the methodically controlled procedures of science is not that the truth that emerges is inaccurate but rather that it "involves a specific kind of questioning which lays open [only] one side of a thing." This one side concerning the truth of the association of safety with rurality is important here because it requires that the researcher re-examine this association in order to recover its deeper truth. This re-examination, however, involves a turning away from one-sided research. This is not a turning to another side of the object; instead "a dialectical hermeneutics opens itself to be questioned by the being of the thing, so that the thing encountered can disclose itself in its being." This fuller disclosure of the being of the claim is possible not because of the "representativeness" of the sample (those talked to), nor because of any attempt to control responses for the influence of class, life-cycle, and so on, but rather because of "the linguisticality of human understanding and ultimately of being itself" (Palmer 1969, 166).

Much of what is laid out in this chapter coheres with certain developments in postmodern and feminist research. In chapter 7 I articulate the broad ontological and theoretical implications embedded in and supportive of the radical interpretive approach. This will allow me to highlight important differences between the latter and certain kinds of postmodern research. In turn this exposition will ground an examination of the limits of phenomenology and postmodernism in terms of the implications these movements/perspectives have for encouraging a consumer relation to place.

It is now clear that the claim for the advantage of rural child-rearing is itself an interpretation grounded in the ability of the collective (i.e., the town) to address and defuse parental anxiety. The conversations I had, both formally and informally, take for granted the responsibility that parenting brings. The social life-world of modern parenting takes as a point of principle (ought) and as a taken-for-granted assumption (is) the responsibility involved in parenting. Given this, the opinion or belief that small-town life is a better environment for child-rearing is really an answer to the question of how we as parents respond to the "enormous responsibility" our culture puts on us as parents: the almost god-like responsibility to raise happy and good adults, when so many forces seem to be working against that aim – not the least of these being the inability of adults to realize the aim for themselves. The solution of the small town is that the mutuality that emerges from high visibility gives the parent confidence to act on the assumption that the town respects this commitment to child-rearing enough to participate in the task. We can now engage the field material more directly, recognizing the social life-world that structures the claims parents make about their setting.

PART THREE

The Prairie Edge Solution to the Problem of Anxious Parenting

CHAPTER SIX

Parenting in Prairie Edge: A Rurban Experience

"To do human science research is to be involved in the crafting of a text," notes Van Manen (1990, 78). This chapter creates a text out of the claims of parents who live in a particular community in Western Canada, with the aim of providing substance for the object which their words identify. Initially, therefore, the interest guiding the creation of the text is descriptive. The description that follows, like all statements, answers certain questions, which at this stage are very ordinary: What kind of setting is Prairie Edge?[1] What did parents say about the benefit of rural child-rearing?

This descriptive interest assumes that the kind of researcher who asks such questions is unfamiliar with the setting and, as outlined in the last section, is able to supply enough goodwill and patience to allow the object, which will remain to be critically and dialogically examined, to emerge. What this reading requires is not the suspension of critical faculties but rather suspension of the rule of doubt and suspicion. Of course, and in a way almost unnecessary to add at this stage, suspension of the rule of doubt and suspicion is required by the rationalities of everyday life if we are to have an object to examine in the first place (Elliot 1974, 21–6; Zimmerman and Pollner 1971, 80–103). Consistent application of the rule of doubt, which even the most rigorous scientific investigation cannot implement fully, does not ensure access to the real or true picture but merely generates an unproductive bewilderment (Garfinkel 1967, 1–75, 262–83). As Gadamer (1989, 55) says, the attitude of goodwill "is essential for any understanding at all to come about. This is nothing more than an observation. It has nothing to do with an 'appeal,' and nothing at all to do with ethics."[2]

THE METHODOLOGICAL
APPROACH

The materials out of which the following description is translated are my own lived experience and observations, the informal, *in situ* conversations with many people (approximately fifty-four predominately middle-class individuals) over the course of five years participation in the community, and the recorded interviews with thirteen people. As the informal conversations of necessity contributed to my own experience, these two aspects were and are important resources for my contextualizing and understanding the material that emerged from the recorded conversations. Therefore, all three aspects work together to help me relate "back to the original communicative situation" (Gadamer 1989b, 36), that is, to the parents' self-understanding of their experience in Prairie Edge.

The difference between the recorded conversations and the informal conversations with others is that for the former a sustained period of time (approximately one and one-half hours) was solely devoted to exploring this question. Where relevant, I talked to husbands and wives together, and several conversations transcribed below show couples conversing with each other. Some of those I talked to were friends who knew me as a sociologist interested in these questions, some were acquaintances, and some I met at the recording situation for the first time. All were chosen for the recorded conversation because they fitted the criteria of being parents who had either lived and parented in a large urban centre or were now parenting in the same setting in which they were raised. After that, if I knew them, they were chosen because I judged them to be direct, forthright about their opinions, and articulate and thoughtful. Again, this is another point where the three elements of the methodology (lived experience, reflective participation, and the notes and transcriptions of conversations) meet.

All of those who were part of the recording, but not all of those I talked to, knew about my research beforehand, and all satisfied the basic criterion of being actively involved in the parenting process.[3] The transcript that is the outcome of the recorded conversations is, in Gadamer's (1989, 35) words, "not simply a given object but a phase in the execution of the communicative event."[4]

The arguments for focusing on the reasons people give to support their belief in rural child-rearing are threefold. On the basis of W.I. Thomas's definition of the situation, if a rural setting is defined as better by parents, then that definition should have real consequences for the practice of parenting. Presumably, parents as parents will be doing things differently than if they were parenting in an urban setting. For example, an inability to be able to support the belief with reasons could lend credence to the interpretation that the belief is merely a bromide or myth that does not correspond to any lived experience. On the other hand, inarticulateness could also point to the unnoticed, taken-for-granted features of the everyday environment. It is precisely at such a juncture that experience and participation are needed. My experience of living and parenting in the community gives me a perspective against which to interpret and understand what the participants said. The interpretive element of radical interpretive sociology is radical because it is so inescapable and all embracing (universal). As the argument of the last chapter shows, the explicit use of and hermeneutic relation to the experience of the inquirer as a resource therefore transcends the epistemological limitations of Thomas's concept.

Second, through an exploration of the reasons various participants offer, I want to recover what urban and rural came to mean for these individuals. For instance, if the parents suggested (and we know from the last chapter they did) that safety was an important advantage for rural child-rearing, then at least impressionistically there is an association of danger with the city. Through an exploration of these reasons I can continue to develop the conceptualization of rurality, now guided by the relevance of the way the rural impinges on the parenting practices of these residents. Lastly and most significantly from the perspective of radical interpretive sociology, exploring the reasons enables the researcher to recover the work of reflection built into any and all self-understanding. The research conversation is a particularly useful procedure to bring this work into the open. As I showed in the last chapter, a researcher who fails to attend to this work may easily miss the point of the issue. Habermas (1988, 159) helps articulate the justification for this procedure: "A series of events attains the unity of a story from the point of view that cannot be derived from the events themselves. The actors are caught up in their histories; when they tell their own stories, they too become aware only after the fact of the point of view from which the events can take on the coherence of a story. The story, of course, has significance only for those who are capable of action in the first place."

Habermas here is explicating Gadamer's argument that "subsequent understanding is in principle superior to the original production" (Gadamer, as cited in Habermas 1988, 154), which is to say that retrospective and reflective accounts are necessarily built into the claims concerning the superiority of rurality for child-rearing. A fuller understanding of the issues involved requires that the researcher attend to and examine the meaning of this reflective work. While the parents I talked to were all at different stages of parenting, the research conversation is the necessary procedure for getting a sense of the meaning this activity has for parents.

This chapter follows through on the problem, identified in chapter 6, of the anxiety associated with modern parenting. Various surveys have established that on the whole a rural setting is preferred for parenting. In part 2 I showed the ground for this preference is the modern parental life world and the anxiety intrinsic to this life world. As various studies have shown (see Hutter 1988, 353–420), parental anxiety is most keenly felt by the middle class (Bonner, 1997). I want to uncover the response given by middle-class or upper working-class parents when asked to reflect on whether and why a more rural setting is "a great place to raise kids."

PRAIRIE EDGE: URBAN, RURAL, OR RURBAN?

Even if what I choose to call "rural" is an urban subculture, there are differences that need a label. Rurban has been suggested but seldom used.

Alex Sim, 1988

Prairie Edge is a community in Western Canada of nearly 14,000. The area was first settled about 1900 and incorporated as a city in 1955. Both legally and according to the criteria of Statistics Canada,[5] Prairie Edge is considered a city and is urban. The question of whether, sociologically speaking, it is a city is still open and was part of the research process. In everyday usage, when local people use the term "the city," they typically and in a taken-for-granted way refer to Edmonton, about one hundred kilometres away. All of those I talked to saw Prairie Edge as more rural than urban (big city) but yet not really rural (i.e., farm). Local informants and the co-conversationalists generally perceived important distinctions between living in a big city and living on an isolated farm, and saw Prairie Edge as different from both, supporting Pahl's (1968) contention that the urban-rural distinction, as a continuum, makes it difficult to recognize significant discontinuities. To distinguish between the *really* rural and the *really* urban, the term *rurban* is useful.

In promotional material from the office of the economic development co-ordinator, Prairie Edge is presented in the following way:

"We're the perfect size to enjoy all of the educational, recreational and entertainment facilities of a thriving city, yet we remain small enough to appreciate the convenience and security of a rural way of life." Along similar lines, a profile in the Alberta Motor Association travel magazine describes Prairie Edge as *"a city that maintains its small town charm"* (*Westworld Magazine* 1990, 17). A theme that emerged in the research was that Prairie Edge "had the best of both worlds" – the amenities and facilities of a city but the character and personality of a small town. Residents tended to describe the place positively (that it has *both* urban and rural characteristics) rather than negatively (Prairie Edge is neither country nor city, neither urban nor rural).[6] Similarly, the promotional material from Prairie Edge does not say, "If you want a small town, come here; if you want city, go elsewhere," or vice versa. This material says, "Whichever you want, we have both."

The term "rurban" has been coined to identify the settlement type that has both rural and urban characteristics, and thus, though it is not an everyday term, it is an appropriate way of indicating the particularity of the Prairie Edge difference. Rurban indicates the modernity of contemporary rurality in a way that bypasses the sterility of deciding whether a place like this is urban or rural; it is particularly appropriate in this case because the meanings associated with rurality, which are recognized from the perspective of the parental life-world, are especially applicable to the new rural communities (Sim, 1988). That is, the association of rurality with notions of safety, of convenience, of reduced parental anxiety, and of high visibility are meanings that are appropriate for rural centres as against farming areas.

In line with the sociological tradition initiated and developed by Tonnies and Simmel and continued by the Canadian sociologist Alex Sim, the town or small city is taken to be the referent for rurality. Prairie Edge can *make an everyday claim* for "small town lifestyle." In the Yerxa survey *Assessing the Quality of Life in Urban and Rural Communities* (March 1992) Prairie Edge was one of the "four rural communities" used to make comparisons between people living in large and in small centres. The survey's approach adds weight to the impression of residents of large centres that "urban" refers to a metropolis and "rural" refers to what is *not* a metropolis. Similarly, in an article in the *Edmonton Journal* (29 April 1992, A15), a columnist refers to the political and social alienation felt by people in Lethbridge (population 60,000) as representative of the "sense of alienation that pervades rural, smalltown Canada." For this columnist, urban is big city and rural is what is not big city (i.e., small cities and towns).[7] This understanding is reflected in a book by an ex-urbanite, Charles Long (*Life after the City,* 1989). For Long, "country places" or "rural images" include small cities (Kingston, 60,000), towns (Perth, 6,000), villages, and what he calls "rural lots." He explicitly excludes farms because real "farms are more places of business than places to live today" (50). All of this suggests that rural is defined in relation to the sense of self-centredness of big cities (not unlike the way the ancient Greeks viewed their cities): what is not another big city is other to the urban. Thus while positivistic sociology shows that "the city today is society" (Pahl 1968, 278), in popular media and in everyday conversation the difference between urban and rural is still meaningful.

In order to describe Prairie Edge in terms of a larger horizon, I will first expand on Alex Sim's description of "the new countryside of Canada" (1988). Because of technological advancements, the globalization of communication, and the mobility of people, companies, jobs, and so on, the "rural experience" is a vastly different experience from what it was a mere fifty years ago (thus the need for a term like "rurban"). An extended quotation from Sim (94) provides an image of the ingredients that go to make up the "new rural community":

Ease of travel and the thrusting of the world beyond into every family circle and individual consciousness by television and other media exert a double or contradictory influence. On the one hand these homogenizing forces have the potential for enforcing uniformity in taste, values, and behaviour. They are the centrifugal forces that weaken community and family ties and lay society open to the influence of political demagogues and television evangelists of questionable worth and taste. On the other hand, the weakening of traditional social controls permits experimentation and diversity. The new rural community contains a rich mixture of old and new drawn from local and distant sources. They may come and go on a daily basis as commuters, or less frequently as circumstance dictates. Members of families move away and then return on visits to stay, carrying with them the pollen of distant experience. The result of all this intercourse is cross-fertilization with the promise of a hybrid vigour.

This mixing has always been present in big cities but, as happens in big cities, the diverse elements are contained in ghetto-like regions ... In the culture of rural places the diverse elements are contained in a smaller vessal. There is more space, greater visibility, less structure, more face-to-face contact. Above all there is the opportunity for individual participation in these smaller units of action.

Sim's solicitous description of "the new countryside" itself supports my claim that the phenomenological concept of life-world can

best help us address the diversity that is now a significant characteristic of the new countryside. I will take this issue up shortly, but for
now I want to remind the reader that the "rurality" of Prairie Edge
no longer rests, if it ever did, on the image of a homogenous, close-
knit, interdependent, and insular community. My own field research
reflects this diversity in that many of those I talked to, both *in situ*
and for the recorded conversations, were ex-urbanites with lived
experience of parenting in an urban setting. These participants help
me test the claim for rural advantage by providing lived-experience
descriptions of both urban and rural settings and also descriptions
of parenting in a rurban setting without the existence of a close-knit
extended family nearby.

Before I engage the ethnographic material, the town of Prairie
Edge has to be understood in terms of these broad changes that have
occurred in the countryside of developed countries in general and
Canada in particular. As a way of describing "the new countryside,"
Sim (1988, 61–94), drawing on a procedure conceived by Weber
(1947), devised four community types which he saw as representative of the different sorts of rural communities to be found in contemporary Canada. These types are pure in the sense that no one
community exactly corresponds to any one type. Rather, the pure
types are a way of theoretically organizing characteristics found in
most rural communities in contemporary Canada, in terms of particular blends and emphasis.

"The identification of these basic or pure types should be useful as
one isolates the factors that make up the blend in any given community and in understanding its characteristics," says Sim:

I have named them: Agraville, Fairview, Ribbonville, and Mighthavebeenville. They represent the four basic elements that are manifest in most rural
communities, each with its own variation of emphasis and dominance.

(a) *Agraville* represents a community based on a rich, productive land
    resource – mining, forestry, fishing, or agriculture. The emphasis here
    will be on agriculture.

(b) *Fairview* represents a community that has important scenic values which
    make it attractive to new arrivals in contrast to its long-time residents
    whose attachment will have less to do with beauty than with economic
    and social conditions.

(c) *Ribbonville* represents a community that is dominated by one or more
    large cities or towns. It still retains much open country around it, and it
    in turn is surrounded by a range of smaller settlements.

(d) *Mighthavebeenville* represents a place dominated by unrealized hopes for
    growth and greatness that seem to burden all small places.

Admittedly all rural settlements have a land base. All have a relationship to one or more urban centres, and most have scenic amenities that make them attractive and desirable. All have unrealized ambitions. But for every 'real' community the weight of each element is different (Sim 1988, 62).

In terms of emphasis, Prairie Edge corresponds most closely to the Agraville type, described by Sim as representing a "community based on a rich productive land resource," which in the case of Prairie Edge is agriculture. These kinds of communities have grown in affluence and size in relation to the demise of the smaller, surrounding villages. In a way that is remarkably similar to Sim's description of Agraville, one sees as one enters Prairie Edge a "commodious shopping mall" enclosed and protected against the weather, a large modern hotel, and several fast food retail outlets. The shopping mall has three of Canada's largest department stores (The Bay, Canadian Tire, and Zellers). As one proceeds toward the town centre, from either end of the highway "automobile dealers and farm machinery agents exhibit their wares in marshalled ranks, decked with fluttering flags and bunting" (Sim 1988, 65). There are several motels as well as many more fast-food outlets of various kinds (e.g., steak houses, pizza parlours, Mexican food) along the way; because Prairie Edge is primarily a service centre, these serve a transient daily population.

As in many prairie settlements, the highway runs right through the town, intersecting with the lower end of the main street. This is wide and spacious, with a distinctly western look. On it the familiar landmarks are to be found: banks (five), Chinese restaurants, pharmacies, variety stores, and clothing shops; some are new and some bear names of established Prairie Edge citizens. Like Agraville, Prairie Edge is a service centre for a wide agricultural region. Its "primary trading population" is 60,000 and its "total trading population" is 90,000. The retail trade (as of 1986) is by far the largest employer (39 per cent) in the town, and this is reflected in a relatively busy main street during retail hours. Again in a way that is remarkably similar to Sim's Agraville,[8] regional offices of the departments of the provincial government, municipal offices, and health clinics are located on main street's west side. Prairie Edge has one full-service hospital, seven public schools, two separate schools, two Bible colleges, and a small liberal arts university. Medical services (13 per cent), educational services (9 per cent), and government (8 per cent), are the leading employment areas after the retail trade, followed by manufacturing (8 per cent) and professional services (7 per cent). The employment picture gives the town a distinctly stable, relatively affluent, middle-class flavour. Unlike some other rural towns which depend economically on a single major resource like oil or nickel, Prairie Edge has not gone through extreme boom and bust economic cycles. The service-oriented nature of the town means that it has a higher than average professional class of doctors, lawyers, teachers, dentists, professors, and so on. Reflecting this, the majority of those parents I talked to were either middle class or upper working class.

On the main street's east side lies a grid of residential streets dating from early in the century with houses ranging from grand to modest. Many have been renovated, adding to the gentrification of this part of the town. Because it is an older area, the trees lining the streets are mature, giving a sense of the bountifulness of nature during the two or three weeks of spring which the northern prairie experiences.

Prairie Edge has the reputation of being a religious community (with seventeen churches, all of various Christian denominations) and a retirement community. This religious and senior ethos make the town a quiet, gentle place for some and a dull, bland place for others. As with the issue of raising children, the horizon or life-world a person brings to a place will structure what that place means. For example, the advertisers' directory of the local 1992 telephone book lists five taverns or nightclubs and five lounges. Describing Prairie Edge to people in Ireland, I often contrast it to my own hometown in Tipperary with a population one quarter the size of Prairie Edge, approximately 3,000 people. The real cultural differences emerge when the ratio of pubs to churches is contrasted: my hometown has twenty-five pubs and two churches. However, the contrast does not stop there: in Ireland people are quiet in the churches and they sing in the pubs, while in Prairie Edge the taverns are low-key and the singing is done in the churches. From the perspective of a relatively homogeneous Irish culture, many shake their heads in wonder at the culture that binds these kinds of practices.

To use another example from the advertisers' directory, under "Dining" there are thirteen entries, while auto-related entries come to seventy-seven. Most of the traffic and business occurs during the day, while in the evenings and at night the streets tend to be quiet, if not deserted. Social life is largely organized on the basis of membership at church, a service club, work, sports activities, or the extended family, rather than through publicly accessible cultural and entertainment facilities. In this regard, rural respondents in the Yerxa survey cited above rated the nightlife and entertainment "as being poor to fair" while people in Edmonton "rated this aspect of the city as primarily being good or excellent" (Yerxa 1992, 8). We used to joke with our neighbours that the idea of the "dead centre" of town was supposed to be a geographic reference point, not a description of the downtown social, cultural, and entertainment facilities. Some took this humour better than others. As we will see, the poor nightlife and entertainment facilities make the town particularly difficult for single people.

When we first arrived from Toronto we were much struck by the privately organized aspect of social life. Particularly for anyone not attached to the community, the town seemed to offer few opportunities to gather in a public place and meet others. One had to belong to a group or organization, a belonging which took a while to establish. Even then, belonging to an organization pulled one into a particular group rather than into the community as a whole. The Elks Lodge and the Moose Lodge show the western side of Prairie Edge, while the Sons of Norway display the importance of the Scandinavian background to the area. The Lions, Kinsmen, and Knights of Columbus are prominent Prairie Edge service clubs that can also be found in many parts of the world. Reflecting the more traditional side of Prairie Edge, many are organized on an exclusively male basis; women belong to corresponding clubs like the Catholic Women's League, the Kinettes, the Women of the Moose, or the Ladies of the Royal Purple. The Rotary club is a prominant exception, having recently agreed to accept women as full members. My point is that, even here, entertainment and community activities are privately organized in private spaces (e.g., Elks Hall), channelling social activities into particular groups rather than the larger community.

The population of Prairie Edge doubled between 1961 and 1981 and is expected to double again in the following fifteen years. The average age of the population is about thirty-three years, slightly lower than the Canadian average of thirty-six years. According to the 1986 Census Area data, 26 per cent are in the twenty-five to forty-four age group, 19 per cent in the sixty-five and over age group, and the rest break down as follows – 17 per cent (forty-five–sixty-four), 13 per cent (five–fourteen), 9 per cent (twenty–twenty-four), 8 per cent (fifteen–nineteen) and 8 per cent (zero–four). As a retirement community, Prairie Edge has a higher percentage of sixty-five and over (19 per cent) than the Albertan average (11 per cent).

Prairie Edge initially developed a reputation as a retirement centre in response to the number of farmers from surrounding areas who choose to retire there. Many facilities (senior housing, a senior centre, and so on) were developed to service the needs of this group and this in turn made Prairie Edge attractive for others outside the immediate area. To this extent the particular reputation of Prairie Edge has more to do with being a good place to retire. Its claim to being a "great place to raise kids" is the kind of claim that many rural centres make. Being a good place to raise a family has more to do with the fact that it is a small town than the fact that it is Prairie Edge.

The influx of people from across Canada for retirement and work purposes emphasizes its character as a Fairview (Sim 1988, 68–77) community. That is, a sizeable proportion of its population (there are no statistics on this) are ex-urbanites.[9] For comparative reasons this group is an important part of my research.

PRAIRIE EDGE AND THE PARENTAL LIFE-WORLD

The vast majority of the approximately fifty-four people talked to informally tended to subscribe to the claim that the rural and, in particular, the Prairie Edge setting was better for child-rearing than a larger centre. The relevant results of the Yerxa survey "considered reliable nineteen times out of twenty, plus or minus 4.9 per cent" (4), are worth citing again:

Comparing Life in Big Cities with Life in Small Towns: ... rural respondents were asked to directly compare their community with that of Edmonton, while Edmontonians were asked to compare their city with that of a smaller rural centre. When asked which community was a better place to raise a family, a dramatically [higher] percentage of rural respondents believed that a rural setting was a better place to raise a family (80.9 per cent). In contrast, only 20.4 per cent of urban respondents believed that an urban setting was a better place to raise a family. Urban respondents were more inclined to state that an urban or rural setting would make no difference in raising a family (15).

The following is the conclusion of the study:

This study found that there are some distinctive contrasts between the ways that people who live in an urban centre perceive of "life in the city" and the way that people who live in smaller towns view quality of life. *Overall, it was found that rural residents were much happier with their communities than urban residents with respect to aspects of everyday life that were very much under their personal control – aspects such as "raising a family," "interactions and communications with other people."* In contrast, urban residents were clearly more satisfied with the city as a place to live than rural residents with respect to the increased opportunities and variety of things to do. These included such things as shopping and entertainment opportunities (movies, live theatre, dining out). Features that remained similar between the types of communities included cleanliness in the community, schools and public recreation facilities. *On the basis of this data, it can be concluded that the rural setting may be lacking wide choices of some activities and entertainment opportunities, but that the quieter and smaller setting was clearly preferred for raising a family and engaging in social interaction.*

Contrasts between urban and rural living became even more important when social problems were examined. In general, urban residents were much more concerned with the impact that crime, violence, and racial/ethnic tensions had on their community than rural residents (who often perceived these problems as having little or no impact on their lives). Moreover, there was a much stronger perception of personal safety in smaller communities than there was in Edmonton. On this facet of social living, rural people are more satisfied with their communities than are urban people" (Yerxa Research 1992, 23–4, emphasis mine).[10]

Most of the people I talked to did not feel particularly strongly about their opinions. Interestingly, many were open to the conclusions this study would establish. They were receptive to the possibility that what they believe might not prove to be true. As with the survey, a minority of parents, all ex-urbanites, did not agree with the claim. Again, except for one occasion, the disagreements tended not to be passionately subscribed to; on that occasion, I was present at an argument when two sets of parents argued vociferously for and against the claim. The argument against was based mostly on the grounds of the sense of social and political regressiveness of the rural area and the narrow exclusiveness and judgmentalism of the smaller community, and the dangers both of these represented to one's social and political development. Such parents feared that their children would turn into narrow-minded "rednecks." I should add that as a rule such parents typically had very young children.

In general, the arguments against living in a more rural setting mirrored those of Marx or Simmel outlined in part 1, and thus the notion of rurality still has a vestigial relation to the meanings developed by sociologists in an earlier era. However, the purpose of this study is not to test for the empirical reliability of the perception of "a great place to raise kids" but to explore and to understand the reasons for holding onto the belief; as it turned out (though this was not explicitly sought), all of the co-conversationalists, in different ways, for different reasons, and with different levels of emphasis, supported the claim. In several cases the claim was tentatively offered at the beginning of the interview, but as the conversation went on, support for it became firmer.

As already shown, the meaning associated with rurality in the claim gets its sense from the parental life-world. According to Van Manen (1990, 78), "To do human science research is to be involved in the crafting of a text. In order to come to grips with the structure of meaning of the text it is helpful to think of the phenomenon described in the text as approachable in terms of meaning units, structures of meaning, or themes. Reflecting on lived experiences then becomes reflectively analyzing the structural or thematic aspects of that experience."

The description of what parents said has been organized around the interrelated themes of safety, convenience, and reduced parental anxiety. Building on what I established in chapter 5, these themes need to be understood as expressions and articulations of the practice of mutuality that is the decisive feature of the greater visibility of the smaller setting. I will demonstrate that the life-world of parenting in this smaller centre enables the development of a "knowing" relation to these particular characteristics of the town and also provides for the interrelation of these characteristics. That of greater safety relates to the reduced parental anxiety as well as to the characteristic of convenience. Most significantly, a knowing everyday relation to these "benefits" is grounded in the social characteristic *par excellence* of town life – high visibility. Following recommendations in contemporary ethnography (Clifford 1988; De Vries and McNab-De Vries 1991) and as a way of drawing attention to the collaborative element involved in ethnographic research, I quote "regularly and at length from informants" (Clifford 1988, 50).

Safety

MOTHER (rural): So one way that the rural place is better than the city is because you feel safer. You feel that there's less harm that can happen to your children – we'll use the example of drugs.

FATHER (ex-urbanite): It's easier, speaking more of the safety factor. Like, in Los Angeles we had difficulties with the children in the school system because there were too many muggings and too many [pause] whatever right in the hallways."

FATHER (rural): If we're talking a city the size of Edmonton, in a way it's kind of intimidating to walk down the street and see some of the people there. It's so different than the people in a small town like Prairie Edge.
INTERVIEWER: In what way?
FATHER: Scarier.

FATHER (ex-urban): Well, we lived for a year in New York, so, although we did not live in Manhattan, we did get a feeling of what it would be like bringing up children there. We also visited friends who lived right in New York City.

INTERVIEWER: And how was that feeling?

FATHER: Awful. It seems like you have to have total control over what your children are doing. Your own freedom becomes very limited by the supervisional needs of your children. And that is one of the reasons why we thought this town would be great. Maybe partially this is an illusion of the small town that sounds wonderful and everybody knows everybody. But it has proven to be correct. In a number of cases where children's behaviour was involved, of slight misdeeds, of not coming home when they were supposed to be home, of going somewhere else than they were supposed to be, or drinking, etc., the smallness of the town has worked as an information system for us. In the sense that without us being there, the kids were supervised by people who we knew.

MOTHER (ex-urbanite): It's very hard for them to get away with something. They can, but it would be difficult. Changing the subject, the crime in cities is really dangerous.

INTERVIEWER: What kind of crime are you thinking about?

MOTHER: Rape, for instance, having two girls. Mugging, robbery, I'm talking about people being victims of crime. If you are talking about a big city like New York, it's very real. If your kids are going to school on the subway and are a half hour late, that may be a cause for real panic. Kidnapping and all sorts of things could happen. So that's not the case here. It's safe for them to be riding their bikes at 11 o'clock at night.

INTERVIEWER: So the difference then is that it makes parenting less anxious.

FATHER: Oh, yes, definitely. You have more time to devote to other things besides the supervision of your children. That also means less anxiety. Last night we didn't know where our youngest [12 years] was, it did not cause us undue alarm. And in fact, we do keep our houses open when we go out. We do keep our cars open when we go shopping in Prairie Edge. So it's not just an illusion. If there were more crime, then we would change our patterns and would put locks on our front doors.

The long selection at the end helps explain the attraction the small town has for parents. To understand this we have to understand how parenting is constituted in modernity. What is unique about the way the family is organized in modern society is the isolation of child-rearing activities from other social activities. Accompanying this isolation is the location of responsibility for child-rearing away from the wider extended family or community and into the hands of one or two people. (Bonner 1997). As LeMasters and DeFrain in their much-reprinted book (1989, 2) note, "Our society puts this tremendous responsibility almost totally on the parent, even though parents, in reality, are only one influence, albeit a major one, among many on the development of children."[11] The parents above all think of themselves in terms of this "almost total" responsibility as providers, protectors, and educators.

As a parent one is not just a protector but, more significantly, a protector of individuals not in a position (because of innocence or ignorance) to protect themselves. As experts are constantly reminding us, "the human infant comes into the world the most helpless of all the primates, and yet its care is less assured than that of any other" (Skolnick 1987, 315). This increases the sense of responsibility and the sense of burden (Skolnick 1987, 305–36) involved in parenting. Children might not recognize when they are in danger, or they might not know what to do if they did recognize it. Because of this aspect of parenting, *the parent's sensitivity to danger is heightened* and, as we know from the last section, the city and sense of danger are intertwined. If one lives in an area that is perceived to be dangerous, as a parent one becomes more anxious.

The city, for example, tempts the father to think that "it seems like you have to have total control over what your children are doing." This in turn makes the supervision of children more demanding in a way that makes parent and child feel less free. In this example, parenting in the city confronts the father with the choice between power and freedom. Because of the child's vulnerability to danger, the perceived requirement of "total control over what your children are doing" is achieved at the expense of the parent's personal freedom. The parent, concerned about the dangerous environment, feels forced to restrict the freedom of the child, an activity that itself restricts the freedom of the parent. On the other hand, the benefit of safety enables this father to choose freedom over the apparently less desirable option of "total control." In the next two chapters I examine the cultural basis for this interest in freedom. For now, the above text suggests that an impression of greater safety is understood by parents to be a major benefit to their everyday practice.

As already established in part 2, attempting to evaluate such reflections against official indicators of safety would be a misinterpretation of what is being said here. These parents are not engaged in neutrally reporting an objective reality. Rather, they are actors in a particular social relation (parenting) who are acting on very particular cultural conceptions of children and parent-child relations. This conception of childhood rests on the idea of a being who is vulnerable and in need of protection. In his famous work *Centuries of Childhood* (1962), Phillippe Aries shows the way this conception of childhood is peculiar to the modern era and in sharp historical contrast to the medieval attitude.

The development of the modern conception of childhood coincides with the rise of the middle classes and the identification of the parent as the agent assigned the responsibility for protecting what is now thought of as an "innocent." Thus the claim for the advantage of rural child-rearing is not articulated in terms of the development of the character, personality, or health of the child. It is not so much that kids are less at risk in this setting than in New York, Edmonton, or Los Angeles; rather, the sense of safety that exists in the smaller setting enables parents to feel less overwhelmed by the normal parental requirement of supervision. Of course, if one were not a parent or if one were indifferent to the tremendous responsibility placed almost totally on parents by society, then the association of rurality with safety would not be as prominent. Life-world analysis is thus crucial to help put a claim like this in its proper context.

The particular social make-up of Prairie Edge contributes to the confidence parents have in their sense that the town is safe. The employment picture behind the town's stable, middle-class character, the demographic picture, and the image of religiosity all work to contribute to the sense of safety. Most of the traffic and business occurs during the day, while in the evenings the streets tend to be quiet, if not deserted. During summer evenings the only form of street life consists of teenagers cruising up and down the main street in their pick-ups and cars (or to use the common Prairie Edge generic term, vehicles). Unlike large urban centres, there is no floating population of homeless people, prostitutes, or drug addicts on the streets. The father in the third example, born and raised in Prairie Edge, describes this element of urban life as "scarier." Though on a per capita basis the incidence of crime between urban and rural settings is not so different as many rural residents believe, the visibility of these populations is what is most striking for those with little or no lived experience of the city.

As the interaction between husband and wife in the last example indicates, the greater sense of safety can mean, as it did for the father, "more time to devote to other things besides the supervision of your children" or it can mean, as it did for the mother, that there will be less "cause for real panic." It means that parenting does not have to be as all-absorbing and oppressive as it might be or it means that parenting is less of an alarming activity. Though the benefit means different things for the mother and father, the consequence for both is that parenting has become more enjoyable. For the mother the enjoyment comes from the relief from panic, and for the father it comes from being relieved of the responsibility of needing to have "total control over what your children are doing."

The strong sense of safety is both nurtured and reproduced in the talk and actions of Prairie Edgers. In the last extract, the father wonders whether this sense of safety is an illusion. He reminds himself of his own practices: "In fact, we do keep our houses open when we go out. We do keep our cars open when we go shopping in Prairie Edge." Reminding himself in this way becomes the ground for his saying, "so it's not just an illusion." The sense of safety in this extract moved from being a possible illusion to a firm fact on the basis of a reminder of everyday practices that affirm a sense of safety. Thus, it is a *sense* of safety that is strengthened through reflection on our everyday practices rather than "knowledge" of safety based on information.

Convenience and Rurbanism

MOTHER (rural): I don't think I'd mind living in some place like Calgary, in fact, I quite like Calgary. But again, it's the size I don't like. You get used to being able to get anywhere in five minutes.

MOTHER (rural to urban to rural): I guess it would be fair to say that we're very comfortable with this size of place. I found that it's just more convenient living in a small town for getting around and getting to places, and our children are very involved and they would probably be in the city as well. But I don't know if we'd have the convenience of having it two minutes outside our door.

MOTHER (rural): We're actually lucky to be in Prairie Edge because we have the availability of just about anything you want within a short time.

FATHER (rural, on his dislike of the city): The busyness, the people, the time it takes you to go from one place to another – even though there's lots of things to do, it always seems like you've got to drive to get wherever that's happening.

… See, here in a small city again, you can go home for lunch. No problem. And the kids can too. And when you got hockey and the kids are involved with that stuff, if you've got to drive them back and forth in the city it takes a lot of time. So I think just the – [pause] you have more time for yourself when you're not running around going to work or from work.

Here again the benefits of the small town's perceived qualities have to be placed in the context of contemporary parenting. An accepted part of it is a concern with occupying children's time and thus parents are often absorbed in facilitating their children's activities. For example, an awareness of psychological development creates a sense that children need to be stimulated, their talents developed, their abilities nurtured. Active parenting is now understood to mean making sure that your children are involved in a variety of activities. One parenting expert argues that "effective parents ... do not bore their children" (White 1975, 147). The advice columns and the "life" sections of newspapers are replete with experts telling parents how important it is to have children involved in different activities. As Arlene Skolnick (1987, 332) remarks, a "concern with child psychology may indeed be a costly luxury for modern Western parents, but it does not make child-rearing any easier. Just as improvements in household appliances have failed to reduce the housewife's working hours, but merely have raised standards of housekeeping, so have child psychology and improved pediatrics raised the standards for childrearing."

This notion of parenting transcends the urban-rural difference. It is almost a taken-for-granted middle-class assumption that responsible parenting means facilitating children's activities. This means that parents will spend much of their time transporting their children from one activity (music) to another (gifted program). In addition to those resulting from the ethic of involving children in educational activities are the activities children generate on their own – meeting friends, birthday parties, and so on. In families with more than one child, such involvements may require considerable parental investment in transportation time. Dropping three children off at three different places at three different times on the same day and then picking them all up, even if a labour of love, is laborious nonetheless!

The lived experience of the town is different from the large city in light of this element of contemporary parenting. While the smaller setting does not have the variety of programs that would be available in the city, the time needed to transport or otherwise arrange the children's activities is minimized. There are two sides to this claim to advantage. First, in isolation, it is understood to be an advantage in itself: the distances and time involved in bringing children to various activities is much less than in larger places. Second, and here we come to the interrelation of these characteristics, because the environment is understood to be safer *and* because the distance is smaller, one can more easily let children go to the activities by themselves. As one parent says (with some exaggeration), one "can be anywhere in five minutes."

Prairie Edge has two main residential areas – a suburb and the downtown area. The suburban area is a five- to ten-minute drive from the downtown area. In between are many tennis courts, parks, baseball diamonds, and an indoor aquatic centre. During the summer, children can ride their bicycles to any part of the town. During the winter, dropping the kids off at different centres is a five-minute task that can be absorbed into one's own ongoing activities. This convenience factor was seen to be important because it makes both the children's independence (they can walk or bike to where they need to go) and the parents' independence possible. As with the previous characteristic, for some parents the convenience of the town meant that parenting is less demanding because they can have time for other things; being an involved adult and being a parent were not seen as mutually conflicting roles – as they would be if facilitating children's activities were more time-consuming. On the other hand, this rural advantage was also interpreted to allow for the possibility of spending more time with the children. Whereas in a metropolis one could end up spending so much time facilitating activities that one actually had very little time with the children, "here in a small city again, you can go home for lunch. No problem. And the kids can, too." The convenience factor frees parents to have more time with their children and/or more time for themselves.

This aspect of convenience is a feature of Prairie Edge that became apparent as my wife and I compared our life in Toronto with our Prairie Edge experience. We enjoyed living and parenting in Toronto, and we were ambivalent about the move. Knowing that we would be moving to Prairie Edge in five months, we discussed what the move would mean for us. Through these discussions we realized that wherever we lived, whether in a city or in a town, much of our non-work time would be taken up with various parenting activities. We thought (perhaps like the urbanites in the Yerxa survey) that living in a town would be neutral with regard to this demand. In fact we found that the claims on our time as facilitators of children's activities were less. I remember reflecting at the end of our first year in Prairie Edge that parenting seemed less demanding (in the overwhelming way that it can sometimes be so) though I was unsure of why this was. In retrospect the convenience characteristic of the town contributed to the reduction of this sense of burden.

An interesting aspect of this convenience factor supports Pahl's (1968) contention that the urban-rural concept, *as a continuum*, hides important discontinuities. It also points to why "rurban," rather than either "urban" or "rural," is a more appropriate denotative term.

Many of the people talked to, and two of the co-conversationalists, had been raised on farms. Their memories of farm life were ones of isolation and inconvenience. Schools and social events were difficult to get to, and they often felt excluded because inconvenience made it difficult to be involved in peer group activities. Along an urban-rural continuum, one would therefore have to argue that the advantage of Prairie Edge (in terms of the convenience of facilitating children's activities) is essentially an urban advantage, and consequently one would have to place this town at the urban end of the continuum. Pahl himself might add that the interest in convenience is a middle-class urban interest.

Yet this is precisely where the continuum fails to throw light on an important discontinuity. As one mother said, neither the large city nor the "really rural" are "convenient." Prairie Edge was interpreted as "a nice balance ... between really rural and really city." On a *convenience continuum* therefore, the town would be at one end, while *farm living and big city living would both share the other end of the continuum.* For these parents *inconvenience* was characteristic of *both the big city and the farm* and was what made the town, in its particular combination of urban and rural characteristics, superior to both.[12] In this way "rurban" as a term for a settlement type combining urban and rural characteristics shows itself to be distinctively different from either a purely urban or a purely rural settlement type.

On the whole and in a way that relates to rurbanism, the co-conversationalists from the larger urban centres did not want to live in any place smaller than Prairie Edge, even if for the time being they thought that a larger centre was disadvantageous. Reflecting the fact that the population of Prairie Edge had doubled between 1961 and 1981, hometowners were inclined to comment on how much Prairie Edge had grown; one parent wondered aloud if it was beginning to get too big. All, however, enjoyed the urban facilities and having access to the facilities of Edmonton, "only an hour's drive away."

According to Pahl (1968, 272–3), this feature would place Prairie Edge in general, and the statements of the informants in particular, in an urban frame. The "essence of the city, to a true urbanite, is choice," which means that this "mobility through the countryside can be seen as an urban pattern." Pahl's idea of choice will be addressed later; for now what my research shows is that such dichotomies (urban or rural pattern) arbitrarily rule out of the analysis a conception of rurality that can be integrated with choice, as well as showing why the term "rurban" is a better analytic choice than seeing mobility through the countryside as "an urban pattern." Ironically, Pahl's criticism of the continuum rests on a requirement to

choose between rural and urban, whereas the term "rurban" identi-
fies what is distinctive about the new countryside of Canada and
overcomes restrictive and now no longer relevant dichotomies.

Less Parental Anxiety

SINGLE MOTHER (rural): I don't worry about the kids riding their bikes or
going places.

FATHER (ex-urbanite): Last night [when] we didn't know where our
youngest was, it did not cause us undue alarm.

FATHER (rural): It's a lot easier for kids to get into trouble in the city than
it is in a place like Prairie Edge as far as drugs, alcohol. I know it's available in Prairie Edge, but I think it's easier for them to get it in the city. [In
the city] I'd probably find myself either over-parenting, being overly cautious, or not being cautious enough. It's a scary situation.

MOTHER (rural): You don't get that underlying fear that something is
going to happen if we don't constantly remind the children.

MOTHER (ex-urbanite): I feel that our children had the opportunity to go
the public library from the time they were six by themselves, with a little
bit of guidance initially from us ... Whether that makes them safer or not,
I don't know, but for us, that's how we felt. So, we're much more low key.

MOTHER (ex-urbanite): "[It's better] because I'm calmer ... I noticed that
when my children were outside playing, I wasn't always in a big panic on
whether someone had come by and picked them up ... I'm a lot more of
a calmer parent.

The interrelation of these motifs is now becoming more apparent.
As shown in the methodology section, the mutuality of town living
and the sense of safety and of convenience together create a feeling
that one is or can be a calmer, less anxious parent. While because of
the way the modernized consciousness is organized, a sense of anxiety accompanies parenting itself, this town creates the feeling that
one neither has to be as watchful oneself nor has "to be constantly
reminding one's children" to be vigilant about safety. According to
these parents, this made parenting less stressful, less fearful, and less
anxiety-provoking, which in turn, made the parents feel more comfortable and confident in their relation with their children.[13] The parents were more comfortable in giving children greater freedom to
move about in their environment without having to constantly
supervise them.

Some parents stated that by virtue of being able to be "calmer" or "low key," they were better parents. Others, more often (though not always) the fathers, felt that their confidence in the safety of the town liberated them from excessive supervision demands. Thus increased parental confidence was seen either to make the task of parenting easier and more enjoyable or to make them better parents on the assumption that calmer parenting is better parenting. Yet what grounds the equation of calmer parenting with better parenting in relation to the lived experience of rurality?

The ex-urbanites who had the experience of parenting in the city remembered the way their fears and anxieties seemed to control their relation to parenting. Others envisioned the way fear and anxiety could dominate their parenting if they were living in the city. Thus the small town is successful in reducing the parental anxiety fed by contemporary society. This reduced sense of anxiety means that one's parenting is less controlled by perceived external factors (the danger of the city), and it can be more responsive to internal elements like one's parenting style or the particular personality of the child. For example, some children are more inclined to stay around the house, while others are more interested in exploring an external environment. If that external environment is perceived to be dangerous, both types of children become subject to a more restrictive and vigilant parenting style. The sense that one is a better parent because one is "calmer" or more "low-key" has a reality when it leads to a greater freedom to exercise practical wisdom (Bonner 1997).

The themes of safety, convenience, and reduced parental anxiety are interrelated. They are collected by the lived experience of parenting in a rurban centre; however, what grounds the interrelation is the theme of high visibility. The lived experience of the small town is the lived experience of high visibility, and this is true not only for parents but for all town residents. This association of rurality with high visibility, first formulated by Georg Simmel (see chapter 1), is an important theme not only for the next chapter but also for when I address the possibilities for community in the "new rurality" in the last chapter.

CHAPTER SEVEN

Smallness, High Visibility, and the Parental Life-World

"YOU PRETTY WELL KNOW WHO THEY'RE WITH ALL THE TIME."

High visibility is the social characteristic *par excellence* of town life. As Hale (1990, 120) remarks, "Smallness results in high visibility, and hence familiarity between residents but this does not necessarily lead to sociability and friendliness." Many of the ex-urbanites I have talked to would agree that "non-urban places are not as friendly as myth would make them out to be ... The rural neighbourhood is less a society of friends, with equal incomes and interests, and more of a mutual-aid society" (Long 1989, 170). The familiarity resulting from high visibility is more likely to lead to an ethic of helping and politeness than, as is often thought, to friendship and intimacy.

As I show in the next chapter, some of the ex-urbanites in this study acknowledged that they did not feel a sense of community in Prairie Edge, although they still felt that it was on the whole a better place to raise their children. In a smaller setting there is much cross-referencing of activities and people: people are more likely to be seen in a variety of settings playing a variety of roles. One is more familiar with more people and, in terms of reciprocity of perspectives (Schutz 1962), one becomes strongly aware of the mutuality of this familiarity. It is this high visibility that gives parents their confidence and sense of safety.

MOTHER (rural): There would be more chances of your parents finding out the trouble you're in ... My kids have a wild party, the neighbour is going to tell me, whereas in the city the neighbour might not even notice, or care.

FATHER (ex-urban): Like if one of the kids were uptown and it started raining or something, the chances of somebody walking home in the rain, of which they would not get to the corner before somebody drove by that they knew and they'd probably have a ride home. And in that minute, they're going to bump into somebody else they know. They'd probably get a ride in a large city, but not necessarily with somebody they know.

MOTHER (ex-urban): I think you would know about it faster, as a parent, if your child was involved with the wrong gang or was being led astray. I think you would hear about it. In the city you would never know, unless there was a teacher or something that reported it. Or you could see it a lot easier – that's just my feeling.

MOTHER (rural): I think another aspect of this, by living in a small place like this, you pretty well know who they're with pretty well all the time.

MOTHER (rural): It makes a difference too that when our kids go to do something, there's probably ten people there that know them, or what-ever, x number of people that know them, and it gives them a little bit more sense of responsibility for their actions, I think. Because when they're going somewhere where no one knows them, who cares what you do, because nobody's ever going to hear about it anyway. And I think they grow up with a different attitude, not that they're being watched, but with a little bit better sense of responsibility for what they're doing.

The above quotations, along with the lengthy statement from the ex-urbanite couple under the Safety category, show that the parents trusted their environment, felt it was safe, and were less anxious about potential dangers to children because children were being raised in a situation of high visibility. It is the high visibility charac-teristic of the town, rather than knowledge of "objective" indicators of crime, that generates the sense of safety and reduction of parental anxiety.

From the parental life-world, the experience of high visibility is really the experience of mutuality described in chapter 5. This mutu-ality increases the parents' sense that they have influence over other agents of socialization, a sense that vestigially connotes a *gemein-schaft*. Westhues (1982, 369), in explaining the decline of parental authority under conditions of advanced modernity, describes the way community extended parental authority. "Parents were once locked in relatively small and stable communities with their chil-dren's teachers and bus drivers, the school principal and the board members, the owners of the local drugstore and the candy shop,

constables and policemen, and the parents of their children's school-
mates. In many respects this community extended the parents own
authority." According to Westhues, a key trend in weakening this
community support is "the increased size of cities and of schools:
today's urban children grow up in settings more anonymous simply
by force of the larger numbers of people within them."

On the other hand, the high visibility feature of the town moves
the parenting experience closer to this older image of community.
High visibility means that there is little opportunity for children to
be anonymous and there is little fear of the perceived dangers of
anonymity on the part of parents. Parents sense that the burden
involved in the commitment to parenthood is shared by others. Parents will hear about the trouble their kids are in or parents know that
their children will get a ride home "from somebody that they know."
But this mutuality does more than increase parental knowledge and
reduce parental anxiety; parents feel that it also has a positive effect
on children's attitudes and character. Being aware that children will
be held accountable for their actions means that they grow up "with
a little bit better sense of responsibility for what they are doing."

Yet this notion of visibility is different from the traditional notion
of the rural community described in part 1. While the parents "pretty
well know who [the children] are with pretty well most of the time,"
this visibility does not take place in the context of the tight-knit,
historically connected, familial community Tonnies describes. High
visibility is recognizable both to ex-urbanites, who are not connected
through history or extended family to a close-knit community, and
to locals who are. What it means for parenting is different for each
group and for parents within the group, but all acknowledge its
importance for parenting.

Interestingly, when parents were asked to reflect on the drawbacks
of raising children in a smaller centre, the ex-urbanites referred to the
way the high visibility impinged negatively on their own freedom.
There was a sense that you had to watch what you said because you
could never be sure that it would not get back to the person being
talked about. ("You're careful what you say about who because you
never know if they're second cousin to my brother-in-law sort of
thing" – mother/rural.) One mother talked about the power of
rumours and reputation and being forced to deal with what others
say about you and your family. All of these drawbacks are due to
high visibility. Clearly, high visibility is not an unqualified good. The
drawbacks connect with Simmel's criticism of the small town (see
chapter 1) as limiting the free development of individual uniqueness,

while the advantage lies in the way high visibility eases the burden of parental supervision; it enhances the power of a parent's vision, thus making *supervision* of the children easier.

In contrast to the locals who take this feature of town life for granted, the ex-urbanites are not as unambiguous. While high visibility creates a history of familiarity and participation for the locals, for the ex-urbanites this characteristic is also very much associated with a lack of privacy. A colleague (ex-urbanite, childless) used to become angry whenever there was a hint that his life and actions were the subject of communal address or gossip. To him it was a "real invasion" of what belonged to him. Another acquaintance, a father and academic who had lived in Los Angeles, Jersey City, and Toronto, also expressed annoyance with the lack of privacy of the town but simultaneously acknowledged being more secure about his parenting. The visibility of the small town, the fact that (as one parent put it) the "town talks," makes him feel more secure about his daughter's movements. Yet this lack of privacy and the sense that *his own movements* are also topicalized (even though "it's none of their bloody business") is what annoys him about the town. In assessing the relative balance of these characteristics, he acknowledges that the sacrifice of greater privacy is compensated by what the small town offers to his parenting. This is a good example of the importance the parental life-world has in the horizon of this adult. Visibility, it seems, makes *super*vision easier, more relaxing, and less of a strain.

To get a sense of the meaning of high visibility, let us look more closely at one conversation between one set of parents:

MOTHER (rural): Like you take [your children]: you know who their friends are and what they're doing. If you get in the city, the kids hop a bus and go across town, you don't know what they're doing. They may be up to absolutely no harm, but then they could be up the other way, too. And you'd never know it.

INTERVIEWER: Knowing more, what does that mean? Does that give you greater security or control?

MOTHER: Control? I think you have more control over them in a smaller place.

FATHER (rural): Yeh, I don't know. Do you mean control? Are you trying to control them, or just trying to supervise them a bit, whatever? I don't know if you really mean control.

The mother describes the rural advantage, saying that in the town you know who the children are with and "know more" about what they are doing. I ask a question of the meaning of this "knowing more" and offer the translation of either security or control. The mother says "control," perhaps meaning that she literally has more control over her children's behaviour or (given the way her discourse connotes a sense of anxiety with "not knowing") perhaps also meaning that she has more control over her own fears and anxieties. However, the father disagrees with the formulation of "knowing more" as control, suggesting alternatively the notion of supervision.

Elaborating later, he says: "So it gives the parents a little bit of a sense of security, too." The "supervision is spread out more;" it does not solely fall on the parents' shoulders and is not there as a "thumbs down thing," expressing a tryannical interest. Rather, it gives the parents confidence to grant more freedom to the children. They feel less pressure to restrict their children's movements because of this "knowing more." Both of these parents were from the locality and enjoyed the sense of belonging that participation in the sense of the town talking created.

When we attend to the way the parents describe the advantage of this sense of high visibility, the terms "knowing who your kids are with" and "hearing what they are up to" are used interchangeably. That is, visibility makes possible a knowledge about one's children's activity which ironically is based *not on what one sees but on what one hears* or "would hear." The capacity for greater/easier supervision is based not on the eye, as in Foucault's (1977) panopticon, but on the ear. The smallness of the town increases the sense that stories and reports about self and other constantly circulate. In the town, people are part of and subject to a particular kind of discourse, and this is so regardless of whether one wants one's life and actions to be so subject. The relevant point here is that this greater capacity for or greater ease of supervision (*surveyability*) is mediated through discourse. It is what we hear or would hear, not what we see or would see. The hearing is necessarily embedded in a social relation, and thus is much more consciously context bound than the apparent detachment of the eye. The hearing is embedded in and expressive of what Hannah Arendt (1958, 181–8) calls the "web of relations," which itself reflects Simmel's formulation of the small-town character of the ancient Greek *polis*. This idea of the interrelation between the town, surveyability, and the *polis* is addressed in a later chapter; here I want to place this material in the context of the modern anxiety about parenting, particularly in relation to the historical development of the isolation of parenting from the wider community.

MOBILITY AND
THE RELEVANCE OF
THE URBAN-RURAL
DISTINCTION FOR PARENTING

What emerges from the research material is the dominance of the modernized consciousness described by Berger, Berger and Kellner (1973) in the third chapter of this text. Social and geographic mobility is either an experience or an assumed fact of modern life. The city, therefore, is not a different and anthropologically strange world but merely a different type of experience (of "diversity," "wealth," "big," "consumerism," "pollution," "excitement," "opportunity," "anonymity," "danger," "crowds," "noise," "pressure," "hostility"). Rural life is neither experienced as primitive nor as radically isolating. It is seen to be safer, more convenient, and familiar, but also, to some, claustrophobic and narrow. Rural is still recognized as being different from urban, but the difference is seen to be one of degree, not of kind. Again, though "rural" was the term commonly used by people I talked to, "rurban" is a term that more precisely denotes the modern town.

Both urban and rural were evaluated in relation to each other in terms of their limitations and drawbacks. All I talked to drew on their knowledge of both city and country when they spoke of the differences. Moving to the city or to the country is not seen as a move from one "way of life" to another but instead is experienced as a move to a different social environment which has significant if subtle differences that are underlined in the lived experience of parenting.

All of the co-conversationalists (rural and ex-urbanite) foresee that their children will live and experience the diversity of the city at some point in their lives. For all of these parents except one (who admitted a "bias against the city"), the children's potential experience of the city was viewed in a positive light. Rural life was seen to be limited in terms of career and educational opportunities, while the city was seen to represent choices, career opportunities, and diversity of experience: it presented "the rich fabric of life that you need in order to make life exciting" (ex-urbanite). City experience was seen as necessary to combat the danger of stagnation that emerges when one is too closely tied to family. One father (ex-urban) said that a risk of staying for a long time in the small town is that people get so wrapped up in a small group (family) that "they have to stay close"; they do not have the freedom to explore different possibilities for themselves. Reminiscent of Simmel's "jealous whole," small-group or family ties can be so interlocking that there is the danger that one will not get to explore and develop one's individuality.

Another ex-urbanite father said that "conformity and stagnation can be the fear of a small community. It needn't be, but you need a lot of extra effort to generate and maintain all those other interesting things yourself." This ex-urbanite also remarked that the choices and options in the city can be "very glitzy ... You can see the worst of our consumer culture when you hit the cities." It was also acknowledged that Prairie Edge has many cultural activities as well as a small university, so that the risk of stagnation is less in this particular town in comparison to other smaller rural centres. It has an arts centre and the university theatre centre; writers' groups, dance classes, and classical and contemporary music lessons as well as many sports activities (skiing, hockey, soccer, baseball, basketball, and so on) are available.

In order to put all of the conversations in perspective, however, it is most important to remember the way everyone accepts that it is the quality of parenting rather than the place of parenting that is most decisive. While Prairie Edge may be a great place to raise kids, it is not a place that can make up for poor-quality parenting. In a taken-for-granted way, everyone recognizes that the decisiveness of the quality of parental intervention supercedes that of the influence of place. Yet this recognition reinforces my claim that rural differences are seen to be real and positively influential from within the life-world of parenting, a difference that may or may not be reflected in any objective indicators.

The importance of the concept of parental life-world for understanding the meaning of rurality in this case is illustrated by the following example. A single mother whose children are now nineteen and twenty-two, said, "Personally, right now, being single and forty-one, I'd get out of here in two seconds if I had a job elsewhere." Here we have a striking example of the phenomenon of separate life-worlds. This individual experiences herself in a double way: as a parent with two children, and as a single woman living in a small town. Because her children are grown, the life-world of the single woman is becoming more relevant; the single woman life-world increasingly begins to dominate the way the town is engaged, measured, and evaluated. Thus she can say that Prairie Edge is a good place to raise children and that she "would get out of here in two seconds" if she "had a job elsewhere." That is to say, the "great place to raise kids" is not necessarily "a great place to be."

PRAIRIE EDGE,
THE PARENTAL LIFE-WORLD,
AND THE BURDEN OF
MODERN PARENTING

As I argued in part 1, the best way to approach and understand these parental reflections is to recognize the predominance of the modern consciousness. One of its defining characteristics is a social life-world that acknowledges, as reality, *the plurality of life-worlds*. Thus, Prairie Edge and the people I talked to do not represent some anthropologically strange community whose language, rituals, everyday practices, and culture are esoteric and difficult to understand. Their consciousness, world view, and life-world are modern. Insofar as the Prairie Edge individuals take the plurality of life-worlds for granted, this sociological encounter is an encounter with the human condition in contemporary society.

Like the single mother above, other sets of parents who had made the transition from urban to rural could imagine themselves living elsewhere after the children had grown up. Unlike the hometowners, who tended to see Prairie Edge as "a great place," period, many ex-urbanites did not feel the same sense of attachment and did not see Prairie Edge in such rose-tinted terms. Whereas for hometowners place, family, friends, and the memories of growing up all interconnected in a way that generated a sense of community and local pride, ex-urbanites saw Prairie Edge's lack of racial and ethnic diversity, the narrowness and conservatism of its population, and the tendency to insularity as disagreeable features. One visitor described Prairie Edge as a typical 1950s US town. For hometowners (as for this visitor), this made Prairie Edge attractive; some ex-urbanites on the other hand, do not see the 1950s as a golden age. Thus, the place in "a great place to raise kids" had a different meaning for each group. Yet given this important disagreement, what is striking is that both saw it as "a great place to raise kids." While some might not like Prairie Edge and others are proud of it, both acknowledge the rural benefit. In the next chapter I address the difference between these groups, but for now I want to emphasize this agreement as evidence of how significant the parental life-world has become in the horizon of modern adults.

The hermeneutic phenomenological research approach (Van Manen, 1990) shows that the recognition of the advantage of the rural setting is not generated from a neutral, objective perspective. It is the life-world of parenting that provides for the recognition and significance of the advantage, and this life-world enables the actor to recognize features of the town to which he or she might otherwise be indifferent. For instance, one ex-urbanite in an informal conversation early in this study argued against the benefit of rural child-rearing by pointing to the dangers of narrowness and insularity. As her child at that time was one year old, the home rather than the town was the decisive environment. Three years later she spoke of the advantages of the town in terms of safety, convenience, and trust in the community. From a static, neutral, and objective point of view, one might argue that these opinions about rural child-rearing are opposed to each other and that given that the same person is talking about the same place, one of the opinions has to be incorrect.

Phenomenology helps us understand that seeking to resolve the correctness of these opposing opinions confuses the matter. Rather, as the life-world of parenting becomes more relevant for this individual, she literally begins to recognize (know and see) features of the town that previously were not noticed or noticeable. It is the life-world of parenting that grounds and organizes a particular relation to the town, and so notions of convenience and safety are experienced socially in terms of a relevant life-world. What is meaningfully encountered as "safe" by a parent may be meaningfully encountered as "boring" and "stultifying" by a single adult or a childless couple. As both understandings are real, the attempt to establish some unitary truth in advance would be both arbitrary and a failure to understand the social nature of experience. This is not to say that different life-worlds cannot themselves be conceptually measured and critically evaluated, but we can only do so after the researcher has identified the object or the "what it is" that is meant by the claim "it's a great place to raise kids." Given that the ground for the claim lies in the significance parenting has for both hometowners and ex-urbanites, understanding the claim requires that this foundation be uncovered.

The claims for the advantage of a setting like Prairie Edge have to be understood against the background of what parenting has come to mean in North America. The very assumption of the decisiveness of parental power and influence has itself created problems that in turn help us understand the meaning of the rural advantage for parenting (Bonner 1997). Recent sociological studies have described the modern parental situation as "disadvantageous and overburdening" (Skolnick 1987, 325–34), as a "crisis" (LeMasters 1957), as the "most difficult task in the world" (LeMasters and DeFrain 1989, 1), as "full of hostility and recrimination" (Lasch 1979, xxii), as "the crucial role transition for men and women" (Hutter 1988, 370), and as "straining" (Rossi 1968). In addressing and summarizing the literature in this area, Arlene Skolnick (1987, 331) summarizes these developments: "Modern parenthood can be a burden because parents lack the support of kin and community ... because children have become consumers of the family's resources rather than productive contributors to it ... [and because] the modern parent is responsible not only for the child's physical well-being, but also for the child's psychological adjustment."

If parenting has become burdensome through the raised standards that parents are expected to meet, an increase in the financial burden of bearing children, and a lack of communal support in the actual practice of parenting, we can now recognize what the claim for the advantage of Prairie Edge means. Prairie Edge seems to address one of the three areas that add to the burden of modern (middle-class) parenting. In this rural centre, parents feel that the burden of parenthood is shared insofar as the need to supervise children is eased. Because you would "hear what your kid was up to," because "the neighbours would tell me," because "you know who they are with" most of the time, the sense is that one is not alone in the task of parenting. The high visibility characteristic of the small town, ironically embedded in the everyday phenomenon of listening to the stories that townsfolk circulate about each other, increases the parents' sense of their own capacity to *supervise* their children.

While the responsibility of the parent is undiminished, the ability to fulfil the responsibility is increased. This increase in ability to supervise is felt not as an increase in power or control but rather as an easing of a burden. The Prairie Edge experience of parenting is liberating for these middle- and upper-working-class parents because they are helped in their responsibility. Thus it can be said that Prairie Edge is a great place to raise kids because it contributes to easing the parents' ability to fulfil the burden of responsibility put almost solely upon them. The benefit of the ease can only be understood against the cultural background of parental responsibility.

This aid is a peculiarly modern version of help. It is aid without being an interference; it helps you supervise your kids without telling you how to raise them or, in the language of sociology, without a "tightening of the parenthood script," as is said to be the case in more traditional societies (Hutter 1988, 353–89; Skolnick 1987, 332). Particularly for the ex-urbanites, Prairie Edge enhances the capacity for supervision without adding the entanglements that come with having an extended family close by; the aid to supervision that Prairie Edge (rurbanism) represents is a modern solution to a modern problem (the almost total responsibility of the parent).

We now have a better sense of the object that the parents of Prairie Edge are "bringing into words" through this research. For these participants the decisive feature of rurality is not tradition, history, isolation, or homogeneity but rather smallness of size. As Hale (1990, 120) says, smallness leads to greater visibility. Within the parental life-world, greater visibility eases the burden of supervision that contemporary society places almost exclusively on parents. To this very particular extent, a place like Prairie Edge lives up to the reputation of the rural advantage.

Yet, despite the use of phenomenology, my analysis so far is bound by the empirical horizon of the other and thus has not gone much beyond mere reconstruction. That is, I have recreated the meaning behind the claim for rural advantage, but I have not allowed that to open other possibilities of meaning: If dialectic is the art of thinking (see chapter 5), then the possibilities intrinsic to the claim have yet to be thought through. This involves bringing up for examination that which was unquestioningly accepted by the interviewee and interviewer. What is it that has still been unquestioningly accepted and therefore is still unresolved? What is the real question here? What has been accepted is the very intelligibility and reasonability of the modernized consciousness. As with the conceptualization of rurality, as with the section on methodology, the history and culture of contemporary society itself needs to be brought into view, as this history and culture is expressed through the particular case of Prairie Edge.

Life-world analysis demonstrates the way modernity both overrides and collects the difference between urban and "rural" settings. In contemporary society, rural no longer references that which is other to modernity, whether that be tradition (Weber) or community (Tonnies); the urban is no longer seen as representative of progress (Marx), capitalism (Tonnies), or anomic social relations (Wirth). Instead, both urban and rural are viewed in relation to size, i.e., as large and small, rather than referring to the particularity of place or way of life. Safety, convenience, and reduced parental anxiety, are all rational (in the Weberian sense of that term) ways of relating to the town. Thus the way persons relate to the town is not unlike the way they relate to the city. The differences that are said to exist between the town and the city are ones that emerge when they are *viewed from a similar modern frame of mind*. It is only because we recognize this frame of mind that we understand the grounds behind the claim that a rurban setting like Prairie Edge is "a great place to raise kids."

What now needs to be done is to examine the particular cultural and historical nature of this frame of mind. If "rurbanism" is a term invented to describe the modernization of the rural, then we need to examine critically the orientation making it possible for such an object to exist. This involves reflecting on the research material in terms of its relation to the larger cultural and historical forces influencing both the research and the researcher. In other words, *the pre-judgments* that allow both the urban and the rural to be seen and evaluated from the same frame of mind now need to be explored. Bringing such pre-judgments into view involves examining the following broader issues: first, the meaning of the "victory of modernity" with regard to the irrelevance of place (Jameson 1983), second, the question of what happens to other(ness) in this victory, and last, the way Berger's phenomenology, though it has been undoubtably useful so far, blinds us to particular ethical and political elements of this "victory." The intellectual problem developed in the course of conceptualizing rurality (i.e., the disappearance of a strong sense of otherness) now re-emerges in this more practical context.

The questions the research project now asks are: Can a place be that "great" if one's relation to it is instrumental? What are we teaching our children when we use a place as a means to an end? What are the ethical and political implications of a theory that uncritically embraces the pluralization of life-worlds? In other words, we now move beyond description in order to engage in ethical, political, and theoretical examination.

The next chapter digresses from the immediate examination of these issues to explicate the theoretic principles requiring this turn in the research project. The digression is necessary because it provides a ground for critiquing certain tendencies in phenomenology and postmodernism. The phenomenology of Berger and the postmodernism of Clifford have been very useful resources for conceptualizing rurality and for articulating the orientation and procedure of radical interpretive sociology. However, in chapter 9 I will show that both phenomenology and postmodernism have ethical and political implications that the self-conscious researcher should be aware of. These implications could unwittingly end up legitimating a consumer relation to the world unless they are self-consciously resisted. The digression seeks to provide the grounds for such a self-conscious resistance.

Moving in this direction, I recognize I am pushing the idea of the research project to a deeper level than usual. The next chapter demonstrates that an oriented and directed research project should contribute not just to knowledge but to understanding and wisdom. If wisdom has as its object knowledge of ethical action (Gadamer 1986), a research project must always be willing to consider and assess the ethical and political implications of its own work. Can this assessment be done as part of the human science research project itself? Or is it merely an adjunct to the research? Can the contribution to wisdom actually further the research, or is it what comes into place after the research is done? Radical interpretive sociology argues for the former because of its recognition that at a deep level "the practical and the theoretical are inextricably joined" in human science research (Taylor 1977, 127).

Whose Side Does the Research Take – the Community of Scholars, the Research Subjects, or the Phenomenon Itself?

POSTMODERNISM AND RADICAL INTERPRETIVE SOCIOLOGY

This is the reason that all understanding is always more than the mere rec-reation of some else's meaning. Asking it opens up possibilities of mean-ing and thus what is meaningful passes over into one's own thinking on the subject ... To understand a question means to ask it. To understand an opinion is to understand it as the answer to a question.

Hans-Georg Gadamer, 1975

Research conducted from within the paradigm of radical interpretive sociology involves acknowledging that the sociologist is of necessity more than a mouthpiece for the member's understanding. Limiting oneself to a representation of the interviewee's self-definition limits the *development* of *understanding* on which the self-definition of Prai-rie Edgers rests. From the radical interpretive perspective, limiting the research project to the recreation of what is meant by the claim is to narrow "the possibilities of meaning" built into the claim. It is to assume that the understanding of this claim belongs to parents in a rural setting.

However, a more ontological approach says that understanding belongs to the being of the object. "Understanding is not an entity in the world but rather the structure in being which makes possible the actual exercise of understanding on an empirical level" (Palmer 1969, 131). Understanding is ultimately and fundamentally a process that possesses us as inquirers as much as we possess it. In this ontological sense, understanding transcends the subject/object (researcher/sub-ject) split. This acknowledgment allows us to recognize the limits of some postmodernist positions on social inquiry.

Poststructuralism (e.g., Foucault 1977; Clifford 1988) shows the way social science research (claiming a transcendental place outside of discourse) is itself shaped by dominant cultural practices (Turner 1989, 13–27) and thus reinforces the very disciplinary society it claims to objectively study. In the area of ethnography, standard scientific studies have the effect of making the culture of the other (e.g., Prairie Edge claims) intelligible to both the scholarly audience and the dominant disciplinary interests. This discursive move makes the other into a knowable object and thus vulnerable to exploitation and disciplinary practices.[1] De Vries and McNab-De Vries (1991) argue that the controlled social scientific discourse of standard modernist ethnographies has the consequence of maintaining barriers between the sociologist and the sociologist's subjects (the members of the particular setting). They see these modernist limitations of scientific discourse, which privilege the academic audience over the self-understanding of the member, being overcome by methods such as participation, recorded interviews, and reciprocity that get close to and preserve the member's interests.

Following this model, my research aim should be to preserve the claims of parents in Prairie Edge against those of positivistic science that prove the claims to be groundless. Poststructuralism sees the modernist relation to research "subjects" as potentially oppressive and exploitative. Here, poststructuralism agrees in spirit with certain kinds of critical theory and feminist principles. For example, "Reinharz describes conventional research as 'rape': 'the researchers take, hit and run. They intrude on their subjects' privacy, disrupt their perceptions, utilize false pretences, manipulate the relationship, and give little or nothing in return. When the needs of the researchers are satisfied, they break off contact with the researched'" (Reinharz 1983, 80 as cited in Lentin 1993, 127).

Accordingly, poststructuralism (and some feminist methodology) seeks to reverse the position here by arguing that research is to be conducted for the research subject and not for an elite scholarly audience or for dominant institutional interests. Empowerment and emancipation (Lentin 1993, 125–6) are crucial elements in this approach. In my case, I should include as part of the research strategy consideration about how my research empowers the voice and situation of the parents who spoke to me. Given the overwhelming oppressive power of urban imperialism, Sim (1988) makes a case for empowerment as a necessary characteristic of all research on and in rural settings (chapter 3). The "distinctive and colonizing force" of the city, he says (23), needs to be counterbalanced. In some ways, what I have done in the previous three chapters could be read in this light. The hermeneutic phenomenological approach requires the researcher to work to strengthen what the parents say, and I have done this by recovering from their talk a conceptual framework (parental life-world) that enables their claims to be recognized as real.

While the postmodern critique and recommendation is an advance on standard social science in the development of a reflexive understanding, from a radical interpretive perspective such poststructuralism still preserves the inquirer/member (subject/object) split on which modernism is founded. Moving closer to describing and empowering the voice of the other still rests on a categorical and interactional self/other distinction. Instead of seeking to describe and even empower the voice of the other, radical interpretive sociology argues for strengthening what the other says by referring to the object being referred to in the talk.

Thus, for example, the issue of the rural advantage is not one of members' claims versus the claims of positivistic science. I am not arguing that the former are right and the latter are wrong. Rather, the object of study is this parental life-world in a rural setting, and the concern is with deepening our understanding of this object. The contributions of positivistic sociology help in the search for an understanding because, for example, they tell us that the claim to rural safety cannot be based on the lower incidence of crime. Such findings tend to surprise rural residents, who take for granted the safety of their setting. Yet this surprise is an opportunity to push for a deeper understanding of the issue and not a mere occasion to correct perceptions. The lived experience (of the researcher, the parents) of rural safety is an essential resource to help push the understanding further. To this extent, getting close to the experience being researched is a shared aim of feminist, phenomenological, and radical interpretive research.

Yet a close relation to research subjects is not the ultimate aim of radical interpretive research. The true situation of social inquiry is ultimately a conversation between self and other, oriented to developing a *shareable understanding of an object* and not simply a therapeutic encounter (concerned with helping Prairie Edge parents understand themselves), a political encounter (concerned with empowering the voice of parents in a rural setting) or even an encounter with a polyphony of diverse voices (Clifford 1988). While these latter are necessary social encounters, they are limited in terms of the aim of social inquiry because they essentially predetermine what the process of inquiry is about.[2]

The very idea of needing to speak for the subjects, to be their representative, or to celebrate the diversity of their voices (De Vries and McNab-De Vries, 1991) demonstrates the failure of the research to achieve a conversational situation and prevents the development of a fuller understanding. While there may be contingent reasons (e.g., the foreignness of speaker or situation) preventing researchers from giving themselves over to the process of understanding, of allowing the conversation to conduct the speakers, the latter needs to be the aim of the analysis. An interpretation that, in preserving the distinction (in its achievement) between the researcher and the subject, even at the point when it reminds itself that it needs to better represent its subjects (informants/the field/the participants), has failed to move and be taken hold of by the object or the *what* of what has been said (the subject matter being discussed). In the language of hermeneutics, such an orientation fails to recognize the analytic thrust of interpretation, that selecting and highlighting is inextricably tied to the process of interpretation and that this selecting and highlighting is oriented by the need to learn about the multi-dimensional reality embedded in the claim "a great place to raise kids." If the aim of this research project is not "to combine the researchers' narratives with those of the informants" (De Vries and McNab-De Vries 1991, 494) or to emancipate rural culture from the threat of urban imperialism (Sim 1988), then what does inspire radical interpretive research?

TRUST, HUMAN EXPERIENCE, AND THE DESIRE TO KNOW

What is necessary and desirable for the knower is that he accept the need and desirability to demonstrate the difference between what appears to be and what is, where that need is unshakeable by persuasion. It is the very unshakeability of this acceptance that empowers that knower to desire discourse that will demonstrate the difference in the case of the particular notion.   Blum and McHugh, 1984

Thus experience is experience of human finitude. The truly experienced man is one who is aware of this, who knows that he is master neither of time nor the future. The experienced man knows the limitedness of all prediction and the uncertainty of all plans.   Hans-Georg Gadamer, 1975

Two principles inspire radical interpretive research. Human experience is fundamentally the "experience of human finitude" (Gadamer 1975, 310–25) and the researcher's recognition that to seek the truth is to accept the deep need for discourse (Blum and McHugh 1984, 123–51). These two principles are like opposite sides of the same coin. The researcher accepts the need for the "knower to desire discourse" precisely as the positive expression of the experience of human finitude. The need to research further, to pursue, for example, other elements hidden in the claim for rural advantage, is the appropriate response to the recognition of Socratic ignorance, that we know we don't know. Both of these principles mean that the understanding that develops through conversation is the means, end, and aim of research (and of living).

What is involved in following through on these principles in a practical research project? Desiring discourse means giving oneself over to understanding the possibilities of meaning behind knowledge of the reasons for a town being "a great place to raise kids." This is a process followed by the researcher. As such the researcher must be able to free him/herself from the unreflective (ideological) hold that pre-understandings exercise in this case. "Allowing oneself to be directed and even possessed by dialectic" is the point where research and thinking meet through the "posing of real questions" (Gadamer 1975, 330). Moving to the level where research and thinking meet means going beyond the mere reconstruction of the understanding of Prairie Edge parents into a deeper understanding of the implications built into the being of the object. In the case of the relation between rurality and the parental life-world, what the researcher does is to allow this to enter his or her thinking. Allowing one's thinking to enter the object through the posing of real questions is to move beyond reconstructing the understanding of the other, thus going beyond what is empirically given. For example, are there other "possibilities of meaning" built into the relation to place than those articulated in the last chapter? What if these possibilities were not considered by the "informants" or co-conversationalists? When the researcher seriously considers what the parents in a rural setting may not have considered, "what is meaningful passes into [the researcher's] thinking on the subject." But this thinking cannot be verified by a return to the "data." As Charles Taylor (1977) clearly demonstrates, verification and predictive capacity are no longer appropriate measures to take account of the research.

The risk the research project runs at this stage is the loss of some listeners whose own life-world prevents them from understanding what is being developed or from needing to understand what is being developed. For example, those for whom knowledge creation and verification go hand in hand may see moving the research project to this level as offering claims that cannot be proven and may not be appreciated. If they can neither be verified nor appreciated, how can this count as knowledge, they may ask. They may add that the difference between "hard-nosed" research and unsupportable speculation is being undermined. Why, therefore, push the research in this direction?

> The practical and theoretical are inextricably joined here. It may not just be that to understand a certain explanation one has to sharpen one's intuitions, it may be that one has to change one's orientation – if not in adopting another orientation, at least in living in one's own way which allows for greater comprehension of others. Thus, in the sciences of man insofar as they are hermeneutical there can be a valid response to "I don't understand" which takes the form, not only "develop your intuitions", but more radically "change yourself." This puts an end to any aspiration to a value free or "ideology free" science of man. A study of the science of man is inseparable from an examination of the options between which men must choose (Taylor 1977, 127).

A "value free" or "ideology free" human science is impossible. Just as humans in community show themselves to be subscribing to some fundamental principles, so too does the researcher. Acting on and subscribing to certain fundamental principles may prevent one from understanding the fundamental principles of another. To use an example cited in chapter 3, the tribal person who believes his deceased grandfather is communicating with him in his dreams will find it difficult to understand that such dreams are merely a result of eating late at night. The modern woman who subscribes to bio-logical understandings of the digestive system may find it hard to understand that her deceased grandfather is saying something to her in her dreams. Each subscribes to a different fundamental principle: the traditional man that he ought to keep in touch with his ancestors, the modern woman that she ought to live as healthily as possible. Each lives according to a different ethos and each understands according to the principles that support the ethos. The issue now is whether there is a way of mediating these two fundamental princi-ples. Is there a way of developing knowledge about the ethical life? To attempt to answer the latter is to disturb the self-understanding of both the modern and traditional persons. Yet the desire for dia-logue and the finitude of human understanding push the researcher to take this risk, one that may mean that both traditional and modern persons will say, "I don't understand."

What further complicates this matter is that the researcher, as a member of a community of scholars, is also subscribing to funda-mental principles in the doing of the research. There is no value-free or ideology-free human science. For example, the interconnection between modernity and science has already been articulated. Thus, a directed and oriented research project would be one that is self-conscious about the fundamental principles to which it subscribes as it examines the fundamental principles inherent in the research subject's actions. Can a research study claim to be fully oriented and directed if it is not aware of the fundamental principles it is implicitly recommending? As Taylor says, "The practical and theoretical are inextricably joined here."

Obviously my understanding of research means that this project subscribes to certain fundamental principles and that it is incumbent on me to articulate these. What principles guide this research? The recognition of the inextricable joining of the theoretical and the practical means that research and what Gadamer calls *Bildung* (1975, 5–39), or self-formation, are also joined. To engage in research is also to engage in a project of self-formation. Hermeneutic phenomenological research is "a form of deep learning, leading to a transformation of consciousness, heightened perceptiveness, increased thoughtfulness and tact" (Van Manen 1990, 163). Engaging in human science research is to engage in a project of "developing one's intuitions," or even "more radically," to "change oneself."

Thus, the purpose or aim of this kind of social research is more than contributing to the store of knowledge. What can be known "cannot be grasped independently of the framework of [the researcher's] own life-praxis ... Gadamer's real accomplishment [is] his demonstration that hermeneutic understanding is necessarily related, on the transcendental level, to the articulation of an action-orienting self-understanding" (Habermas 1988, 160–2). Therefore, for radical interpretive sociology, research and the creation of knowledge are deeply pedagogical undertakings, involving both learning and teaching. In doing research, one is involved in turning attention "to principles recommended for acceptance" (R. McKeon, as cited in Blum & McHugh 1984, 3). Self-formation (*Bildung*) is the standard against which radical interpretive research must ultimately be measured. Of course, given that all research at some level shows the community of scholarship it belongs to, and thus the fundamental principles it subscribes to, radical interpretive research self-consciously addresses this universal aspect of research.

The radical (i.e., rooted) position of radical interpretive sociology is that *all* research findings are forms of interpretation and that accepting certain conclusions is a simultaneous acceptance of a way of relating to the world. What has to be brought into the research project for examination are not the conclusions by themselves but the way the methods and the theorizing that generate conclusions are grounded in a way of "being in the world." The issues of "knowl-edge" and "truth" are essentially and intrinsically related to "an examination of the options between which men must choose" (Taylor 1977, 127). This principle means that the sociological researcher is more than a neutral witness (detached observer), more than a sym-pathetic listener to the claims of everyday members (participant observer), more than an expert offering explanations about social phenomena, but is also a self-conscious theorist showing or exempli-fying a "possible society" (Blum 1971) or "the agreement of an ideal community" (Gadamer 1975, 36). All lay and professional investiga-tions, whether quantitative, qualitative, interpretive, or analytic, are forms of theorizing. The different methods each perspective espouses are different ways the theorist has of composing him or herself – as his or her way of showing not only the world in which one happens to live, but, insofar as the life of examination is (necessarily) part of this world, the principles one chooses to recommend. The dialectical analysis component of radical interpretive sociology is oriented to providing a way the inquirer can take responsibility for this choice.

"What an inquiry inquires about (its concrete topic) is not its ana-lytic end, because we locate that end in its aim to create acceptance of its principles. These principles constitute principled ways of for-mulating and conceptualizing a topic and can be seen as an author-itative way of discussing or discoursing about a topic ... A communicative end is not merely a "goal" of inquiry, but it also impregnates the very constitution of inquiry as its foundation" (Blum & McHugh 1984, 3). That is, the concrete topic ("a great place to raise kids") and the analytic end (what fundamental principles are worth recommending) are explicitly integrated in an oriented and self-directed human science research project. Obviously different tra-ditions of research take different stands with regard to the necessity and desirability of doing research in this way. In so doing, these traditions implicitly (and sometimes unwittingly) but necessarily turn attention to different principles recommended for acceptance. Are these principles worth recommending? Worth accepting?

To summarize, I argue that the issue of sociological inquiry into any specific part of social life is not only a matter of methodology but also a matter of seeing (perspective), knowing (epistemology) and being in the world (ontology). While these issues are bound up with every study, a strongly oriented and directed research project requires engaging such issues explicitly as part of the particular project under consideration.

Thus, though my immediate concern is with the claim for the superiority of raising children in a more rural setting, that concern cannot be divorced from broader *praxis* concerns of what a good relation to place looks like and what a good relation to research looks like.

The demand that "deep" concerns be theorized does not mean that the very particular issue of parenting in a smaller centre has to be set aside. Rather, what I seek to show is that thoroughly engaging particular concerns requires having the analytic nerve to pursue them to their deep/broad implications. The next chapter undertakes to recover for critical examination the socio-historical influences that sustain a consumer relation to place and the theoretic perspective of Berger's phenomenology. My analysis is not only concerned with the actualities of meaning (in relations between self and other, parents and children, people and place) but also with "possibilities of meaning." These seemingly theoretic and general concerns have very specific implications for *praxis* in a rural setting.

As a way of engaging these issues, I want to return to the research material to address and examine a small (but significant) difference between the reasons hometowners and ex-urbanites offered for the benefit of a rural setting. This difference refers to the level of importance each group gave to the value of living close to the extended family. In terms of the research conversations as a whole, whether formal or informal, the emphasis on this value is small and subtle. It would not emerge as remarkable in any objective, formal coding of the interviews; yet the difference is significant because it points to a vestige of resistance to modernity. Attachments to the wider kin (who share the same place of residence) is considered a significant part of a pre-modern orientation to family (Skolnick 1987, 123). This small difference will be explored and examined as a way of critically resisting the particular character of recent developments in contemporary society, i.e., consumerism. Parenthetically, these last two chapters re-engage, re-think, and re-integrate themes developed in parts 1 to 3.

PART FOUR

Postmodernism, Finitude, and the Problem of Community

CHAPTER NINE

Postmodernism and the Consumer Relation to Place

This book is about deciding where to live. About choices. It is in fact about the choice between city and country living. But more than that, it's about the very fact that the choice exists ... There are some broad reasons a former necessity has become a choice: the dispersal of industry and jobs away from city centres and the technical revolution that has decentralized access to information, the economy and even the culture. The sum of these changes is the end of rural isolation as we know it.

Charles Long, 1989

At some point following World War II a new kind of society began to emerge (variously described as post industrial society, multinational capitalism, consumer society, media society and so forth). [It was characterized by] new types of consumption; planned obsolescence; an ever more rapid rhythm of fashion and styling changes; the penetration of advertising, television and the media generally to a hitherto unparalleled degree throughout society; the replacement of the old tension between city and country, centre and province, by the suburb and by universal standardization ..."

Frederic Jameson, 1983

As described by Baumann, and also by Jean Baudrillard ... the postmodern order is one that privileges consumption rather than production. The consumer society is one of rapidly changing fashion, the constant creation and obsolescence of goods, and a society 'without history'. The objects with which consumers are surrounded are not grounded in historical tradition and have no particular relation to the past.

Giddens *et al.*, 1994

The three authors above refer to the "new kind of society" in which we now live. My own field material and lived experience in different ways express the nature of this society. In these pages so far I have acknowledged the "dominance of modernity" by showing the way it pervades the attitude of all parents with regard to the advantage of rural child-rearing. The above authors suggest that modernity has moved into a new phase of postmodernism or consumerism. As we know from the conceptualization of rurality, and, in particular, from the works of Marx, Tonnies, Weber, Wirth, and Redfield, the urban-rural difference was generally thought of in terms of the modernism of the city and the traditionalism of rural life. With the terms *gemeinschaft* and *gesellschaft*, Tonnies conceptualized the difference as referencing not just place but also a way of life. Rural and urban were understood to reference different organizational and political communities (*gemeinschaft* a pre-voluntary co-operative community, and *gesellschaft* an association based on rational and instrumental calculation of individual advantage).

Now, it is argued, we live in a new era, in which, as Long says, choice has become universal. Parents can think of small town life in terms of the advantage to themselves, instead of, for example, advantage to community as a whole (loyalty), or in terms of the disadvantages of *gesellschaft*. In the words of Jameson, the "old tension between town and country" has been replaced "by the suburb and by universal standardization." In his colloquial way, Long provides support for Jameson's thesis: "It may be true that where we live matters less than what we make of it. And it is certainly true that if we are not wholly mobile, then the rest of the world is – McDonald's and Mitsubishi will come to us no matter where we are" (1989, 11). By taking for granted that "the world" means McDonald's and Mitsubishi, Long confirms Jameson's claim that we now live in a consumer society. Because of the universal standardization of consumer society, place has become irrelevant to where we eat (McDonald's), what we watch (the fall of the Berlin Wall), what we worry about (the environmental crisis), or drive (a Japanese car). Consumer society is everywhere. Giddens (1990, 108–9) refers elsewhere to this relation to space as a "disembedding of the primacy of place."

At a deeper level, universal standardization references the idea that the particular standard or principle one uses to relate to the world has become an empirical universal. This standard is modern in the sense that individuals evaluate their relation to the world (city, country) in terms of personal advantage. It is postmodern insofar as such an orientation is no longer confined to the city. Pahl (chapter 2), operating within a modern scientific epistemology, said the city references choice and the country references isolation. Yet the modernity of that recognition is now being replaced by the "new kind of society" that began to emerge after World War II. Thus, for a single mother (chapter 7), the small town is advantageous while her children are young but disadvantageous when her singlehood takes on more prominence. This is what Long means when he says that now "a choice exists between city and country living."

In this new kind of society, individual choice and the creation of ever more opportunities for choice is decisive.[1] It is "about the very fact that choice between city and country living" exists. Country living no longer takes the choice away from individuals (*gemeinschaft*); city living is no longer a decision forced on people because of employment or careers. Recent technological changes have made it possible to choose between city and country living without having to sacrifice the benefits of modernity.[2] Because this is a recent development in modernity, I will, following Jameson and Baudrillard, refer to this as a postmodern movement. For Berger, Berger and Kellner (1973), this loss of a centre raises the spector of homelessness, a phenomenon to be lamented and corrected. For Long (1989, 15–18), in true postmodern spirit, the reality of a loss of centre is an occasion for celebration, for this opens the opportunity to choose between city and country without having to make a fundamental sacrifice (career, income, access to culture – in short, modernity itself).

In this section I take up the term "postmodern"[3] as a way of specifying a particular consumer relation to place, a relation addressed by Jameson and exemplified by Long. I do this by using the different understandings that the hometowners and ex-urbanites attach to living with the extended family and simultaneously use these understandings to recover a living relation to Tonnies's distinctions of *gemeinschaft* and *gesellschaft*. I then show that the practical orientation displayed by ex-urbanites is legitimated (unwittingly) by the theoretic orientation of Berger's phenomenology. As stated in the last chapter, radical interpretive research recognizes the inextricable intertwining between the practical and the theoretical, between having an instrumental relation to place and the theoretic position that posits the primacy of the subjective realm of desires and moods over the objective realm of place and world. These practical/theoretical tendencies, I argue, have troublesome ethical and political tendencies.

Overall, the material is now engaged so as to provide an opportunity to theorize certain important contemporary concerns (consumerism) and, in Gadamer's terms, to comprehend the way Berger's phenomenology comprehends the world. That is, through an examination of the postmodern ethos, I aim to show that the seemingly empirically neutral phenomenology of Berger and his associates carries cultural and ethical implications which need to be critically examined. In the process, I aim to *exemplify* the possibility of a strong relation to self-resistance which the very terms of *gemeinschaft* and *gesellschaft* sought to initiate. Therefore the categories of hometowner and mobile ex-urbanite are not descriptive terms; they do not describe different types of people: rather, they are ways of conceptualizing different relations to place.[4]

THE EXTENDED FAMILY: THE TIES THAT BIND

Certain descriptions by the people who themselves were raised and were now raising children in their hometown (hometowners) can be used to make relevant Tonnies's understanding of *gemeinschaft* as itself referencing the interconnection of family attachment and community. The themes of family, community, and town emerged in the conversations with these individuals. Raising children in one's hometown and among brothers, sisters, and parents was a decisive lived experience inseparably linked to the way the town was known. This experience means that the parental life-world of the hometowners has a different horizon than that of the ex-urbanites, because choosing to parent in the town is bound up with the decision to parent beside the extended family. This interrelation of family, town, and community moderates and resists the instrumental relation to place. Said one father: "If I had a choice, I'd definitely choose [to be beside family] – I want my children to know my family – because I think it's a good family. I wouldn't want to take them away from it because I think there are positive things they can learn from my parents and brothers and sisters." Similarly, the mother added that being beside family was "awfully important ... because I like my family."

Another couple said that the presence of family was a major factor in their decision to stay in their hometown. The mother said: "That's a whole side of parenting, to have family involved, to know the grandparents, to know the aunts and uncles, to set up those type of relationships ... Family support is pretty nice for the kids to have."

Here we get an image of parenting in which the town, the family, and the community all interrelate, and this interrelation is part of the reason for claiming that rural life is beneficial. While the extended family no longer centres economic activity (unlike the precapitalist/ *gemeinschaft* communities), it remains very important for sustaining a sense of belonging, security, and stability, the terms these people used to translate the meaning of community. This coheres with other research that shows that "the rural family … is … increasingly becoming more important as a source of emotional gratification to its members" as it is "no longer able to maintain its solidarity based on the common occupation of all members on the farm" (Dasgupta 1988, 145).

Despite this modernization of the relation to the extended family, the interest in the attachment itself helps us understand the premodern. For Tonnies, an essential aspect of *gemeinschaft* is its prevoluntary character; it pre-exists conscious choice. The family can be understood as a group that exists prior to a child's conscious choice (children do not choose their parents, brothers, or sisters). In the case of the images above, we have people who acknowledge the option to live away from their extended family, but who choose to stay in the hometown. This suggests a choosing of what they have been given. Unlike modernity with its vision of a perfectible world (enlightenment and progress), premodernity is oriented by the concern with developing a relation to that which precedes conscious choice. For the premodern as against the modern, value does not solely reside in what is consciously chosen, or in what is made by human artifice; there is also a sense of value in that which one inherits, precisely because it is inherited. In this case, the hometowners do not understand themselves to be passively and fatalistically complying with a given and accepted way of life (S.D. Clark, 1978);[5] rather, they reason that family ties in particular make the rural type of setting more choice-worthy with regards to their parenting practices. In Heideggerian terms, they choose to live and be in a place that represents the world into which they were thrown.

When they were asked about the particular virtue of the extended family, the following images suggested themselves. One mother says family represents the value of "unconditional love. You don't have to win friends or win approval, it's just there, they're just there and just being there. Knowing that if something comes up, I can call my sister across town and say, 'Can you watch the kids for a couple of days, we have to – whatever – 'and in 20 minutes, you're on a plane somewhere if you have to be."

Another father volunteers a similar response: "It's nice in the time of emergencies if you ever need it. Unless you have some very good friends and you had to run to the city for whatever reason, you can just, we can pretty well drop everything, phone my father and he can come and check the house and make sure – and he'd do the lawn, and I guess you don't feel – even though you are – that you're imposing as much when it's family as much as you would with a friend."

Both of these hometowners see relations with the extended family as ends in themselves. The ties are intrinsically valuable. "Knowing aunts and uncles," "knowing one's family," "knowing family is 'just there'," refers to knowledge that is pleasurable and valuable in its own right. Yet when asked to articulate the meaning of this value, the hometowners give examples of utility. Tonnies (1960, 37–40) says that in *gemeinschaft*, recurring acts of mutual aid build up substantial psychological bonds. I have shown in chapter 1 that this understanding of the premodern – despite Tonnies's apparent championing of this way of life – is grounded in, and limited by, a nineteenth-century scientific epistemology. His formulation of this kind of relationship tends to be reductively psychologistic, in the sense that he would understand the above relations as expressions of the "Natural Will."

An alternative and more particular (radical in the sense of rooted) interpretation of such self-understandings is the sense of acknowledgment of the security and trust generated by a commitment to "being there." As the mother above says, the virtue of (parenting in close proximity to) the extended family is "it's just there, they're just there and just being there." The extended family points to an unconditional commitment to "being there," and the help or aid offered in an emergency is merely an example or expression of this commitment. To the hometowners, family is not a mere means to mutual aid which could be substituted by an impersonal but efficient government agency: mutual aid is the expression of a relationship based on the shared commitment to "being there." *It is the sense of commitment itself rather than what the commitment delivers that is decisive.* This is not to say that this relationship is irrational; rather, it is not a relationship based on instrumental rationality.[6]

It is in this sense that the claims being made for the advantage of child-rearing in a rural centre can be understood as *gemeinschaftlich* claims. "Family life is the general basis of life in the *Gemeinschaft* ... Here original kinship and inherited status remain an essential, or at least the most important condition of participating fully in common property" (Tonnies 1960, 228). *Gemeinschaftlich* relations refer to an image of community built on personal relations that start in the immediate family and continue into the extended family and further into the community. In a *gemeinschaftlich* social organization, there is a continuity rather than a discontinuity between relations inside the immediate family and outside the immediate family, and it is on the basis of this continuity that a *gemeinschaft* is established.[7] In the statements of the parents cited above, the children and the house represent two kinds of common property (Collins 1982). The children can be spontaneously dropped off with a sister, or the father can come

over and make sure the house is secure. That is, the discourse of the
hometowners reveals an understanding that the extended family
participates in the common project of child-rearing.

Because of the self-understanding of shared commitment to "being
there," the request for aid is not felt to be an imposition. More importantly, it is because the extended family has a "being there" character
(for the children or house) that the parents do not have to *be* there.
Their project (i.e., house/children) will go on even if for some unan-
ticipated reason they cannot go on. Their connection with the past
(the extended family) simultaneously connects these parents with a
future (their child-rearing), providing a practical example of
Arendt's claim (1968) that having a worldly relation to the future
requires having a real relation to what we inherit. While the above
expressions refer to ordinary interruptions ("on a plane somewhere"), the connotation of the fatal interruption would certainly
add to the security the presence of the extended family offers concerning the anxiety of parenting. That is, the "being there" of the
extended family nurtures a sense of permanence with regards to
one's projects (raising one's children) that transcends the instability
inherent in human mortality.

THE EXTENDED FAMILY: LIBERATION FROM THE TIES THAT BIND

In contrast to the hometowners' stated preference for the benefit of
parenting close to the extended family are the preferences of those
who moved to this town from a larger urban setting. Mobility is part
of these individuals' lives, both socially and geographically. Some
were born and raised in cities; others were raised in a rural setting
and lived much of their adult single and married life in the city. One
couple moved to Prairie Edge from a larger setting precisely for the
perceived benefits it offered for child-rearing. All tended to view the
world from the perspective of the *life plan*.[8] From this perspective,
"the basic organizing principle for biographical projects is one's job,
and other career projections typically revolve around and depend on
the job" (Berger, Berger and Kellner 1973, 72–3). That is, one's own
career rather than the importance of relations with the larger family
is the principle used for organizing one's relation to place. All of
these couples were in Prairie Edge because of their jobs and
acknowledged the primacy of career in choosing a place to live. Even
the woman (of the couple) who explicitly chose the town because of
its conduciveness to parenting acknowledged that "if a person has a

good job opportunity, I think they're going to be willing to take it and make the best of where they are ... We were sort of in a different situation because we were looking for a place to start our job."

If *gesellschaft* points to the prominence of organizing relations on the basis of rational means-end deliberation, then these couples could be said to display this consciousness. For example, two sets of co-conversationalists did not deliberately choose a smaller setting over a larger one; rather, they were in Prairie Edge because their jobs brought them here, thus acknowledging the primacy of career in the life plan. Others did choose the place, but not because of any history or ties to family: they chose not so much a place as a size. They preferred a place where small was a decisive qualifier. Smallness of size rather than particularity of place is what rural was taken to mean by these ex-urbanites. While place points to particularity and history, size is more formally universalistic in conception; size is not tied to place but is rather a way of relating to *any* place. This orientation instantiates Giddens's (1990, 18) argument about the separation of space and place in modernity.[9]

The hometowners expressed sentiments that suggest that their relation to the town could be characterized as a *gemeinschaftlich* relation. For the two parents quoted on page 157, the children and the house represent two kinds of property, and in each case the extended family participated or could potentially participate fully. In contrast, the geographically mobile families are, in this respect, more like Wirth's description (chapter 2) of families in the city, "emancipated" from the larger kinship group characteristic of the country. This means they are free, at least as a nuclear family, to pursue interests that diverge from the interests of the larger extended family. In this regard, when asked about the preference for living beside the extended family, one father said, "Well, I'm surely glad that we have distance, and that we are in the kind of situation where one can overcome the distance, if need be or if the wish is there. The fact that we have had three of the relatives' children here staying with us for an extended period of time, and we have gone over there visiting – all that is great; but I'm not at all missing the situation where my sisters are just around the corner."

While this father desires to be able to be in contact with family, he is also "surely glad" he has the distance. This points to a feature of the postmodern situation that makes the experience of the rural different from what it was for the early moderns. Mobile couples evaluate their decisions, actions, and beliefs in the context of the fact that we live in a technological and media-influenced world.[10] Whereas for Wirth the modernism of the city involved emancipation from the wider kinship groups, now moving no longer means losing contact with kin and, as Long states above, with technology (communication and transportation) distance does not mean isolation. In contemporary society, contact with extended kin can be maintained because technology transcends the limits of space. If the city formerly referenced the "emancipation" from the extended family, leaving the place of birth no longer means saying goodbye forever. The "old tension between city and country, centre and province," between the tradition of the rural and the progressiveness of the city, no longer applies.

In comparison with the father's statement above on the benefit of distance from family, other statements suggest a little more ambivalence about this emancipation. Such ambivalence itself instances the postmodern condition.[11] Some wanted distance but, as the three following quotations indicate, did not like the family too far away.

MOTHER: In a way, I wished that maybe they lived closer. I'm not sure I want them right in town. We've got too big a family. You know, I come from a family of six and he comes from a family of five, and there's a lot of inter-involvement and they all know each other and you know, I don't know what it would be like.

MOTHER: I would rather choose not to be in the same town [with the extended family]. An hour's drive would be quite wonderful, two hours. I would be happier with a little distance.

MOTHER: My mother is living with us for four months right now and we've never had the situation where we have lived close to family. I was really happy to get away from the town I grew up in. I never wanted to move out next to family, I wanted to leave. In the years since, I'd like to have my family around, in the same town.

This last statement generated the following marital exchange:

FATHER: But you never wished to move back to the town you came from. I was not allowed to look for a job there.
MOTHER: We've really been spared a lot of family feuds by not living right close to our family.

In contrast to the hometowners of this study, many of the ex-urbanites want distance though not complete isolation from the extended family. They value the presence of the extended family but also value the independence distance makes possible. The ties to the clan that Tonnies talks about are not only experienced as making harmony and cooperation possible but also as entangling. Family feuds, inter-involvement, the obligatory Sunday dinner, and so on all represent a tie which, while making stability and security possible, limit freedom and personal development. The postmodern wants to be able "to overcome the distance if need be" but also wants the independence which distance gives. Foucault has shown the way the independent individual is a construction of modern society (Foucault 1977; Turner 1989); consumer society is organized around providing the means (technology) by which this individual's choice and desire can be satisfied. When freedom and individual uniqueness are deemed desirable, then, as we know from Simmel, the community based on the extended family is understood to be oppressive.

For the ex-urbanites a rural setting is not chosen because of the presence of the extended family, who aid and support one's own parenting. Neither is a rural setting automatically associated with community. In fact, some of the ex-urbanites found that they did not experience a sense of community in Prairie Edge, as the following exchange suggests:

MOTHER: I think a sense of community is, for me, the feeling that you are not out there alone, that there are other people who care for you, that you care for other people. That you are actually part of something, and there's a sense of caring for one another and helping each other … [This town] does not measure up to that sense of community.
FATHER: Well, there is a lot of that sense of community here because the families are all interrelated. So they are all relatives in this town. If you are a latecomer, like we are latecomers, it is very hard to break into that community.

This couple experiences a weak sense of community precisely for *gemeinschaftlich* reasons, that is, because of *the difficulty entering a community which is based on kinship.* In this regard Tonnies (1960, 228) says: "Strangers may be accepted and protected as serving members or guests, either temporarily or permanently. Thus, they can belong to the *Gemeinschaft* as objects, but not easily as agents and representatives of the *Gemeinschaft*." According to Sim (1988, 68–94), the ex-urbanite (who is now a "new ruralite") is often ignored in the new environment. Such individuals do not feel they belong because of the indifference a community based on kinship and with a sense of history can show to the stranger; they are excluded in a way that makes the woman, in this case, feel she is not actually "part of something." The resulting sense of self is of one who is an outsider to a closed or tight-knit group.

The temptation of the hometowner is therefore the classic temptation of insularity, which equates (or confuses) interest with self-absorption. Because kinship is treated as all there is, the message given to the stranger is "be us or be nothing." That is, the hometowner is in danger of reproducing an indifference to the difference of the stranger which, reminiscent of Redfield's folk society, begins to look like an indifference to difference itself. The ex-urbanite, on the other hand, knows difference by virtue of being confronted with this difference of insularity. The ex-urbanites know they can never really be part of someone else's kin group and can be disappointed, angry, or even contemptuous of the community that is unable to engage the challenge the stranger brings. The ex-urbanite's acknowledgment of the indifference to difference this insularity exemplifies echoes the more sustained criticism of rurality provided by Marx and Simmel.

CONSUMERISM AND PLACE AS COMMODITY: THE PRACTICAL EXAMPLE

One might hypothesize that this sense of disappointment, anger, or contempt would lead to a negative evaluation of parenting in a rural setting – in the way, for example, that James Joyce has the character Stephen Daedalus reject Irish nationalism and Catholicism in *Portrait of the Artist As a Young Man*. Yet as we know from chapter 6, all the co-conversationalists and most of the other participants claim that the town was beneficial for their parenting practices. Some claimed this while simultaneously claiming a critical reserve on Prairie Edge:

MOTHER (ex-urbanite): I don't think any of us feel particularly proud of Prairie Edge ... because we're quite critical about [it] in terms of its architecture, the street coming in, it's just the ugliest thing going. So I'm not sure [the children would] be particularly proud of Prairie Edge, or feel that they're Prairie Edgers.

The evaluation that Prairie Edge is good for child-rearing does not necessarily lead to positive emotional feeling toward the town. In precisely a way that is difficult for a hometowner to do (because the town, one's own upbringing, and attachment to the wider family are all intertwined), the ex-urbanite can evaluate Prairie Edge child-rearing as positive while not feeling in any way attached by way of loyalty or emotion to Prairie Edge. The town does not (as in Tonnies, and vestigially with the hometowners) instance a sacred attachment to the land or the ineffable attachment to the larger family. Rather, rural life is talked about in much the same way any environment is talked about.

Charles Long in *Life after the City* (1989, 8) says he came to the conclusion that rural life was the best place for his family on the basis of two realizations:

The first is that you don't have to live in a place to enjoy it. In my eyes, Venice is the most charming city in Europe, but those who live there year round must worry about rising tides, eroding foundations, hordes of tourists and the stench of canals in the summer. The second realization, the one that took the longest to see, is that Utopia does not exist. A tropical climate includes tropical insects. A mountain view is at the end of a mountain road … Sooner or later, most of us have to settle down some place, any place, and live our lives. The best we can do is choose one of the pleasant places and keep most of the things we love within reach.

Both of these realizations reflect a postmodern sentiment. In fact, they seem extensions of each other, because Long's use of Venice as an example has the same discursive structure as his tropical climate example. The fact that Venice has a dark side mirrors the tautological recognition that "Utopia does not exist." The first realization reveals its postmodern character in taking for granted the existence of technology ("keep most of the things we love within reach"), while the second does so by acknowledging the limitation of the modern project in *its* attempt to eliminate ambivalence ("choose *one* of the pleasant places").[12] For the postmodern, the urban-rural difference no longer represents the choice of either community (*gemeinschaft*) or progress but is instead an instance of choice among the diversity of choices, a diversity both within as well as between the urban and the rural. A condition of maintaining a diversity of choices requires an ability to keep one's options open. Closure is therefore a limit that is decisively resisted. On the other hand, a committed relation to place means that it has to mean more than "one of the pleasant places to live." Can being a pleasant place to live really be "a great place?"

Unlike the modern who rejects or holds in contempt the rural other (as exemplified in the language and orientation of Marx in chapter 1), the postmodern is able to recognize the benefits rural life can offer through the use of a means-end rationality. The postmodern does not feel obliged to choose between progressiveness (of the city) and regressiveness (of the rural) or between the community of the rural and the association of the city. As Long (1989, 15) says, "The nut of the thing is that we no longer need to be places anymore." Places "are becoming unnecessary."

This orientation challenges Tonnies's opposition of *gemeinschaft* and *gesellschaft*. As discussed previously, Tonnies's distinction was a modernist attempt to resist the excesses of modernity. He thus generated an opposition between a premodern and a modern way of life. The postmodern, personified in the image of the consumer, resists such either-or oppositions by making the difference between the city and the country itself not a choice to be with other people (community) or with a progressive project (modernism) but rather a personal/lifestyle choice. It is this notion of lifestyle that makes place seem unnecessary. To use Tonnies's terms, the postmodern has a *gesellschaft* way of relating to *gemeinschaft*, that is, he or she relates to the benefits of the new rural community in a rational and instrumental way.

If "postmodernity means coming to terms with ambivalence ... and with the indeterminacy of the future" (Baumann 1994, 350), this orientation is expressed by a new relation to place. Being mobile, the postmodern does not see the beneficial aspects of Prairie Edge as arising out of or leading to any sense of loyalty to or pride in place. For example, many of the ex-urbanites imagine themselves moving on to another place in the future. Bringing this interpretive frame to the example of the single mother who is now ready to leave, we can recognize that benefits and disadvantages are suspended by the social situation of the actor. In another example, a mother who had lived in the town for ten years said, "I could see myself living here for the rest of my life, and I could see myself moving in a year." There is nothing about the benefit of the object that leads to a lasting tie; one is not attached to the object (the place); the place has status only *vis à vis* the ex-urbanite as a floating consumer. In Baudrillard's terms (1994, 349), the objects (city, town, village, or rural lot) "gain their desirability from their position in the mosaic of other commodities." Place has now become one of those other commodities. If it is a commodity, can it be that great a place?

In terms of the parenting life-world, the ex-urbanites feel that the small town is on the whole better than the large urban centre. Yet from the perspective of an aesthetic life-world or a single adult life-world or a sense of community, they can be quite critical of the town. The acceptance of pluralization of life-worlds *as reality* means that there is no felt need to reconcile these potentially opposing and diverse views on the same object. As in Meno's definition of excellence (*The Meno*), the town can be known and evaluated in different ways dependent on the particular life-world of the knower. This is not to say that, from the perspective of a pluralized life-world, anything can become anything. Rather, the object is known and evaluated in a modern, instrumental fashion, in terms of costs and benefits to the ex-urbanites with respect to their parenting activity.[13] From within this life-world, the town has more benefits than costs. But knowing and evaluating the place as positive is conditional on viewing it from the perspective of the parental life-world.

Recognizing the primacy given to the life-world of parenting makes it possible to specify the underlying principle that made the connotations of rurality with safety, convenience, and reduced anxiety intelligible. Though the participants (myself included) evaluated Prairie Edge positively, the principle that made such an evaluation possible is the commitment to parenting rather than to place. *What is valued as an end in itself is the parent-child relation.* It is this latter commitment that subverts and resists an unregulated surrender to the instrumental reasoning. What this intrinsic virtue of the parent-child relation actually means is another project (Bonner 1997); for now I merely want to point out the unquestioned assumption of the ex-urbanites in this study. They acknowledged a willingness to leave (abandon) the town but would be shocked at the idea of leaving (or abandoning) their children. Yet it is possible to imagine a life-world with the opposite relation to place.

Socrates (*The Apology*), for example, when faced with the choice of escaping death by escaping from both prison and Athens, chose not to leave. That choice meant his death and, as he was reminded, the leaving of his children. For Socrates, his love of Athens and his commitment to moral action superceded his love of his children; for the parents in this study, love of their own children supercedes and structures their relation to place. This is another way of saying that the value of the place is only relevant insofar as it relates to the life-world of parenting. As such, the value of place as an end in itself does not get to be developed. Again, what example do we show our children when this is our relation to place?

Of course, a stronger relation to place, one that treats it more than a means to another end, does not mean having to love a place that is unlovable. One characteristic of Prairie Edge is that it conceives of itself as a commercial centre; it promotes itself as a commodity. The street coming into Prairie Edge, beckoning with the signatures of national and global capitalism (Canadian Tire, McDonald's), may be "the ugliest thing going." Such things may make it hard to love the particularity of place; yet one can develop a critical relation to one's place as a way of keeping alive, if only by implication, the importance of a non-instrumental relation to place.

For the hometowners, town references place, and place is particular. This place in turn becomes an object with which one has to come to terms for good or ill. For the postmodern, on the other hand, this town could be any small town, because what is important is not the town but the small. Small is both a more comparative and a more abstract concept than place because it is a way of collecting and organizing space. It leads rather to an intellectual and abstract relation to an object than to a particular and emotional relation. According to Tonnies, this is precisely a *gesellschaft* mentality, yet it is practised in a way that recognizes the value of a *gemeinschaft* setting. More importantly, this mentality is transferable. While there might be only one Prairie Edge, there are many small towns. If one is more interested in small than in the town itself, then one can preserve one's relation to an object while retaining the possibility of mobility (Giddens, 1990).

Neither the pre-modern notion of loyalty to place nor the modern universalist commitment to enlightenment and progress are real issues for the consumer. One is never required to think in terms of commitment to place as a particular other, nor in terms of "constructing a better, reason-guided and thus ultimately universal order" (Baumann 1994, 352), because what one is committed to is a general idea that can accommodate a variety of places as the occasion arises. This orientation means that place can be treated as "some place, any place" (Long 1989, 8). One is not required to think in terms of resisting a commitment to place in the name of progress and enlightenment. The postmodern can be with the other (place, people, community) and yet not be with that other at the same time. Is this ambivalence, however, merely a way of avoiding the question of how a great place (to raise kids) is not such a great place?

When one likes a town because it is small, one does not have to think about or come to terms with the particularity of the town, because what is attractive about it only incidentally belongs to it. Thinking about a place in this way allows one to keep one's options open – a method for keeping the possibility of mobility alive. Thus one can like the smallness of Prairie Edge without liking Prairie Edge, as smallness is not unique to Prairie Edge. The postmodern can like being in Prairie Edge and still be ready to leave because what is appealing about being in Prairie Edge (its size) is not necessarily something that must be left behind. For example, size allows one to think in terms of actions that benefit one's own family and not, for instance, the relationship that would collect self with a community. What this analysis is beginning to bring into the open is a potentially dangerous temptation built into contemporary praise for the importance of parenthood. It is becoming apparent how the important commitment to the other, which contemporary parenting references, can be structured by modern consumerism into an extension of self interest (i.e., what is good for *my* children).

For some, Prairie Edge may be "a great place to raise kids," but it is not such a great place. The latter is due in part to the insularity that belongs to any self-interested community, but it may also be due to the particular way Prairie Edge conceives of itself. If its self-conception is primarily as a commercial centre, then the commodification of place is built into the identity of the town. The issue for parents, however, is: What relation to place do we teach our children when we say a great place to raise kids is not such a great place? Are we unwittingly encouraging a nomadic relation to the world? Of course, the problem of the consumer relation to place is not just a problem for mobile professionals: the problem also lies in the way we construct our theories. The practical and the theoretical are inextricably intertwined.

PHENOMENOLOGY AND
THE WORLD AS COMMODITY:
THE THEORETIC EXAMPLE

As an alternative relation to place, think of the more traditional idea of loyalty to one's country, or of the reputation for loyalty and pride that some places in the world generate. While it is possible to think of developing an instrumental relation to New York, Rome, Dublin, the American South, Newfoundland, or Montreal, to name a few examples, such places connote images of loyalty and pride. And while the suburbs are invented precisely to allow for an instrumental relation to place, it is for this very reason of instrumentality that the true city resident does not consider the suburbanite a fellow citizen. As Jameson says above, the prominence of the suburbs in the city symbolizes the consumer relation to place. They are removed from the productivity of industry and the sociability of the old town centre. As such, the suburbs have the appearance of being anywhere, and all suburbs everywhere look alike.[14]

The true representative of the place (e.g., the Dubliner) demands that the resident earn the city/country name. These are places that voice the demand that the resident come to terms with particularity. They are not necessarily convenient, or safe, or anxiety-reducing places, but they do have an identity, whether frustrating or attractive, that demands that the resident develop an intrinsic relation to it. Whether the requirement to come to terms with the particularity of place be infuriating, charming, annoying, or inspiring, it is a relationship that requires some ecstasy (Berger 1963), some act of moving outside oneself to know and truly live with an other. This necessarily involves some resistance and in turn acceptance of the principle that developing this kind of relation to place requires self-resistance. The place that requires a commitment to its particularity creates an openness to resisting narrow self-interest.

In the context of a genuine encounter with the other, place has the possibility of becoming an end in itself: to develop a positive relation to place, self must recognize its intrinsic value and move to conserve it, to take responsibility for it. For that to happen, however, place has to become an end in itself and not a mere means for satisfying private, individual, or familial (*my* children) desires. In this way, as Arendt (1958, 173–96) says, the culture of the place can be what we receive from our ancestors and seek to hand on to our progeny. But engaging the world in this way is precisely to resist what is most seductive about the postmodern extension of modernism – that is, that the world is there to satisfy the individual's life plan (Berger *et al.* 1973). This orientation is the reason McDonald's and Mitsubishi will seek us out.

Consumerism panders to a fantasy of paradise, and it is successful because it tells and retells us that the world can be arranged so as to satisfy private desires. "Thorough, adamant and uncompromising *privatization* of all concerns has been the main factor that has rendered postmodern society so spectacularly immune to systematic critique and radical social dissent with revolutionary potential" (Baumann 1994, 359). Berger *et al.* (1973), in describing the life plan as the basic organizing principle of individuals, *not only describe the modern consciousness but also unknowingly legitimate a consumer relation to the world.* The pluralized consciousness prepares us to be seduced by consumerism: "Because of the plurality of social worlds in modern society, the structures of each particular world are experienced as relatively unstable and unreliable … Put differently, the individual's experience of himself becomes more real to him than his experience of the objective social world. Therefore, the individual seeks to find his 'foothold' in reality in himself rather than outside himself" (Berger *et al.* 1973, 77–8).

We have already seen examples of instability and unreliability in the usages above. The town is good for a single mother, yet she would leave "in two seconds" if she could. For another parent, Prairie Edge is good (for child-rearing) and bad (aesthetically ugly). A couple view Prairie Edge as good for their children, and yet they will not be named by that experience because they are not Prairie Edgers.

Here we have examples where the individual's experience of self in parenting is more real than the experience of the objective social world.

The theoretical description that Berger and associates provide is not as neutral and objective as it first appeared. They seem merely to describe the modern individual as one who "seeks to find his 'foothold' in reality in himself rather than outside himself." Yet their theoretic position coheres well with a consumerism that privatizes individuals through an appeal to their private desires or fantasies. Of course in these fantasies there is always a desire for what is good. In the ex-urbanite case, we have parents who desire the good for *their own* children. Again, the parent-child (self-other) relation provides a site where what appears to be good (a commitment to parenting) can be thought about, worked out, and developed rather than merely being offered as one consumer good among an array of others. To the extent that abandoning one's children is not an option, consumerism is being decisively resisted. Therefore, *what is problematic is not the desire to be good parents* per se *but rather the surrender to the privatization of desire.* This leads to contradictions like "we are here and not here," and "we are from Prairie Edge and not from Prairie Edge."

In the case of the phenomenology of Berger *et al.*, we have the aim of the good description. That is, they aim to describe a world and absent their own description from being implicated in the world they describe. In describing the modern world as pluralized and then failing reflectively to take responsibility for choosing to look at it in this way, they show pluralization to be the seduction of consumerism. Neither the unworldliness of the actor they theorize nor the unrealistic aim of his sustaining a "foothold" in reality in himself is resisted. As Bergerian phenomenology shows (1963, 93–122), reality and identity are socially sustained, and the contradiction between what this actor seeks and what is possible for this actor is not discursively examined.

As we know from the Socratic Dialogues, from Hegel, and from Marx, being in a contradiction can be treated as an opportunity to re-engage and transform one's relation to the object. But the contradiction offers the potential for development only when it is consciously recognized, and when the ethical and political implications of the contradiction are subjected to dialogical examination. Acknowledging the contradiction is an acknowledgment of the reality of other, an other that challenges self to move outside itself. This ability to move outside of particular self-interest is required for self-formation (*paideia*). The consumer orientation makes the principle of self-formation, recommended in the last chapter, difficult if not impossible to achieve. What is needed, therefore, is a critical and knowing resistance to the life-world that Berger and associates merely describe and, by implication, legitimize. That is, Berger's phenomenological description of modern consciousness, while insightful, can now be recognized as reproducing the very attitude it sets out to describe. The Bergerian description of the "objective social world" *itself* reproduces a sense of "unreliability and instability."

Given my analysis of their theoretical orientation, it is easy to see why Berger and Kellner (1964, 6–7) would describe modern society in the following way:

The public institutions now confront the individual as an immensely powerful and alien world, incomprehensible in its inner workings, anonymous in its human character. If only through his work in some nook of the economic machinery, the individual must find a way of living in this alien world, come to terms with its power over him, be satisfied with a few conceptual rules of thumb to guide him through a vast reality that otherwise remains opaque to his understanding, and modify its anonymity by whatever *human relations* he can work out in his involvement with it.

Here the authors seem to be offering their description of social life in modern society. The modern individual is alienated from "public institutions" and therefore seeks "to modify [their] anonymity by whatever human relations" he or she can work out. Intimate relations in general, and parenthood in particular, are instances of such modification. However, their subsequent conclusion looks more like a legitimation of this life-world than a description:

It ought to be emphasized, against some critics of "mass society," that this does not inevitably leave the individual with a sense of profound unhappiness and lostness. It would rather seem that large number of people in our society are quite content with a situation in which their public involvements have little subjective importance, regarding work as not too bad a necessity and politics as at best a spectator sport. It is usually only intellectuals with ethical and political commitments who assume that such people must be terribly desperate.

It is worth noting that it is Berger and Kellner who assume that the happiness or desperation of people is the issue and by so doing displace what is precisely an ethical and political issue (what relation to place/community should we have?) with an empirical issue (are most people happy?). Their own phenomenology prevents them from recognizing the way all understanding is influenced by culture and history, and thus this phenomenology is unable to free itself from domination "by the ruling preconceptions of the moment" (Gadamer 1989, 289). In this case a very definite political and ethical position (consumerism) is (implicitly) legitimated on the grounds that a "large number of people are quite content" with the situation – as though if everybody is doing it, it must therefore be okay.

Here we have a clear example of why ontology is important for sociological inquiry. The epistemological and methodological position of Berger's phenomenology has very definite implications for being in the world (ontology), and it simultaneously shows why sociological inquiry, when it is limited by empiricism, can end up legitimating a political and ethical position *without offering any political or ethical justification*. The very thing that needs to be examined is unreflectively assumed and concealed by an empiricist epistemology. Bergerian phenomenology, like all theory, (implicitly) turns attention to a principle recommended for acceptance. Is the principle of attaching "little subjective importance" to "public involvements" worth accepting? Surely "a study of the science of man is inseparable from an examination of the options between which men must choose" (Taylor 1977, 127).

As Gadamer (1975, 333–41) argues, unless the analysis undertakes to comprehend the way it comprehends, which means taking into account the influence of history, culture, and community on inquiry, such "possibilities of meaning" will remain concealed. While Berger's phenomenology goes some way towards helping us understand the modern life-world, its failure to account for its own grounds leaves it open to criticism. Here we see this in the case of Prairie Edge. The temptation of the ex-urbanites to treat place instrumentally makes sense when one recognizes that the parental life-world is being privileged. But the temptation also displays a postmodern prejudice when other (the town) is evaluated in terms of one's own private interests. Thus the very assumption that modern reality *necessarily* means *the pluralization of life-worlds* must be called into question, not in terms of its empirical justification (because it does accurately describe much of modern society) but in terms of its ethical and political implications. The self-formation principle of radical interpretive sociology requires that such a phenomenology be critically resisted. Here the practical and the theoretical intersect because within a form of life which assumes as fundamental that reality is the pluralization of life-worlds, it becomes very difficult to imagine a relation to place driven by something other than consumerism. If small size is the object that parents see as good, we need to be able to recover a relation to that object that does not view it as a mere means to a private and narrow end.

PRAIRIE EDGE AS A
COMMERCIAL CENTRE

In the sociological tradition, Tonnies's *gemeinschaft* and Weber's traditional society were constructed precisely in resistance to the modern vulnerability of being unable to acknowledge an other that challenges self. For the modern consciousness, as constituted by Bergerian phenomenology, the objective world has become unstable and unreliable: reality is felt to reside inside oneself, and the outside has become merely a means for self to satisfy internal desires. Of course, such a way of relating to the world is a self-deceit, because all social practices require communal and political organization in order for them to exist. Consumerism, the orientation that the world is there to satisfy private desires, is an example of postmodernity's surrender to its own destructive impulse, its fascination with its own power to satisfy that desire. Consumerism panders to the self-deception that the self is a private possession rather than seeking to expose it. "Consumer freedom means orientation of life towards market-approved commodities and thereby precludes one crucial freedom: freedom from the market, freedom that means anything else but the choice between standard commercial products. Above all, consumer freedom successfully deflects aspirations of human liberty from communal affairs and the management of human life" (Baumann 1994, 360). Likewise, a phenomenology limited by a commitment to scientific empiricism is ironically unable to "see" the way it participates in legitimizing this way of being-in-the-world.

Arendt says (1968, 208–11):

An object is cultural to the extent that it can endure; its durability is the very opposite of functionality, which is the quality which makes it disappear again from the phenomenal world by being used and used up. The great user and consumer of objects is life itself, the life of the individual and the life of society as a whole. Life is indifferent to the thingness of an object; it insists that everything must be functional, fulfill some needs ... The point is that a consumer society cannot possibly know how to take care of a world and the things which belong exclusively to the space of worldly appearances, because its central attitude toward all objects, the attitude of consumption, spells ruin for everything it touches.

I am no longer describing (à la phenomenology) the empirical threat of any ex-urbanite in my study. The ex-urbanite experience, after all, names my own entry into this narrative. Rather, I am interpreting and formulating the particular and lively life-world of consumerism constantly promoted in contemporary society even in rural centres like Prairie Edge. As members of this society, we cannot but be vulnerable to this socialization. We cannot avoid *being tempted* to measure and know the place in which we live (the city, the town) in an instrumental fashion. As Jameson indicates, the phenomenon of the suburb has already institutionalized this relation for the city. The "new ruralite" is in danger of repeating this process for the small town. So, in contrast to Simmel's description of the small town denying freedom, the ex-urbanite has found a way to enhance individual freedom. The method is to nurture an instrumental relation to place, an instrumental relation that is facilitated and enhanced by modern technology ("Miss the city? It's only an hour's drive to … all the amenities of city life. But you don't have to live there") and by mass communication (Meyrowitz 1985).

In 1997 we are very aware of the danger of consumerism for the survival of the earth. But the problem is more than a technical matter of reduce, re-use, and re-cycle. The three-R response, while necessary for survival, can be grounded in the same instrumental means-end relation to the world that brought about the problem in the first place. In and of itself, survival is part of the same life process that makes consuming necessary. We need to consume in order to survive, but do we want the earth to survive in order that we can consume? We need an image (form of life) of something other than survival if we are to do more than consume. This form of life has to have the potential to resist an unlimited interest in survival.

Unfortunately, if a town sees the good of its size in terms of a great place to (a) raise your productivity, (b) raise your profits, and (c) raise your kids, then, ironically, it embraces and nurtures the very *gesellschaft* society it understands itself as not being (the big city). If Prairie Edge considers itself primarily a commercial centre, then the instrumental attitude of the newcomer is precisely what is invited. To resist instrumentalism, a place needs a story about itself, a sense of its identity, which invites participation in other than commercial ways. Failure to generate such a story, failure to bring to life such an identity, means that the instrumental newcomer and the commercially oriented town suit each other. In this case one can legitimately ask: what is so great about this kind of place?

If, as Tonnies (232) says, "the city is typical of *Gesellschaft*," it is because it "is essentially a commercial town." For *gesellschaft* to happen, place has to be erased of its particular tradition and conceptualized in terms of size (where ten minutes gets you anywhere in town, where "rush hour" lasts five minutes). A method (instrumentality) is then formulated, which provides a way of relating to size (the best of both worlds; raise your productivity, your profits, your kids). The victory of *gesellschaft* is therefore assured; there is no tangible other on the horizon. The intellectual problem, formulated through an examination of the literature in part 1, can now be recognized as a particular ethical and political problem: the other that self needs to engage (for self-formation) has been eliminated.

The postmodern ambivalence that can relate positively to the size of the town without relating positively to the town itself expresses a particular socio-historical attitude. Depending on the town's own self-understanding, this ambivalence to place may reproduce the relation that the town, as a *gesellschaft*, has invited them to produce. That is to say, any town that wants to resist being treated instrumentally by its citizens must provide something other than a commercial ethos.

If consumerism nurtures an instrumental relation to place, resistance to such an orientation requires an image of a world that inspires a sense of responsibility. We need an image of something other than survival (of the individual, the family, the society, the earth) to provide the positive basis to resist unregulated self-interest. Given that high visibility is the characteristic *par excellence* of small towns, I will seek to develop the virtue or excellence of this characteristic. It is the task of the concluding chapter to develop an image of community in contemporary small towns that enables the town and its participants to resist the claims of consumerism.

Understanding the Whole and One's Place in It: The Panopticon, the Polis and Radical Interpretive Sociology

Postmodernity is a site of opportunity and a site of danger: and it is both for the same set of reasons.   Zygmunt Baumann, 1994

The new rural community contains a rich mix of old and new drawn from local and distant sources ... In the culture of rural places the diverse elements are contained in a smaller vessel. There is more space, greater visibility, less structure, more face-to-face contact. Above all, there is the opportunity for individual participation in these smaller units of action. In a world of uncertainty and danger, small communities can be places for social pioneering, as indeed they have always been.   Alex Sim, 1988

[T]he ancient *polis* seems in this regard to have had a character of a small town ... The tremendous agitation and excitement, and the unique color-fulness of Athenian life is perhaps explained by the fact that a people of incomparably individualized personalities were in constant struggle against the incessant inner and external oppression of a de-individualizing small town.   Georg Simmel, 1971

In the last chapter I developed a critical perspective on the way consumer society socializes us to relate to place, and simultaneously showed how an otherwise productive approach to social inquiry (the phenomenology of Berger *et al.* 1973) blinds us to this phenomenon. In so doing, I sought to give one image of the direction a research project takes when it aims to be oriented in a principled way. This direction involves, in Gadamer's words (1989, 289), elucidating "the ruling pre-conceptions of the moment" that operate even in a science that aims for empirical objectivity. These preconceptions are cultural and historical; they have a hold on people/researchers by virtue of the way the new kind of society is practically and cognitively organized.

In short, society's problem is also the theorist's problem. The practical and the theoretical are, in a deep sense, intertwined.

In this concluding chapter the radical interpretive position on the creation of knowledge ("anything known requires a knower"), as *both* a theoretical and a practical issue, is more explicitly addressed. In practical terms, I show the way a small community enables the development of the skill of surveyability. In theoretical terms, I show that this skill is also a research skill; it relates to the ability to take the whole into account. The broad implications of these issues concern the interrelation of society / community and the kind of theorizing (*logos*) that society privileges.

For example, consumer society actively encourages us to disregard the particularity of place through the universal standardization of size. Grant (1965) lamented this development and saw in it the disappearance of the place called Canada. In this study I show a local example of the process, where the relevance of Prairie Edge for child-rearing was grounded not in the place (particularity) but the size (generalizability). I show that this orientation can be seen as an invitation by a certain local self-understanding (the town as a site of commerce) and as an ex-urbanite response to that invitation. Moreover, science in general, and the social sciences in particular, have not been innocent bystanders in this modern development (Grant 1969, 15–40, 111–33); they have paved the way for technological thinking by virtue of their orientation to the calculability of problems. As Blum and McHugh (1978, 323) remark in their paper on Grant, total calculability requires that everything be judged by a single standard, and thus makes of all difference only a technical difference: "What is particular to the particular is lost in the domination of the single standard of sameness." Thus, social science in general, and Berger's phenomenology in particular, despite its *epistemological advance* on conventional sociology, are both a product of and contributors to a consciousness that promotes an abstract and instrumental relation to place. An oriented research project requires this kind of reflexive otherness *vis à vis* the methods it uses to understand a problem if it is to free itself from "the ruling pre-conception of the moment."

Yet consumerism and instrumentality are not the only possible relations to size. While size (small or large) is both more abstract and more manipulable, there are other possible and actual social relations to the smallness of the rural than the consumer relation. Baumann hints at this in saying that postmodernity is a "site of opportunity" as well as "a site of danger." It is the idea of opportunity that I want to develop here. Sim says that the "greater visibility, less structure, more face-to-face contact" of the "smaller vessel" provides "an opportunity for participation" not necessarily available in the city. Both of these comments connect with a point made in the conceptualization of rurality when Simmel's work was addressed. There I took his understanding of the *polis*, quoted above, as offering a positive image of resistance between self and other, the individual and the town, or reason and spirit. Simmel, I said earlier, shows the possibilities for collaborative resistance, a resistance that makes "the tremendous agitation and excitement, and the unique colorfulness of Athenian life" a reality.

What opportunity does smallness offer? In this concluding chapter, I recover possible social relations to small size, re-engaging the work of Wirth and Simmel and introducing the work of Aristotle. I develop the possibilities for community and character that are involved in nurturing a positive and active relation to the condition of smallness. My concern here is to engage the field material and literature in order to develop an image or a form of life of the social possibilities available for the "new rural community." My intention is to develop an image that decisively resists the form of life (pluralization of life-worlds) that makes the practice of consumerism seem reasonable. If a "study of the science of man is inseparable from an examination of the options between which men must choose" (Taylor 1977, 127), then a directed and oriented research project needs to develop an image of community that makes a defensible claim to being a more reasonable or choice-worthy option than consumerism.

SMALLNESS AND THE VIRTUE OF DEVELOPING A CONCEPTION OF THE WHOLE

Ever since Aristotle's *Politics*, it has been recognized that increasing the number of inhabitants in a settlement beyond a certain limit will affect the relations between them and the character of the city.

Louis Wirth, 1938

Wirth, in his famous and much-critiqued essay, makes size one of the three key variables that, according to his scientific perspective, determine the nature and quality of social life, and the character of the city. He conceptualizes size solely in terms of population numbers and treats as incidental the concern with area or with history; the empirical, universalizing interest of science requires that these aspects of the size of a community be seen as local and incidental. Though area is necessarily implicated in the category of density, and history is involved in the act of understanding itself, Wirth's conceptualization of size solely in terms of population is reductionist and deterministic. That is, size is treated as determining social relations independently of the way size is interpreted by social actors. Conceptualizing a place in terms of population (size, density, heterogeneity) alone limits the way smallness can be understood as a sociological concept.

Yet despite the many critiques that Wirth's paper generated (see chapter 2), he understood *the need* for a sociological conception of size. That is, he understood that size has to be conceptualized differently for sociology than it is for demography, statistics, administration, or urban geography. A sociological conception of size should clarify the way the character of a rural town (or that of a neighbourhood in a city) will differ because the condition of smallness is recognized as an opportunity.

Wirth conceptualizes the urban-rural difference in terms of "ideal typical polar concepts" (1969, 166). A large population will inevitably lead to "the superficiality, the anonymity and the transitory character of urban social relations ... The contacts of the city may indeed be face to face, but they are nevertheless impersonal, superficial, transitory, and segmental" (1938, 12). The polar opposite of urbanism is a community where individuals can know each other as "full personalities" (12), "can know one another and be assembled in one spot" (13), where relationships are mutual and close (14), and so on. In other words, Wirth thinks of social relationships in terms of the continuum between the poles of intensive intimacy and impersonal anonymity, with size being the determining variable. But this is a logical rather than a socio-logical conceptualization; it is merely logical because subjective understanding has not been taken into account (Weber 1958)[1] and because it is blind to the dialectical character of human life (Gadamer 1986, 122).[2] The irony of Wirth's formulation of the city is that despite the vast amount of empirical evidence upon which he based it, further empirical evidence falsified his thesis. Thus, as we now know, we can have intimate neighbourhoods and communities in the city, and impersonal and anomic relations in the country.

Yet if we set aside the issue of empiricism and work with the spirit of Wirth's text, the issue becomes one of recovering the problem or question to which his text responds. What is the analytic problem for which the city is a metaphor and to which the metaphor of the smaller size of the rural responds?[3] Wirth (1938, 13–14) says:

In a community composed of a larger number of individuals than one can know one another individually or can be assembled in one spot, it becomes necessary to communicate through indirect mediums [sic] and to articulate individual interests by a process of delegation ... The individual counts for little, but the voice of the representative is heard with a deference roughly proportional to the numbers for whom he speaks ... [In the city we] see the uniform which denotes the role of the functionaries and are oblivious to the personal eccentricities that are hidden behind the uniform.

These characteristics of the city lead Wirth (1938, 17) to conclude, "There is little opportunity for the individual to obtain a conception of the city as a whole or to survey his place in it." All of the quotations are taken from Wirth's description of the effects of the three different variables of size, density, and heterogeneity. Despite the fact that they fall under different categories, they share a similarity of tone and focus. The danger of the city (as a metaphor) is that it undermines the possibility of knowing another as an "individual," it creates an obliviousness "to the personal eccentricities" of people, and, most important of all, this leaves little opportunity for the individual to know "the city as a whole or to survey his place in it." What is involved, both in terms of the limits of human understanding (ontologically) and in terms of our relations to each other (sociologically), in being able to develop a conception of the whole and one's place in it? Why is this important, and what opportunities do the smaller community create for developing this capacity?

The analytic concern for Wirth is with the individual as a particular knowable and knowing actor, and with the kind of communities that seek to develop or inhibit this actor. For Wirth a community is superior when it makes this kind of actor possible. The principle implied or recommended here is the importance of knowing other as a particular individual who in turn has the opportunity to develop a "conception" of the whole and of his/her own part in it. The notion Wirth seeks to articulate is the idea, in Raymond Williams's terms (1973, 165) of a "knowable community – a whole community, wholly knowable." It is this idea of a knowable person who simultaneously has the capacity to "survey the city as a whole and his part in it" that motivates Wirth's analysis of the city.

The practical and theoretical principle which he sees as needed is what I call the "capacity for surveyability," the capacity to obtain a conception of the whole and one's place in that. While he does not develop the reasonableness of this principle, it is the ground from which he speaks, "the principle recommended for acceptance" in his work. Presumably if it is a reasonably important virtue, it is worth nurturing in the young. Yet to nurture it one would have to understand and be able to recognize a community that exemplifies it. What ethical and political reasonableness can be developed to ground this claim? Could such a discourse recover a sense of the experience of living with others that undermines or resists the pluralization of life-worlds? In what way can an interactionally intimate relation to the whole resist segmentalization and the pluralization of life-worlds? Wirth provides us with one requirement: for such a relation to the whole to be possible, the number of people who are members of this whole has to be small.[4] The smaller community, it seems, provides its members with an opportunity "to obtain a conception of the [community] as a whole [and] to survey [their] place in it." (Wirth 1938, 17). I now return to the field material in order to tease out and examine statements that help in understanding this opportunity and what is involved in acting on it.

THE CONDITION OF SMALLNESS AND THE CHARACTER OF RESPONSIBILITY

The public character of the small town imparts a different sense of responsibility over time. Behavior has to be more considerate. It is one thing to lose your temper with the clumsy waiter who spills soup in your lap in the city. A quick retort, a curse on all his children, gets it out of your system, and it's done. It is quite another thing to behave like that in a small town. There, you'll likely see the waiter on the street for the next 20 years or see him grow up and marry your daughter, or you'll sit next to his brother at the Rotary luncheon: "You know, old Harold still talks about the day that he spilled the soup in your lap and you cursed him out like a drunken sailor."

Charles Long, 1989

FATHER (ex-urbanite): People from one situation all of a sudden end up being whatever, you're now, camp leader or whatever ... or they run the church camp or something. So again, that same point of the multi-dimensionality of people becomes more visible here ... [And you learn] that you still can live with them, even if you have strong disagreements with them.

MOTHER (ex-urbanite): And it may be while you also see your effects, you also see when you're being inconsistent, or shallow about your commitment or consistency because that becomes much more apparent, too ... So if you screw up you may just be much more accountable to take responsibility, apologizing, whatever it is. And I find that sometimes uncomfortable in a small community, I don't find that always easy, but I think it's probably good for me.

The above quotations point to the sociological difference (effects on social relations and on the character of the town) that small can make. According to Long, "behavior has to be more considerate" because "the small town imparts a different sense of responsibility" over time. Long's understanding includes a sense of history, because this is a responsibility developed "over time." An intimate relation to the whole does not mean, therefore, that friendship and intimacy are fostered. Rather, what can be nurtured is a different sense of responsibility, which requires taking one's own behaviour into consideration. In the city, Long says, the waiter can be reacted to solely in response to the anger his clumsiness has brought about. This cursing does not reverberate back into one's life: You "get it out of your system, and it's done." In the small town, however, you are "likely to see the waiter on the street for the next 20 years, or see him grow up and marry your daughter." This means that the small town makes it difficult to escape dealing with the consequences of one's actions. This does not mean that one does not get angry with waiters; rather, it means that one has to be prepared to face consequences that recall the original action.

The "smaller vessel," as Sim (1988, 94) calls the rural community, tends to enhance consciousness of the intersubjectivity of social life; one's deeds are not forgotten because the context is historically intersubjective. The angry customer does not just orient to the waiter's mistake but also to the way the waiter orients to the customer's anger and to the way that the waiter's orientation can become part of the mythology of the town. In the small town one acts in the context of a history of having one's actions taken into account by others. Unlike consumer society, a society without history, the small community creates the opportunity to make the past a continuous topic of conversation ("old Harold still talks about the day … you cursed him out like a drunken sailor"). What an individual in the small town continually has to take into account is that his or her actions are always taken into account and that this account becomes part of the discourse of the community. It is the continuous experience of this mutuality that "imparts a different sense of responsibility." What are the consequences in terms of the development of character of being in a situation where one has to deal with the consequences of one's actions?

One possible consequence is enforced politeness. Because one is aware that even an apparently minor event can reverberate throughout the community, a safe option may involve consciously supporting the community norms and mores, thereby supporting the small town's image of passivity and conformity. To new ruralites, the polite and deferential aspect of the small town often appears to be both dominant and oppressive. Being aware that any talk or action can return to haunt the actor can be an intimidating prospect. It is for this reason that action in the smaller community is felt to be more restrictive and why, according to Simmel (1971), there is more freedom to develop one's individual uniqueness in the city. The oppressiveness of politeness, deference, and conservatism is all the more empirically likely if the rural community does not contain "a rich mix of old and new drawn from local and distant sources" (Sim 1988, 94). In such cases the narrowness of the rural community can be felt to be overwhelming and incorrigible. Yet as Prairie Edge contains the mix of old and new characteristic of the new countryside of Canada, another relation to the condition of a smaller community is possible.

As the above speakers suggest, the condition of smallness can also impart a different sense of responsibility. This may be "sometimes uncomfortable," but such discomfort is that which comes from being forced to reflect on one's own commitments: "If you screw up you may just be much more accountable to take responsibility." Smallness makes it harder to hide from the consequences of one's deeds, and thus, *when the condition of smallness is befriended*, the understanding of actions in terms of such history is nurtured.

The value of befriending the condition of smallness resides in the virtue of a certain kind of self-consciousness, in the need to take into consideration one's own behaviour. This does not have to mean that one cannot argue or be angry with waiters. It can also mean that "you can still live with them, even if you have strong disagreements with them." The need to take one's own behaviour into consideration means that one has to live with the effects of one's conduct, and it is this "living with" that needs to be given consideration.

The very phenomenon of understanding one's actions within a historical frame itself subverts the tendency to pluralize life-worlds. A community that requires taking one's own behaviour into consideration is very different from one that encourages an instrumental relation to behaviour. In the first instance, one's conduct is less easily privatized (privatization is the condition of consumerism [Baumann 1994]). Secondly, this kind of socialization requires that one think of one's actions in terms of others in the community, particularly in terms of others' ability to hold one accountable.[5] Because of the reduced ability to privatize one's life and the awareness that the smaller community has a memory, life-worlds have a greater possibility of intersecting. Such intersecting undermines the tendency to segregate consciousness according to the roles one plays (Berger 1963, 108) and to hold rigidly to an orientation that reality *is* the pluralization of life-worlds.

Complaints about the lack of privacy common to my participants and the image of rural life can now be interpreted in light of what the mother means when she says, "I don't find that always easy, but I think it's probably good for me." Taking other into account is not now based on an abstract ethical command nor on an altruistic impulse. Rather it is based on the capacity of the other to respond to one's actions so that the need to be aware of taking the other into account becomes part of the ethos of the community and thus intrinsic to socialization into that community.

Analytically speaking, the visibility characteristic of smaller communities encourages, as an ethos, taking an overview with regard to one's actions ("obtaining a conception of the ... whole or to survey his place in it"). Taking such an overview can have many different empirical consequences; it may encourage passivity, or encourage learning that one "can live with people with whom one disagrees," or encourage recognition of the need to "take responsibility for inconsistencies in one's actions," and so on. Not all of these responses are equal in terms of their ethical and political implications. A community that values responsibility would make room for, even privilege, disagreements that one can live with, and privilege the practice of being held accountable for inconsistencies in one's commitments over the practice of mere agreeable conformity to community norms. That the latter occurs more often does not deny the possibility that the former can and should be the case.

In the small town, Long says, behaviour has to be "more considerate" or tactful. Tact is a social skill that, according to Gadamer (1975, 10–19), is also central to the mode of knowing which belongs to the human sciences: "By 'tact' we understand a particular sensitivity and sensitiveness to situations, and how to behave in them, for which we cannot find knowledge from general principles. Hence an essential part of tact is inexplicitness or unexpressibility" (16). Tact is the art of making sure distinctions and evaluations in the individual case; it is needed for interpretive sociology, and it is needed to help in dealing with waiters who spill soup on your lap. It is both a theoretical skill and a practical skill.

Tact says something and always leaves something else unsaid. As Gadamer (1975, 17) says, it is not so much an averting "of a gaze from something" as a watching it "in such a way that rather than knock against it, one slips by it." In the example of the clumsy waiter, who might be your neighbour's son and on his first day on the job, it would be tactless to treat the soup spilling in isolation from its context and oblivious to the nervousness and remorse of the waiter. Rather, tact calls on us to say something that both acknowledges and transforms the situation created by the waiter's blunder. If polite response merely averts one's gaze from the blunder, and anger clumsily (and egocentrically) knocks against it, the tactful response watches the blunder "in such a way that ... one slips by it." Tact and humour have a similar artful structure; for example, if this were the waiter's first day and his eagerness to please (by providing fast and efficient service) led to the soup spilling, one could respond, "I wasn't that hungry." Of course, if it turned out that the waiter was irredeemably clumsy, it would be tactless for anyone to politely encourage him to keep a position for which he is unsuited. Tact, therefore, requires good judgment as well as artfulness.

Tact is the art that can be developed by recognizing that behaviour has to be considerate. It is the art of being sensitive to the context and history of the action and the actor, an art crucial for the cultivated person and for the person who wants to understand action. It has both practical and theoretical implications because it is one important instance of showing "a conception of the whole" and surveying one's "place in it." It is for this reason that the self-cultivation required by phenomenological hermeneutic procedures (Van Manen 1990, 2–34) is intertwined with the self-cultivation required by a community that says behaviour must be considerate. "Hermeneutic phenomenological research edifies the personal insight, contributing to one's thoughtfulness and one's ability to act toward others, children or adults, with tact or tactfulness. In this sense, human science research is itself a kind of *Bildung* or *paideia*; it is the curriculum of being and becoming" (Van Manen 1990, 7).

The meaning of the capacity to obtain a conception of the whole and one's place in it as it interrelates with the high visibility characteristic of smaller towns still needs further development. Exploring this meaning provides opportunities to collect various motifs woven through this project so far. I ground the way the small town reduces parental anxiety (see chapter 5), and I develop the difference between the visibility of the *polis* (Arendt 1958) and the visibility of the panopticon (Foucault 1977). Most important of all, I continue to develop and demonstrate the recommended principle that theoretical issues are also practical issues.

THE ANXIETY OF PARENTING AND THE FACULTY OF SURVEYABILITY: FOUCAULT'S PANOPTICON OR ARENDT'S POLIS?

The notion of surveyability is addressed by Aristotle's argument (*Politics*, IV.1–14–V.1–4) of why size is relevant to the character of the city state. For Aristotle, size has two aspects: number of people and size of territory. The issue of the most appropriate size is judged according to the criterion of "surveyability." That is, members should be able to take an overview that will enable them to form a judgment about the whole, leading to an understanding of appropriate action (*praxis*). Aristotle considered this faculty particularly important for the health of a democracy in a city state because it enabled a citizen to form a fuller picture of the others ("know one another's character" [*Politics* IV, 12]) with whom power and responsibility was shared.

This capacity for surveyability is developed in a smaller community *precisely because* of the high visibility characteristic of the small town. As the term itself suggests, high visibility not only means that one's deeds are visible to the community but also leads to a greater ability to see and evaluate others' actions. *Surveyability is the human skill that high visibility strengthens.* To talk about the small town merely in terms of high visibility without addressing its corollary – enhanced ability of greater surveyability – is a passive understanding of the sociological experience of the small town. As I show, such an understanding collapses the important differences between the visibility associated with Foucault's panopticon and the visibility of Arendt's *polis*. It is my contention that Arendt's is a more appropriate model to help understand the possibilities for self-cultivation in smaller communities. Ironically, it is Aristotle who (in drawing on surveyability as a theoretic capacity i.e., a practical wisdom) reminds us of the need to preserve or, more accurately, recover the oriented actor's experience of the small community.

Surveyability is a particularly relevant skill for parents of young children. As we know (chapter 5), contemporary parenting is an anxiety-generating activity. For example, in crowded situations parents are fearful of losing their children. The solution in the city involves some attempt to maintain a tight rein on children so they do not wander off. As a parent myself I am familiar with how much small children resist this rein as overly restrictive, yet it is often necessary in the city. Two of the more frightening memories I have of living in Toronto concern losing our youngest child in a crowd. We found him, but the experiences were traumatic, reinforcing the necessity of close surveillance.

In chapter 7 we saw the way the visibility of the small town allowed parents to give their children more freedom. Aristotle's insight into the human capacity for surveyability can now aid us in formulating the basis for this reduction of anxiety and enhancement of confidence on the part of the parents. The confidence of rurban parents is based on their enhanced capacity, which the smallness of the town enables, for surveyability. From the perspective of the parental life-world, high visibility is the objective description of the subjective experience of an enhanced capacity to survey. The parent is in a dialectical relation with the social environment, and high visibility creates the opportunity for taking an overview of one's situation and community. This itself supports Gadamer's claim that social life is inherently dialectical and therefore can best be understood through the application of dialectic.

Let me return to the example of the mother who described most of her friends as single mothers, and remarked on how many of them moved from the city to raise their children in the town. She said that this involved a cost, because "there's nothing here for single people." When asked why they moved back, she said, "because it's a good place to raise your kids, it's small enough, you can't get lost, you know you can locate your kids within a few minutes, family. They come back to raise kids." The smallness, the impossibility of getting lost, and the ability to locate kids within a few minutes are interrelated. All are outcomes of the enhanced capacity for surveyability that the high visibility of the town nurtures. Because this capacity is a sense that is nurtured in a taken-for-granted way, one becomes simultaneously nurtured in the capacity to "obtain a conception of the ... whole" and "to survey" one's place in it.

Another couple raised a different aspect of this capacity:

FATHER: Well, I think one of the things was we have two kids, and one of them was – they were only five or ten minutes from the countryside, which to me was quite important.
MOTHER: Go out and build a fort, or whatever, the freedom of living in a small town.
FATHER: You know, they have parks and stuff in the city that are beautiful, but a lot of them, do you want your children to be there unsupervised because of who else is in those parks?
MOTHER: It was mostly freedom to be natural.
FATHER: For kids to be kids, I guess, without having to just go to movies, go to the community centre, having those kinds of things – just go out.

Here we see cases of parents referencing different aspects of surveyability. In the first case, the single mother describes the benefits of a size that is easily surveyable if her child gets lost, because intrinsic to parenting a smaller child is living with the anxiety of losing one's child. In a smaller setting you know you can locate your child in a few minutes, a knowledge that serves in turn to reduce anxiety. The resulting sense of security means that one can be more free, both with the child and with self. The enhanced ability to survey the environment means that *both* parent and child have greater freedom. The child is not subject to a tight rein, and the parent is not restricted by the need to restrict the child's movements. In this sense the parent/child relation is less of a Hegelian master/slave relation.

In the second case, the parents address an implication of the sense of security that emerges from surveyability. If a territory is small enough to enable locating a child within minutes, it is also small enough for the child to explore. That is, surveyability is a skill both the child and the parent get to develop when the condition of small-ness is befriended. The mother translates this freedom as the freedom to be natural. Children, endowed with a natural sense of curiosity, can explore, wander, build a fort, or "whatever." The small-ness of the territory is large enough to nurture this curiosity, but small enough to allow this nurturance to be done without the constant gaze of the parent. Parent and child are not just two separate actors joined together by their interaction; they are now understood as collected by *the shared capacity to develop or to exercise the judgment that is based on taking an overall view.*

Smallness in territory is important because it is surveyable. This does not mean, as it does for scientific geography, that it has to be surveyed in detail. Rather, smallness allows for the knowledge that you can survey the territory, if necessary (emergency, curiosity). This means that a small size makes a particular kind *of knowledge* possible, which in turn leads to a sense of confidence and trust in one's immediate environment. This knowledge is neither cognitive nor scientific in nature nor is it based on detached and detailed observation. Rather, as already stated, it is more related to feeling, to (in Gadamer's – who follows Aristotle in this – terms) tact, judgment, and taste (1975, 5–38), because it is intrinsically related to membership in a community or culture. These are faculties that are developed and operate in community, but – what is most decisive – they are not subservient to the community. If this is so, then to critique this kind of knowledge as a misperception (e.g., because it does not correspond to "the facts" about crime, safety, etc.) is itself a misinterpretation.

To get a better sense of the embeddedness of this knowledge, I will turn to a second aspect of size, i.e., numbers of people, alluded to by parents:

MOTHER: I think you would know about it faster, as a parent, if your child was involved in the wrong gang or being led astray. I think you would hear about it. In the city, you would never know unless there was a teacher or something that reported it. In a town, the town talks and I think you would hear about it.

MOTHER (ex-urbanite): Like you can't run an errand in five minutes in Prairie Edge, because invariably you are going to run into ten people that you know in that space of time ... I mean it's a very odd day that you would go downtown and not see a familiar face. Whereas in the city, my goodness, that was something of a miracle if you were downtown and saw any face.

As Simmel noted in *Metropolis and Mental Life*, this visibility is central to the *polis*-like character of the small town. Your words and deeds are highly visible and quickly become the property of the town. The first mother says that the "town talks." The smallness of the community creates the effect that your actions are being observed and commented on by the town. One father who grew up in the town commented on the experience of being subject to this form of observation:

FATHER: [As a boy] you were very careful what you did down on Main Street because you never, you know, even if you met the principal or a teacher from the school and saw them on holidays, you always behaved, because they had no qualms about phoning your parents and this was not the way that people should act. When I got older, with a driver's licence, of course you wanted to go to another town to your dance and stuff because you didn't care who saw you because no one knew you.

What is being referred to here is the awareness of knowing and being known by the other. That is, the capacity for surveyability is developed *in the context of high visibility*. This connects with but is different from "panopticism" (Foucault 1977, 195–228). Foucault (201) describes the panopticon in this way: "Hence the major effect of the Panopticon: to induce in the inmate a state of conscious and permanent visibility that assures the automatic functioning of power. So to arrange things that the surveillance is permanent in its effects, even if it is discontinuous in its action; that the perfection of power should tend to render its actual exercise unnecessary." This visibility resonates with the recollections of the father above: he is "conscious" of the "visibility" that seemed to assure the "functioning" of his parents' power. However, unlike Foucault's inmate, as he moved into the teenage years, he could escape from this visibility "to another town" where "you didn't care who saw you because no one knew you."

Modern society, according to Foucault, has developed unprecedented power to subject individual members to discipline and control.

The panopticon is the symbol of this power that induces in the individual "a state of conscious and permanent visibility." The social sciences have not been neutral observers of this development. Rather, by contributing knowledge of the way individuals act and think, they have bolstered the capacity of modern society to engage in the "surveillance and discipline" of its members through the specific interlocking of knowledge and power.

On the surface it seems that modern society has merely exaggerated this power to subject individuals to a consciousness of being visible – a power that was already present in smaller communities. Yet there is an important difference that makes the visibility of the small town experientially and conceptually distinct. In the system of the panopticon (Foucault 1977, 200), the individual "is seen, but he does not see; he is the object of information, never a subject in communication."[6] In contrast, the above excerpts suggest that the visibility of the small town is more like the *polis*. Where the panopticon develops an image of an observed person who does not observe ("the inmate must never know whether he is being looked at at any one moment; but he must be sure that he may always be so"), the *polis* addresses the phenomenon where one is both seen and sees, observed and observer. Using Foucault's terminology, the individual, seen through the medium of communication, is always "a subject in communication." The experience of visibility in smaller communities is mediated through communication, and simultaneously expresses community ("the town talks"). It is a capacity developed in and through community as both the surveyor and the surveyed are embedded in a communal discourse. This experience of seeing and being seen more closely approximates the image of a *polis*: "The *polis*, properly speaking, is not the city-state in its physical location; it is the organization of the people as it arises out of acting and speaking together, and its true space lies between people living together for this purpose, no matter where they happen to be" (Arendt 1958, 198).

The faculty of obtaining a conception of the whole and one's place in it is developed through participation in community. The actor who possesses this art will be not one who stands above and outside community but who is simultaneously a member of and actor in the community being conceptualized. In fact, it is only through reflection on the relation between the intention and consequences of our action that one gains a sense of the whole and one's place in it.

Because embeddedness references a community, surveyability is developed in a context of accountability. While surveyability gives an actor greater freedom and confidence, accountability means that "people who see you and know you" hold you responsible for your actions. This is the tension of the *polis: the freedom of exploring the meaning of the whole is developed and exercised in the context of the limitation represented by accountability.* This tension is enhanced by modern conditions, that is, by the fact that the new rural community contains a "rich mix of old and new." The diversity that was the hallmark of the city is now part of the new countryside of Canada. As well, the pervasiveness of consumerism, as one of the ways postmodernity expresses the desire for freedom, is limited by the way the small town watches over the deeds and actions of individuals.

It is in this sense that the small town has the possibility of being a *polis*, a public space where one sees and is seen by others. In other words, what the small size makes possible is a *polis* not in the sense of a city but rather in the sense of a community where one's actions and speech become part of the common property of the town rather than the private concern of the individual. It is as though the community itself were watching "over the deeds, the conduct of life and the attitudes of the individual" (Simmel 1971, 333).

Simmel pointed out the way that this *polis* factor can have either positive or limiting consequences. Negatively, it operates to oppress because of its de-individualizing effect. Yet a commitment on the part of individuals to freedom and uniqueness will mean undertaking to struggle with this tendency of the smaller community. In turn, such a struggle can bring about the energy, excitement, and unique colourfulness that typified Athenian life. Such struggles will obviously increase the tension in small towns. The piety of the old ways will be challenged by newcomers for whom such ways do not make sense. Newcomers will be seen to be disrespectful, impatient, rude, naive, and even disloyal; hometowners will be seen as conservative, irrational, stuck in their ways. Yet such tension expresses the fundamental relation between the desire for free individuality and the needs of community. The tension between the accountability intrinsic to a smaller community and the freedom of (post)modernity is not a problem to be eliminated but a particular opportunity to be developed. Without the tension, one is left with two problematic options: the oppressiveness and de-individualizing tendency of the small town or the consumer freedom of postmodernity.

ACCOUNTABILITY AND THE LIMIT OF HUMAN MASTERY

I have sought to unfold the way the condition of smallness can be positively and actively developed (befriended) in a way that creates opportunity for collective living. I argue that the quality of high visibility, when it is embedded in a community, must be understood as simultaneously developing the human capacity to take the whole situation or community into account. This capacity involves tact, judgment, and taste, capacities collected by the virtue of practical wisdom (Gadamer 1975; Bonner 1997), and they inform action and speech in the very communal situation through which they are developed.

Parent and child are now understood as collected by the interest in and need to develop this capacity for action that takes the whole into account. The whole is not now any one empirical community but any community that brings together the qualities of visibility and surveyability: this bringing together, this integration, issues in a strong sense of accountability. Whereas Wirth's formulation suggests the development of some technical capacity (and thus becomes that which supports the surveillance society Foucault critiques), a more precise understanding shows the way accountability becomes a social practice. Accountability provides a specific resistance to the privatization of the interest in freedom which consumerism represents, while that interest in freedom resists the potential oppressiveness of the de-individualizing effect of the small town.

To what does the *polis* aspect of the small town make one more accountable? The comments of one ex-urbanite are telling in this regard:

FATHER: I don't know whether being unconventional [in the city] is really a way of challenging a convention when it [being unconventional] is already tolerated [as a subculture]. In the smaller community, everybody will talk about it, and you have to live with that, and then you really are unconventional.

If you want to make people responsible in the sense of being responsive to actual people, that's what responsibility, I think, is. It's not some sort of guilt feeling, but can you respond, can you act, face the consequences of your action? Or see that other people act, and they live with their consequences, and you have to interact with them? I think that is better done in a smaller community again where you have more levels of face-to-face contact. Because otherwise you could simply label and dismiss people.

With this understanding of the notion of responsibility, I can formulate the practice of accountability further. In a *polis*, one is accountable in terms of being required to face the consequences of one's actions as these return in the form of rumour and reputation. In the town "you can act, [and] face the consequences of your action. Or see that other people act and that they live with their consequences and you have to interact with them." What has to be taken into account is that one is interpreted, literally speaking, known, in terms of the history of one's words and deeds, and this is so regardless of how one wants to be understood. One has to interact with those who have a different understanding from oneself about who one is and what one is doing.

Arendt (1958, 182–3), in developing her understanding of the human capacity for action and speech, describes this aspect of action: "Since this disclosure of the subject [speaker or doer] is an integral part of all, even the most 'objective' intercourse, the physical, worldly in-between along with its interests is overlaid and, as it were, overgrown with an altogether different in-between which consists of deeds and words and owes its origin exclusively to men's acting and speaking directly *to* one another." Arendt (183) calls this reality "the 'web' of human relationships, indicating by the metaphor its somewhat intangible quality."

Accountability means that people are going to hear about and ask you to account for your actions. Returning to the example of the clumsy waiter, ten or twenty years later "you'll sit next to his brother at the Rotary luncheon" and be told, "'old Harold still talks about the day he spilled the soup in your lap and you cursed him out like a drunken sailor'" (Long 1989, 45). This incident is a good example of an everyday version of accountability. The angry customer now is required to develop a relation to and give an account of his or her anger. The very raising of the issue at the Rotary luncheon is implicitly asking for an account. It is not that the angry customer needs to be sorry. Rather, the stories that one's actions generate have to be taken into account. The angry customer is called to remember that a minor incident in his or her life is a major event in Harold's life.

In a deeper way, what one is called to remember is the boundlessness of human action. Says Arendt (1958, 184), "It is because of this already existing web of human relationships, with its innumerable conflicting wills and intentions, that action almost never achieves its purpose; but it is also because of this medium, in which action alone is real, that it 'produces' stories with or without intention." In this case, one could end up with a reputation of acting like a drunken sailor. Given that the anger is a response to the clumsiness of the waiter, it is ironic that the customer ends up with the drunken sailor reputation. The "existing web of human relationships" ensures that "action almost never achieves its purpose."

One's words and deeds become real and capable of resisting self-understanding ("I don't act like a drunken sailor") because they are seen and interpreted from within this web of relationships. What

Arendt is referring to here is that the story or discourse that reveals an individual's uniqueness is neither authored nor controlled by that individual. This "disclosure of the subject" which "is an integral part of all" intercourse is developed in the stories we tell of each other's actions. Accountability in this sense means needing to come to terms with the account others have of who one is and what one is doing, an account that inevitably resists and provokes self-understanding.

Simmel, writing at a time when the small town represented the tradition of the rural as against the modernity of the city, suggests that this very prospect of accountability, of having to face the consequences of one's actions, has a de-individualizing effect. On the other hand, the example of Athens shows that by directly challenging this de-individualizing tendency, excitement, agitation, and a unique colourfulness can emerge. This is the inherent promise built into the idea of the *polis*. It is also the promise that the new residents (ex-urbanites) bring to the contemporary Canadian town (Sim 1988, 68–96). While oppressive conformity might be more typical, empirically speaking, it is not *the necessary* outcome of the *town*. Oppressiveness is a consequence when the accountability that the *polis* demands is responded to in a timid, passive, and unimaginative way. But such a sense of oppressiveness also reminds us of why courage, that now-archaic virtue, was so important for the creation of the original Greek *polis*. Courage and imagination were necessary virtues for transforming the hierarchical household structure into a *polis*. Courage was what an actor needed in order to leave the security of the household for the freedom of the *polis* (Arendt 1958, 28–37). Tact, courage, and imagination are needed if the tension between the desire for freedom and the need of community is to be developed into colourfulness and excitement instead of degenerating into the segregated and ghetto-like factions of the metropolis or passive, de-individualizing deference of the small town. With courage, tact, and imagination, it is possible to develop a strong relation to accountability.

This is the promise of excellence built into every *polis*, even if it is rarely realized. Yet this kind of excellence can become one reference point or guide for smaller communities and, in particular, for the new rural Canada struggling to integrate diverse people and voices into a community of weakened "traditional social controls" (Sim 1988, 96). The promise lies in the realization that the development of the individual is conditional on the development of the community, that through one's actions one not only changes self but simultaneously changes the community, which will reflect back (both positively and negatively) that change to self. According to Hannah Arendt (1958), this relation to community is truer to the original image of what democracy is all about, an image that has been all but erased by the interest of the modern state in household activities. While she articulated the concept of the *polis* in terms of its embodiment in the ancient Greek city state, here we are reminded that the *spirit* of the *polis* is an ever-present possibility.

THE LIMITS OF ACTION AND THE LIMITS OF UNDERSTANDING

This enduring potential of the *polis* can only develop through the understanding of that which limits human action and understanding. At this highest level, what we learn here points to a condition that must be admitted rather than transformed. This limit is as true for inquiry as it is for action and, though Arendt develops only the latter, we have here a particularly strong example of the radical interpretive principle that theoretical problems are also problems of *praxis*.

Because of the accountability that the web of human relations weaves in the *polis*, we cannot be masters of the way our deeds and our words are interpreted and understood. What we say and what we do are responded to by others, who themselves have the capacity to interpret and respond in ways we cannot control and may not desire. Living with the consequences of action means in turn that the limit on one's desire to be understood and interpreted according to one's own wishes must be lived with.

This limit to human mastery not only has to be taken into account as a practical problem in the strongest sense of that term; it is also a theoretical problem, again in the strongest sense, because what is true for human action is also true for human inquiry. If we live with others who interpret our deeds and words differently from the way we do, we also live with the condition that *our understanding of others' understanding* is fundamentally limited. This is as true for scientific and philosophic understanding as it is for everyday understanding and, as such, is the reason why Gadamer fundamentally rejects the manipulating and controlling character of scientific method for social inquiry. "Method is an effort to measure and control from the side of the interpreter; it is the opposite of letting the phenomenon lead" (Palmer 1969, 247), letting what has to be understood lead the inquirer. A formulaic following of method is incapable of embracing the deep limit to which human understanding is subject. Therefore the problem of the limit of the human condition of action (that our actions are subject to the conditions of irreversibility and unpredictability) and the recognition of the finitude of human understanding are as much issues for the community of researchers (in this case sociologists) as they are for the people of Prairie Edge. But precisely because they concern the human condition, they are also an issue for every human community and so, therefore, for Prairie Edge.

This issue of limit and finitude allows us to recognize the flaw in Wirth's idea of obtaining a conception of the whole and one's place in it, and the idea of a "whole community, wholly knowable." Both are fundamentally illusory in any final sense. Both represent dreams and hopes concerning the highest possibility of human mastery, but to treat them as achievable is to deny the negativity inherent in human experience. To retain them as realizable goals no longer merely expresses the ambition of modernity; it more precisely shows that the holder is in the grip of an illusory dogmatism which, in the case of the urban-rural discourse, led to the elimination of the very other it sought to engage.

The experience of human finitude involves the recognition that humans can be "master neither of time nor the future. The experienced man knows the limitedness of all prediction and the uncertainty of all plans" (Gadamer 1975, 320). To put it more formally, language both pervades and escapes any one speech about language (e.g., obtaining a conception of the whole and one's place in it); and thus any understanding of the whole, whether sociological, scientific, or philosophical, has to include in it a recognition of the essential incompleteness of any (including this) speech. In Gadamer's terms (320), the knowledge that emerges from "real experience is that in which man becomes aware of his finiteness. In it are discovered the limits of the power and the self-knowledge of his planning reason." Thus real experience has to include a "fundamental sort of openness" (325). "Openness to the other then includes the acknowledgment that I must accept some things that are against myself, even though there is no one else who asks this of me" (324). The awareness of the accountability element intrinsic to smaller communities can nurture a receptiveness to this acknowledgment. On the other hand, the depth of the meaning of this acknowledgment appears when desire (for freedom, for a conception of the whole, for discourse) is pursued to its limit.

The interest in engaging otherness and questioning limits, the informing interest of the urban-rural discourse, now means that the person in a genuine human relationship (and this includes the relationship between inquirer and interlocutor) must put him/herself in a position where what the other says can become a claim on self. Knowing (recognizing) the principled limitations of humanity requires such openness. Engaging otherness therefore means listening to the other in as much an attitude of openness as is humanly possible – recognizing that what one learns through that openness is the difficulty of being genuinely open to understanding the other. This is a challenging demand on us as human beings and as inquirers engaged in oriented and directed research. Seeking to meet the challenge cannot be developed without simultaneously developing the self-understanding involved in the arts of tact, judgment, and taste. Oriented and directed research involves the self-formation of *Bildung* or *paideia*. Taylor (1977, 130) summarizes the theoretical issues involved in developing these practical skills:

There are good grounds both in epistemological arguments and in their greater fruitfulness for opting for hermeneutical sciences of man. But we cannot hide from ourselves how greatly this option breaks with certain commonly held notions about our scientific tradition. We cannot measure such sciences against the requirements of a science of a verification: we cannot judge them by their predictive capacity. We have to accept that they are founded on intuitions which all do not share, and what is worse that these intuitions are closely bound up with our fundamental options. These sciences cannot be "wertfrei"; they are moral sciences in a more radical sense that the eighteenth century understood. Finally, their successful prosecution requires a high degree of self-knowledge, a freedom from illusion, in the sense of error which is rooted and expressed in one's way of life; for our incapacity to understand is rooted in our own self-definitions, hence in what we are. To say this is not to say anything new: Aristotle makes a similar point in Book 1 of the *Ethics*. But it is still radically shocking and unassimilable to the mainstream of modern science.

The problem of engaging otherness and questioning limits is now no longer just a problem of the urban-rural literature, no longer just a problem for methodology, no longer just a problem of even modernity itself: it is all of these insofar as these are instances of a "genuine human relationship," where "belonging together always also means being able to listen to one another" (Gadamer 1975, 324). To seek to differentiate the theoretical from the practical, or the ontological from the sociological, would, at this level, be an exercise in abstraction.

WHAT IS DESIRED AND WHAT NEEDS TO BE KNOWN

[T]he transition from country to city – from a predominantly rural to a predominantly urban society – is transforming and significant. The

growth of towns and especially of cities and a metropolis; the increasing
division and complexity of labour; the altered and critical relations
between and within social classes: in changes like these any assumption
of a knowable community – a whole community, wholly knowable –
became harder and harder to sustain. But this is not the whole story, and
once again, in realizing the new fact of the city, we must be careful not to
idealize the old facts of the country. For what is knowable is not only a
function of objects – of what is there to be known. It is also a function of
subjects, of observers – of what is desired and what needs to be known.

Raymond Williams, 1973

Educators ... stand in relation to the young as representatives of a world
for which they must assume responsibility although they themselves did
not make it, and even though they may, secretly or openly, wish it were
other than it is. This responsibility is not arbitrarily imposed upon educators; it is implicit in the fact that the young are introduced by adults into
a continuously changing world. Anyone who refuses to assume joint
responsibility for the world should not have children and must not be
allowed to take part in educating them.   Hannah Arendt, 1968

Raymond Williams articulates the radical interpretive principle used
as a resource and explicated as a topic throughout the discussion.
What "is knowable is not only a function of objects – of what is there
to be known. It is also a function of observers – of what is desired
and what needs to be known." Arendt, on the other hand, talks
about the responsibility imposed on us as educators of the young.
We must assume joint responsibility for the world and the child.
   "What is desired and what needs to be known" has been subject
to continuous discursive examination in this research project. For an
oriented and directed research project, every stage, from the conceptualization of rurality to research design, from what is to be investigated to who has to be understood, from engaging principles of
knowing to engaging parents in Prairie Edge, from the experience of
the researcher to reflection on that experience, and from the data to
the organization of the narrative, is continuously subject to this question. My argument throughout is that radical interpretive sociology
is equipped for this task.
   It is especially interesting that Williams's articulation of this principle is developed (recommended for acceptance) precisely around
his examination of the urban-rural discourse in English literature. As
he says, the transition from country to city, the urbanization of society, is transforming and significant. The belief that a more rural
centre is a "great place to raise kids" is an idea that gets its practical

intelligibility and its prominence as a consequence of this transformation of society.

The transformation is not only a matter of demographics but also of consciousness, influencing not only where we happen to live but also what we think "we need to know." This is as true for the researcher as it is for the parent who makes such a claim. This transformation means that the conceptualization of rurality itself must be examined. One important example of the modern transformation in consciousness, in "what is desired and what needs to be known," is the interest in engaging otherness and questioning limits. Ironically, as the otherness of the rural in western society began increasingly to disappear, the hegemony of the scientific orientation simultaneously made it difficult for sociology to recognize the problem. The concept of the life-world provides for the possibility of incorporating reflexivity into sociological procedure and thus allowing the question of the otherness of rurality to again become a practical matter.

Is the small town (Prairie Edge) a great place to raise children? What is desired and what needs to be known in order to respond to this question in a strong way? What needs to be known is the importance of the parental life-world in providing context and horizon for asking and answering this question. Parenting, in late modernity, is a particular way of organizing and knowing the world. From within this life-world, the social organization of the small town is successful in reducing the anxiety and burden associated with modern parenthood. When the researcher recognizes that the object of analysis is not children *per se* but parental anxiety concerning the almost total responsibility for the life of another being, then safety, convenience, and sense of mutuality of the small town can be recognized as real.

But is this all that "needs to be known" here? Might the place in the "great place" be used in an instrumental way? It is great merely because it is great for my parenting? On the other hand, what if the place invites itself to be treated in an instrumental manner? Both sides of this concern are seen in this study, and both are deeply indifferent to the identity of place in "a great place." Can a place like this be such a great place?

Our modern age invites a consumer relation to place. This invitation is unwittingly legitimated by a phenomenology that does not ask itself the questions "What is desired, and what needs to be known?" Thus reflexive research has to be pushed to its root. The reflexivity needs to be radical. This is as true for parents as it is for researchers. Despite the genuine commitment to being a good parent, are we refusing "joint responsibility for the world" when we exemplify an instrumental relation to place – even when "we wish it were other than it is"? How do children develop a love of the world when those charged with educating them see it as a means to an end? According to Arendt, such people "should not have children and must not be allowed to take part in educating them." What needs to be known is not only what is a good place but also what is good parenting: according to Arendt, one cannot be a good parent without also developing a good relation to the world.

What are the possibilities of taking joint responsibility for our place and for our child, when, empirically, McDonald's and Mitsubishi dominate the horizon? What are the possibilities of developing a good relation to place when the place itself appears to be indifferent to this need? What is desired and what needs to be known cannot be limited by knowledge grounded in empirical verification. Rather, the researcher has to draw on the very tact, judgment, and taste that are themselves developed within community. These moral and political faculties enable sure distinctions and evaluations about appropriate action, distinctions that cannot be cognitively demonstrated.

What needs to be known, therefore, is the ideal community to which the cultivated researcher can give agreement against the tyranny exercised by the dominance of consumerism or the tyranny of the indifference of a place. What is desired is an image of what an ideal community looks like. This image, which must be fashioned out of the possibilities of meaning inherent in existing communities like Prairie Edge, is the other that must now be engaged, and the empiricism of fashion (McDonald's, the commercial town) is the limit that must be questioned. Engaging otherness and questioning limits is educational when the other is constructed in such a way that it can challenge, motivate, and inspire action and understanding. Taking joint responsibility for the world and the child includes providing images for the child of a world worth acting in, preserving, and handing on. In the end, this is what we as parents and researchers hand on to the future.

Epilogue

My wife and I were having lunch in January 1995 when the phone rang. The vice-principal of a local Prairie Edge grade school spoke to my wife. He informed her that there had been a shooting the day before, that the police had been called, and he was asking permission for the police to interview our youngest child. A boy of thirteen, it seems, had taken a couple of shots with a .22-calibre rifle in the presence of a group of boys, one of whom was our son. We were shocked. Our youngest had not said anything about this to us the previous day. I remembered him complaining about his physical education teacher being sexist because she made boys do full push-ups while girls did push-ups from the knees. This complaint absorbed our conversation. There was no indication that he might have been shot at that day.

It was hard to know how to take this news. When our son came home from school, we asked him why he had not told us about the incident. He said he did not know that the thirteen year old was using a real gun. He and his four friends had a teasing friendship going on with this boy. They teased him; he tried to bully them. They had numbers on their side, he had age on his. This kind of banter had happened often, and yesterday's encounter was part of it. I asked my son exactly what had happened.

"He started beating up on one of our friends," he said. "We started making fun of him. He started beating up on the friend again, and we made fun of him again. It kept going like that until all of a sudden he brought out a rifle. He fired a shot in the air, I thought he was pretending, and I said: 'Oh come on. Is that your best shot?' He went back in and came out. He aimed the gun at me. Then he suddenly turned and shot at the garbage can. We didn't think the gun was real."

It was clear that our son was now becoming scared. The interview with the police had jolted him. He was upset and unsure whether he had done something wrong. He asked me if we were angry because he now has a police record.

"What do you mean?" I asked.

"The police told me that the statement they took was for the record."

I reassured him that he did not have a record and explained what the police meant. He was confused and disturbed by the seriousness of the new meaning yesterday's incident was taking on.

I did not know what to think. My wife was very frightened. The penultimate version of this manuscript, *A Great Place to Raise Kids*, was being reviewed by the Aid to Scholarly Publications Programme in Ottawa. Yet it seemed our son had had a very serious encounter with a shooting incident. And what kind of gun is a .22-calibre rifle? Surrounding this incident was the debate about the new gun-registration law in Canada.

We tried to piece the story together. None of the boys realized that the gun the thirteen year old used was real. But a neighbour saw what happened and told her friend who was a teacher's aid at the school. The teacher's aid told the principal, who called in the police.

That evening I spoke to one of the officers investigating the incident. They had had run-ins with the thirteen year old before. I had heard a rumour that he was mentally unstable. The police officer thought not; he said the kid had a chip on his shoulder. He also explained to me that a .22-calibre rifle is a powerful weapon that could kill a moose at that distance.

We did not know the kid nor his parents. We heard that the mom and dad had just split up, and the gun and ammunition belonged to the father. I tried to imagine what was going through the boy's mind that he somehow saw that the solution to the teasing was to use a gun.

The next day the police asked my wife to accompany our son to the scene of the crime. They re-enacted the scene to the best of our son's memory. It seems that his playful challenge ("Is that your best shot?") turned him into a target. As they re-enacted the scene, my wife heard one of the police officers say, "It looks like he was shooting to hit." There was a bullet-hole in a metal garbage can between the ten year olds and the thirteen year old. A pretty back lane now took on ominous overtones. The frightening prospect began to sink in more. My wife later showed me the lane and the garbage can with the bullet-hole in it.

We talked about the incident to our friends but not in front of our son. The principal had told him to keep the matter confidential until it was cleared up. He was also embarrassed about it in a way that neither he nor we really understood. I could not figure out what the incident meant. What did it mean about the claims to safety discussed in the book? Why our son? I did not revise my opinion about the school, the neighbourhood, nor even that now-infamous back lane. None of them were places to be avoided for reasons of safety. Did the idea of the town as safe have to be revised? How did the thirteen year old get his hands on a rifle? I thought writing it down it would help me understand. Here is what I wrote that day:

Jan 20, 1995

Today Margaret and I went to view the scene of the crime. I still feel as if the whole event is unreal. Trying to imagine that our ten year old and his buddies, in Prairie Edge, could be shot at by a thirteen-year-old school rival. The whole event is so absurd, given our setting. It is so absurd that he did not realize that it happened. On Tuesday 17th of January, our son and his friends were fired at twice by a thirteen-year-old acquaintance with whom they have an ongoing rivalry. They did not think that it was anything remarkable: they thought the gun was a toy one and that this was a normal part of the rivalry between this boy and his four friends. So, when he comes home that afternoon he does not mention the

I stopped there. I couldn't write any more. The whole event was too emotional for me. I felt myself starting to cry. The prospect of my son being killed was too terrible to contemplate. Every parent knows how hard it is to imagine their lives without their children. The potential trauma of a tragedy was itself traumatic and too difficult to think about. That day the *Edmonton Journal* published a short article on the incident.[1] The local newspapers also gave the story space, though, ironically, they reported it in a shorter and more bureaucratically anonymous fashion.

Considering the seriousness and unusual character of the event, it did not get much coverage locally.[2] One of the weeklies has a policy of avoiding or downplaying "bad-news" stories. The opening of a new supermarket in town gets much more coverage than this incident did. This reaction is one reason why smaller towns "feel safer" – incidents like these are played down in the local media whereas in the city media they are blown up. Incidents like this offend the image of the smaller town and, in a setting where many people know many others, there is a risk that someone, some family member or friend, will be offended. Local newspapers, dependent on local advertising, try as much as possible to avoid offending their customers. Yet such things happen in small towns, and one such incident had happened here. While we were more aware of this kind of danger when we lived in Toronto, it had never happened to us there.

So what does this happening mean in terms of this book? I did think it highly strange and ironic that such an incident happened after I completed a version of this book. When we got some distance on the shooting, when we realized that we were fortunate that in the end no one was hurt, we saw the humour in the paradox of the relation between the book and the event. We played around with a *Saturday Night Live* routine and proposed ending the book with an epilogue that reports on the incident and then says about the thesis, "Never mind."

Yet the incident does not lead me to change anything concluded in the book. Neither has it changed our relation to parenting in a rural setting. Our children, and especially our son, still roam the town freely. As I have developed, it is both safe enough and convenient enough to allow for that. The incident did not point to a pattern either missed or emerging in the town. It made me more of a supporter of the new law requiring registration of guns in Canada, not a popular position in rural Alberta. Existing laws covered this case, however, and both the thirteen-year-old boy and his father were charged.

My wife went to the boy's court case. It was a classic rural scene: we knew as a friend the lawyer who defended the boy. He was surprised and even a little embarrassed to see my wife at the court case. Given that there was no one else she knew there, he invited her to sit beside him and the boy. She declined. The boy was charged not with attempted manslaughter but with possessing and using a dangerous weapon. His defence was that he was on medication at the time, and he had forgotten to take it. He was given a community-service sentence and ordered not to handle a firearm for ten years. On Canada Day I saw him helping at the annual fund-raiser for the local Boys and Girls Club, a plastic duck race. My wife pointed him out, and it was weird seeing the kid who could have shot our son in a communal and celebratory occasion. The anomalies of the event were again underlined for me. He has since left the town.

In some ways the incident and its reverberations remind me of the richness of the themes raised here. For example, the episode brings home an issue addressed in chapter 5, that there is no real difference between rural and urban settings in terms of the "objective" indicators of safety. Although we were much more aware of the danger of something like this happening in Toronto, it never did. On the other hand, the idea of something like this happening in a rural setting did not cross our minds, and yet it happened here. But that this incident has not led to any drastic change in our parenting practices and the sense of freedom we as parents have in a small-town setting also demonstrates my claim that the rural setting successfully redresses the fears and anxieties of the parent. In some ways, it is almost a test case.

What is interesting to me is the way this event, though it happened, might have disappeared if the neighbour had not seen it and reported it to a friend who reported it to the principal. If that neighbour had not seen it, or had seen it but did not report it, or did not report it to a person who would inform the appropriate officials, we would not know that this had happened. The ten year olds did not recognize the event for what it was, and the boasting of a thirteen year old with a chip on his shoulder might have been dismissed. The key characteristic of the small town – high visibility – enabled this event to become a story, to enter into the communal conversation, and thus become real. Without that witness who chose to tell someone, no one, not even the children, would have realized what had happened. They did not think the gun was real, remember, and so there was nothing "remarkable" about the event for them. It demonstrates the hermeneutic principle of how talking and stories make an event real: the phenomenon becomes real and re-cognizable when it is "brought into words" by people who act and speak in response to happenings in a community. In evidence here are both visibility and surveyability, as these are developed within the demand of the small town that one be accountable for what one sees and does.

Also interesting are the different ways in which people responded when I told the story. All acknowledged the awful brush with tragedy we had just experienced. Then each went on to assign cause or blame depending on their ideology. Those who were for the new law requiring the registration of all guns saw it as further evidence of the need for such a law. Those on the more conservative side who were against the new law saw it as evidence of the decline of family and the laxity of legal institutions in punishing law-breakers. One police officer said to me, "It's not guns that kill people, it's people that kill people." Another person, suspicious of the influence of the media in society, assigned blame to the media's glorification of violence. A relative said, "See what your son risks for being such a 'smart alec'?" ("Is that your best shot?") Perhaps one of them is right. Perhaps all in different ways are right. For me, all of these interpretations reinforce the radical interpretive claim that "different observers will see different things in the stream of events because they assign different meanings to those events and conceptualize them in different ways. What mediates between a knower and known, then, is a perspective, and knowledge is always coloured by that perspective" (Littlejohn 1989, 9).

Most of all, what this event reinforces is the importance of the parental life-world as a way of knowing and re-cognizing a place. Our life has been transformed by our children. If something awful happened to one of them, our life would be again transformed, this time traumatically. If a tragedy had happened, the question of whether this town is "a great place to raise kids" would be absurd and even offensive. Because of the significance parenting has for us, our whole lives, including our relation to this small town, would be changed drastically. This event brings me a step closer to the lived experience of parents who have experienced such a tragedy.

When I try to formulate the overall meaning of the event, I note that I used the word "absurd" twice in my first attempt to write about it. It still has that absurd sense. "Absurd" means that it is ridiculously unreasonable: the event makes no sense in terms of the order and meaning of our lived experience. It reminds me that the order and meaning of our existence is vulnerable to the absurd, whether it be in Dunblane in Scotland or a small town in New Zealand. This lived experience of absurdity, in turn, reminds me of the fragility of meaning and of our mortality. The overwhelming ordinariness of everyday life can lull us into a forgetfulness of this fragility. Remembering it, on the other hand, reinforces for me both the challenge and the significance of developing a strong relation to the meaningfulness of life. This is the continuous challenge facing the theorist.

The Radical Interpretive Research Approach to the Question of Rural Merit

Using a configuration of phenomenological (Berger and Kellner 1964; Berger *et al.* 1973; Garfinkel 1967), hermeneutic (Gadamer 1975), and dialectical analytic (McHugh *et al.* 1974; Blum & McHugh 1984) methods and theories (i.e., radical interpretive sociology), a radical interpretive project would want to recover, address, and understand first the nature and meaning of "rural" as this is constituted through and by the urban-rural discourse in sociology; second, to understand what is involved in the process of understanding what parents in this study mean when they refer to the benefits of parenting in a more rural setting; third, to understand the meaning this kind of claim has for those of us who base it on our own lived experiences (parents who now live in rural settings); and last, to critically engage the above reflections in dialogue in order to bring into the open various cultural understandings (*life-world*) of "better" and "worse" with regard to parenting, from which the above claims derive their significance. The research project, therefore, would have three interrelated components: the theoretical and methodological debates concerning the nature of this kind of examination, the relevant classic and contemporary literature, and the lived experience of the inquirer coupled with formal and informal conversations of parents from the same setting.

Because radical interpretive sociology influences every stage of the research process (the evaluation of the concept of rurality, the methodology, engaging the field material, the experience of the researcher, the analysis of the material in relation to contemporary socio-historical influences), the nature of the perspective needs to be developed throughout the study.

Radical interpretive sociology draws on the theories and methods that acknowledge "the linguistic turn" (Dallmayr & McCarthy 1977); this is to say that the materials (language, beliefs, reasons, statements, evidence, etc.) we use to understand and represent who we are and what we do are linguistic, public, and shared by both the inquirer and the subject of inquiry (Habermas 1988, 89–170). This makes reflexivity an essential component of this research project. As the inquirer takes into account reflections (by sociologists, parents, popular culture) on this issue, he or she must also be able to take into account the inquirer's reflections on these reflections. In Gadamer's terms, the inquiry must be able to comprehend the way it comprehends its subject matter (1975, 333–41).

A sustained summary of the actual approach I take runs as follows. This summary can only be artificial, given the influence of the radical interpretive approach over the whole project. However, it provides the reader with some sense of the direction my research takes. I assess the relevance of various representations of rural life in the classic literature as they pertain to the current literature and the radical interpretive perspective. Acknowledging the poststructuralist critique of modern thinking (Scott 1990, 134–48), this assessment does not attempt to develop an "essentialist" definition of rurality. Rather, my analysis of the meaning of the various attempts to develop a unitary concept of rurality involves teasing out the way the negations and oppositions, suppressed in the concept, operate in specific texts. As this analysis proceeds, I show that the meaning of rural is constituted by a modern discourse that has as its interest a concern with engaging otherness and questioning limits. The problem, which is both concealed in and revealed by this discourse, is: What is interest in, meaning of, and way of practising an engagement with otherness, when the apparent other is the "rural"?

In part 2, I address and examine what is involved in making the claim for the benefit of parenting in a more rural setting an object of study. That is, I address and examine the "authority" and relation to the "truth" that various theoretical and methodological perspectives display, as these impinge on the examination of the claims parents make. Because any and all examination can only be undertaken from a particular position, this research project privileges questioning and dialogical examination. As stated, the position from which this study is undertaken draws on a particular configuration of phenomenology, hermeneutics, and especially dialectical analysis, which I call radical interpretive sociology. I demonstrate that this perspective (*praxis*) best helps us to examine and to sociologically understand the various meanings behind the claim that a rural setting is better for child-rearing. All knowledge, whether of the everyday member or the sociologist, is shaped by history, culture, and community. Gadamer (1975, 267–74) calls this axiom the principle of "effective history." I show the way the axiom operates in the claims parents make for the benefit of rural child-rearing and the way it operates in the social science literature that seeks to investigate objectively such claims.

The third section describes, understands, and analyses the kinds of reasons given to support the truth value of the claim(s), by working with the "data/usage" made available primarily by the methods of what I call reflective participation. The material out of which an understanding is constructed is my own lived experience and observations, the informal and *in situ* conversations held with many people (approximately fifty-four predominately middle-class people) over the course of five years' participation, and the recorded "sustained conversations" with thirteen people. All of the "data/usage" is used to help articulate and understand *the reasons* given to support the claim. These reasons are elicited from the subjects in order to recover the self-understanding that grounds the reference for rural child-rearing and the actions that follow from this preference. These reasons are described, critically evaluated, and analysed with reference to the way culture, history, and community influence conceptions of parenting in the late twentieth century. The relevance of the concept of "rurbanism" to describe the new rural community in contemporary Canada is developed. Critical and dialogical examination is my way of bringing into the open (language) the various meanings "better" and "worse" both have (actuality) and can have (possibility) for our times and culture.

In the last section, the arguments that we are living in a new era of postmodernism and consumerism (Baudrillard 1994; Baumann 1994; Jameson 1983) are addressed and examined as these reflect and are reflected by the new rural community of contemporary Canada (Sim 1988). The issue of the relevance/irrelevance of place to parenting, and the possibilities for and dangers to community that postmodernism and consumerism represent, are developed.

Finally, the visibility characteristic of the smaller community is analysed, in terms of the way it can enhance the specific skill of surveyability and in terms of the way this visibility relates to (and is different from) both Foucault's "panopticon" (1977) and Arendt's *polis* (1958). The *polis*-like possibilities inherent in the diversity that is now part of the new rural community are developed in a way that seeks to understand simultaneously the possibilities and limits of social inquiry itself.

Notes

INTRODUCTION

1 Shortly after we applied for a SSHRC grant, Rod Michalko moved to another city. Though we have continued to discuss the project and share ideas, distance made the planned collaboration largely impossible. But the project would not exist without Rod's initial work and his continuing support. He drew my attention to relevant literature, commented on, responded to, and critiqued my research, and encouraged me in my efforts to complete the project. The original interest behind the project was to do collaborative research. In this sense this work is the product of two people, but because circumstances prevented us from realizing this interest, the adequacy of the research and the direction of analysis is the author's responsibility.

CHAPTER ONE

1 "The process of industrialization generated increasing *urbanization* – the movement of the population into towns and cities, away from the life on the land. In 1800, well under 20 percent of the British population lived in towns or cities having more than 10,000 inhabitants. By 1900, this proportion had become 74 percent. The capital city, London, held about 1.1 million people in 1800; it increased in size to a population of over seven million by the beginning of the twentieth century. London was at that date by far the largest city ever seen in the world; it was a vast manufacturing, commercial, and financial centre at the heart of a still-expanding British Empire."

"The urbanization of most other European countries, and the United States, took place somewhat later but in some cases, once under way, accelerated even faster. In 1800, the United States was more of a rural society than were the leading European countries at the same date. Less than ten percent of the population lived in communities with populations of more than 2,500 people. Today, well over three-quarters of Americans are city dwellers. Between 1800 and 1900, as industrialization grew in the United States, the population of New York leapt from 60,000 people to 4.8 million" (Giddens 1990, 676).

The following graphs visually illustrate the similar process that happened in Canada.

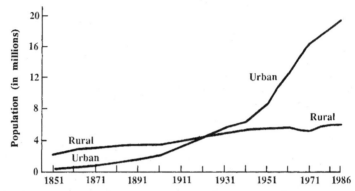

Graph 1
Changes in rural and urban populations, 1851–1986. (GiddensCanada, Canadian Supplement for *Introduction to Sociology,* 32)

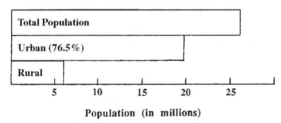

Population (in millions)

Graph 2
Urban population compared to rural and overall populations, 1986. (GiddensCanada, Canadian Supplement for *Introduction to Sociology,* 32)

2 For Marx, freedom is understood in terms of emancipation from conditions that prevent humans from realizing their full potential. That is, freedom is essentially understood as a liberation. For a perspective that distinguishes between freedom and liberation in order to make room for the concept of action, see Hannah Arendt (1963, especially 29–33).

3 It is interesting that two words with the same connotation of laziness are used. Marx and Engels do not just say "sloth" but "slothful indolence," not just "indolence" but "slothful indolence." It is as though

they wanted to convey through repetition the dangerous nature of the ethos of rural life. The root meaning of sloth is slow – OE *slaeth* – and the root meaning of indolence is not to feel pain – Lat. *in-*, not; *dolere*, to feel pain.

4 This is a distinction developed within the "analysis" tradition in sociology – a tradition called here dialectical analysis to distinguish this perspective from similarly named perspectives in science and philosophy. The distinction appears throughout in the works of Blum and McHugh but is most clearly developed in *Self Reflection in the Arts and Sciences* (1984).

5 It is ironic to note that as both the sociological literature and modern society develop, "the rural" becomes less possible to conceptualize as even a mere empirical possibility.

6 As such, Marx's position is dialectical in a Hegelian rather than a Platonic way (Gadamer 1975, 325–33).

7 Though Tonnies's perspective is closer to a political economy than a functionalist perspective (Hale 1990, 135), it is not completely accurate, as this section goes on to show, to see him (as Hale 1990, does) as a spokesperson for liberation. As Liebersohn (1988, 32) remarks, Tonnies "did not restrain his disgust toward the liberties permitted in a *gesellschaft*."

8 *Gesellschaft* moves toward decadence, and thus is itself ultimately doomed to collapse. Unlike Marx, Tonnies saw the potential for self-destruction rather than self-transformation inherent in the modern moment.

9 It is the need to get at the ground and not merely the preference itself that makes the "sustained conversation" (see part 2 and the beginning of part 3) the most appropriate sociological procedure.

10 He says this is necessary because "of all communities, the social constitution of rural districts are the most individual and the most closely connected with particular historical developments" (363).

11 Dasgupta in his book *Rural Canada: Structure and Change* (1988, 12) describes the modern farmer in this way: "A farmer in an industrial society is a commercially oriented rural villager who produces food and other articles of consumption by his family but to make a profit. His productive activities respond to supply and demand, and fluctuating prices in the marketplace." To Weber this definition itself means that the qualifier "rural villager" is not sociologically relevant as it does not indicate an alternative "society."

12 Dasgupta, by virtue of his focus on structure, is not sensitive to the subjectively meaningful character of social action. So at the end of his book (1988, 192–3) he acknowledges that contemporary Canadian rural society "increasingly resembles the urban population in sex and dependency

ratios, rate of divorce, level of educational attainment, and ethnic composition ... The contemporary rural life in Canada thus has attained many features which are typical of an urban society. Its structure is increasingly *gesellschaft* with the use in the number of secondary groups" (189–90). Yet Dasgupta goes on to say that rural society is not in the process of extinction because the population is no longer declining – thus (from Weber's perspective) confusing a technical point (demographic trends) with a sociological point (social action). Weber in his argument here foreshadows the debate by Gans, Pahl, and others (1968) about the need to scrap as sociologically (as against demographically or geographically) irrelevant the urban-rural distinction. I will demonstrate how phenomenology enables us to rescue the urban-rural distinction as sociologically relevant.

13 Dreyfus and Rabinow go on to argue (1982, 166) that Foucault's "genealogical analytics" avoid such paradoxical dilemmas by "taking the best" of the positions of Weber, Heidegger, Adorno, and Merleau-Ponty in a "way which enables him to overcome some of their difficulties." These difficulties will be articulated and examined in more detail in chapters 4, 5, and 7. What is being pointed out at this stage of the narrative is the principle of radical interpretive sociology, that theory, methods, and relation to the field of literature, research, and analysis are all inextricably interrelated.

CHAPTER TWO

1 Stein (1967, 101) describes the urban context of Park, Wirth, and their colleagues when they were developing their ideas about urban life: "According to the 1950 *World Almanac*, the population of Chicago grew as follows: 1860, 112,172; 1900, 1,698,575; 1910, 2,185,283; 1920, 2,701,705; 1930, 3,376,438. Cold figures alone cannot suggest what it must mean to people living in a city when the population swells at a rate of about one-half million per decade for three consecutive decades. Small wonder that the Chicago sociologists focused on the absence of established institutional patterns in so many regions of the city, stressing that the neighborhoods grew and changed hands so rapidly that sometimes the only constant feature appeared to be mobility. If to this is added the fact that much of the incoming population consisted of foreigners arriving in the heavy wave of immigration to America during the first quarter of this century, while most of the rest were farmers as unaccustomed to city ways as their foreign-born neighbors, it then becomes clear why 'disorganization' accompanied 'mobility'."

2 "The advent of modernity increasingly tears space away from place by fostering relations between 'absent' others, locationally different from any given situation of face-to-face interaction" (Giddens 1990, 18).

3 Wirth's critique of number as a merely administrative rather than a truly sociological criterion for characterizing a city is as true today of Statistics Canada's (and for that matter, all governmental/administrative) definition(s) of urban and rural, as it was true of the United States in 1938 (and still is).

4 As we see from this quotation, Wirth is not, as he is sometimes taken to be (Hale, 109–12), developing a theory of the city as a physical entity.

5 "Wirth's conception of the city dweller as depersonalized, atomized, and susceptible to mass movements suggests that his paper is based on, and contributes to, the theory of mass society" (Gans 1968, 96).

6 One colleague responded to Wirth's conceptualization of the rural in this way: "The statement works for those who are willing to be rural idiots. Those who espouse practices or belief that jar the prevalent ideology must keep such thoughts and behaviours secret or accept ridicule or ostracism. One doesn't have to look far. Feminists, pagans (wicca), homosexuals, animal rights activists, socialists, do not enjoy 'permanent, personal and complete relations,' because rural society doesn't accommodate the novel, the unique, or the unusual. The assumption too that because in the city, one is able to meet in groups for a specific purpose, the relations are fragmented (not the whole person) also seems odd. If one can meet in a 'special interest' group where one can be candid and show the self without censure, isn't it more likely that such disclosure will lead to more 'personal, permanent, and complete relations'? One could say that rural society encourages hiding, superficiality and incompleteness."

7 For example, in his *Rural-Urban Differences* paper, the reader constantly gets the sense of his frustration with the dichotomy. ("The difficulties … are many," "Unfortunately this evidence has not been accumulated," "What is even more regrettable," "One looks in vain in the textbooks," and so on.)

8 To deal with the issue of the interrelation between the knower and the known requires coming to terms with the reflexivity inherent in knowing, a requirement pointed out and resolved with the development of phenomenological sociology.

9 "Ethnographers who have read Foucault lose their innocence. The pre-Foucauldian ethnographer could easily understand himself as one who resisted ethnocentrism, detaching himself from the prejudices of everyday life and treating the life-world as the site of scientific inquiry. But to read, for example that 'the appropriate application of correct punishment required an object who was fixed as an individual and known in great detail' and that this motivated an important step in the growth of the sciences of society … is to be made uncomfortably aware that one's 'science' was conceived in suspicious circumstances and its birth attended by concerns which cast doubt on its purity … Sociological

inquiry itself can easily be located here as one more source or valida-
tion of the distribution of categories which function to 'control', that is
to punish, cure, rehabilitate or recuperate individuals and populations.
'The field', then, which is no longer that unselfconscious designation
of a place where the life of the other can be objectively investigated,
but becomes assimilated to disciplinary technology" (Turner 1989,
13–14).

10 "The development of 'empty space' is linked above all to two sets of
   factors: those allowing for the representation of space without reference to a privileged locale which forms a distinct vantage-point; and
   those making possible the specific substitutability of different spacial
   units. The 'discovery' of remote regions of the world by Western travel-
   lers and explorers was the necessary basis of both of these. The progressive charting of the globe that led to the creation of universal
   maps, in which perspective played little part in the representation of
   geographic position and form, established space as 'independent' of
   any particular place or region" (Giddens 1990, 19). My argument is
   that sociological concepts like the folk society not only do not objectively describe the difference between modernity and tradition – they
   further the "emptying of space" process. It would be another project to
   address what kind of furthering Giddens's own concepts are doing.

CHAPTER THREE

1 This point is very relevant when we come to examine the field material in the third section.

2 "Dorothy Smith (1987, 9) willingly admits that her method 'does not
  come from nowhere' and that she has learned above all from Mead,
  Merleau-Ponty, Marx, and Garfinkel, as she 'could not imagine beginning all over again'" (Lentin 1993, 123).

3 "Enthusiasm for the American city has not been typical or predomi-
  nant in our intellectual history. Fear has been the most common reaction. For a variety of reasons, our most celebrated thinkers have
  expressed different degrees of ambivalence and animosity toward the
  city ... We have no persistent or pervasive tradition of romantic attachment to the city in our literature or in our philosophy, nothing like the
  Greek attachment to the *polis* or the French writers' affection for Paris"
  (White & White 1962, 1–2 as quoted in Hutter 1988, 42).

4 I thank Bob Moore for these observations.

5 These studies show that Wirth's claim is not empirically correct. They
  do not show that these urban "kinship groups actually influenced
  socialization and the transmission of culture ... It has been asserted
  that kinship studies call into question the isolation of the family in

nuclear society; but this issue cannot be resolved by a study of kinship. The question is not whether the nuclear family is isolated from
the extended kin group, but whether the family as a whole, as an insti-
tution based on 'ascription' upholds values or works on principles
opposed to the ones that prevail elsewhere" (Lasch 1979, 143). Lasch
shows that he recognizes the issue (of the possibility of society engaging otherness and questioning its limits) implicit in this debate, though
his recognition is structured by the discourse of the critical school. The
relevance of his recognition will be taken up when we address the
"data" emerging from the project.

6 "Statistical uniformity is by no means a harmless scientific ideal; it is
the no longer secret political ideal of a society which, entirely sub-
merged in the routine of everyday living, is at peace with the scientific
outlook inherent in its very existence.

"To gauge the extent of society's victory in the modern age, its early
substitution of behavior for action and its eventual substitution of
bureaucracy, the rule of nobody, for personal rulership, it may be well
to recall that its initial science of economics, which substitutes patterns
of behavior only in this rather limited field of human activity, was followed by the all-comprehensive pretension of the social sciences
which, as 'behavioral sciences,' aim to reduce man as a whole, in all
his activities, to the level of a conditioned and behaving animal. If economics is the science of society at its early stages, when it could
impose its rules of behavior only on sections of the population and on
parts of their activities, the rise of the 'behavioral sciences' indicates
clearly the final stage of this development, when mass society has
devoured all strata of the nation and 'social behavior' has become standard for all regions of life" (Arendt 1958, 43–5).

7 "This insight cannot be communicated by the gathering of brute data,
or initiation in the modes of formal reasoning or some combination of
these. But this is a scandalous result according to the authoritative conception of science in our tradition, which is shared even by many of
those who are highly critical of the approach of mainstream psychology, or sociology, or political science. For it means … that some differences will be nonarbitrable by further evidence, but that each side can
only make appeal to deeper insight on the part of the other" (Taylor
1977, 126–7).

8 This concept of the life-world has proven to be a decisive idea for contemporary social theorists, including Berger et al., Blum and McHugh,
Gadamer, Garfinkel, Habermas, and Schutz.

9 "Phenomenology means letting things become manifest as what they
are, without forcing our own categories on them. It means a reversal of
direction from that one is accustomed to: it is not we who point to

things; rather things show themselves to us. This is not to suggest some primitive animism but the recognition that the very essence of true understanding is that of being led by the power of the thing to manifest itself. This conception is an expression of Husserl's own intention to return to the things themselves. Phenomenology is a means of being led by the phenomenon through a way of access genuinely belonging to it" (Palmer 1969, 128).

10 Hansen & Muszynski (1990), in following Giddens, recognize the importance of ontology for sociological analysis, but also in following Giddens, have a literal and unontological understanding of ontology: an "ontological perspective" is a contradiction in terms.

11 As they remark (12–19), phenomenology, unlike positivistic social psychology (behaviourism), enables the description of the structures of consciousness "from within" and, unlike the "culture and personality" perspective of American clinical psychology, enables the description of the relationship between the objective structures of consciousness and social institutions.

12 "All forms of naturalism and logical empiricism simply take for granted this social reality, which is the proper object of the social sciences. Intersubjectivity, interaction, inter-communication, and language are simply presupposed as the unclarified foundation of these theories. They assume, as it were, that the social scientist has already solved his fundamental problem, before scientific inquiry starts" (Schutz 1977, 229).

13 In saying this they build on Schutz's work on multiple realities, and, in so doing, show a similarity with Habermas's (1988) analysis of late capitalism, though for him this feature of modern life is precisely what is problematic about our times. Wallace & Wolf (1991, 128) summarize Habermas's position in the following way: "Habermas argues that, as social evolution progresses, there develops a 'system' of institutions – markets 'steered' by money and state organizations 'steered' by power. It is then possible for more people to be involved with each other *without sharing meanings or the same lifeworld* ... Lifeworlds get more provincial as the social system gets more complex."

14 Hutter's review of the agreement among social historians about the specific changes the family went through with the rise of modernity adds historical support for this phenomenological claim: "Historically, the family has served as the very foundation of social life and the center of the institutional order. There was no segregation between the family and the totality of institutions in the society. It is precisely this change in the texture of private family life and the family's involvement in work and community that is seen as the outstanding feature of the contemporary family" (Hutter 1988, 84–5).

15 These possible responses are not intended to prejudge the actual responses. Rather, in Garfinkel's words (1967, 38), they are intended to "produce reflections through which the strangeness of an obstinately familiar world can be detected."

16 For the urban-to-rural interviewees (ex-urbanites), mobility was a lived experience. For the rural respondents, mobility was a lived experience in terms of mass transportation. There is a relatively large city (population 680,000 – 1992 census) about one hundred kilometres from Prairie Edge, and all interviewees talked about the accessibility of "the city" (their term) for short trips. Automobiles and highways reduced the distance between Prairie Edge and "the city" to a little over one hour. The "city" is thus within the horizon of everyday experience for the parents of the study.

CHAPTER FOUR

1 Thus, for example, the US study by Helge (1990, 3) cited in the introduction about rural children faring worse than non-rural children in terms of being "at risk" students itself rests on the arbitrary definition that "rural" is an area of less than 2,500 population. It does not speak to the increasing recognition that villages, towns, and small cities are viewed and view themselves as rural areas. Similarly any "facts" about rural life that come from Statistics Canada are based on studies done on areas with a population density of less than 1,000. Citing these "facts" without describing the method that enabled their production is an arbitrary rather than oriented relation to the truth.

CHAPTER FIVE

1 According to the 1991 annual report of the chief of police, Prairie Edge is a "very safe community." Also, the "crime rate in Stony Plain – and other communities – is lower than in Edmonton, according to a 1989 Uniform Crime Report compiled by the provincial government. Edmonton's Criminal Code crime rate per 1,000 population is 154.62. Other crime rates in surrounding communities range from the low-end in St Albert of 65.2 to Devon, at 132.71" (*Edmonton Journal*, 11 May 1992, B1). I am not addressing the issue of accepting police statistics as true indicators of the level of crime in a community. The statistics only measure what particular police in particular communities decide to measure.

According to the General Social Survey of Statistics Canada, urban "victimization rates were higher for most types of crime and for most age-gender groups. Consistent with this, urban residents indicated more fear of crime, and were more likely to perceive crime as higher and increasing in their neighbourhoods" (Norris & Johal, in Bollman 1992, 367). According to this survey, claims that rural places are safer have a statistical basis. Thus there is some dispute over the relative safety of the town or rural area. Obviously some towns, perhaps a majority, have a lower crime rate than some cities, but also some cities have a lower crime rate than some towns. Ultimately, I accept Garfinkel's argument (1967, 186–207) that records produced by an organization are better understood as contracts rather than objective descriptions of an external reality. My main purpose in this chapter is to address the way science in general assesses the truth value of any and all claims.

2 "Like Heidegger, Gadamer is a critic of the modern surrender to technological thinking, which is rooted in subjectism – that is, in taking the human subjective consciousness, and the certainties of reason based on it, as the ultimate point of reference for human knowledge. The pre-Cartesian philosophers, for instance the ancient Greeks, saw their thinking as part of being itself; they did not take their subjectivity as their starting point and then ground the objectivity of their knowledge on it. Theirs was a more dialectical approach that tried to allow itself to be guided by the nature of what was being understood. Knowledge was not something that they acquired as a possession, but something in which they participated, allowing themselves to be directed, even possessed by their knowledge" (Palmer 1969, 164–5).

3 It is for this reason that I prefer to use the term "research conversation" rather than interview. More on this term in ch. 6, n. 2.

4 Which, not incidentally, overcomes the problem of "subjectism" (Palmer 1969, 124–222).

CHAPTER SIX

1 The particular community is Camrose, Alberta, situated approximately one hundred kilometres from Edmonton. I use the pseudonym "Prairie Edge" not only according to sociological convention but also to underline that this study is not an ethnography in the ordinary sense of that term. Rather, I aim to draw the reader's attention to the universal characteristics embedded in the relation between modern rurality (rurbanism) and the parental life-world.

2 Gadamer (1989b, 55) continues: "Even immoral beings try to understand one another. I cannot believe that Derrida would actually disagree with me about this. Whoever opens his mouth wants to be understood; otherwise, one would neither speak nor write. And finally, I

have an exceptionally good piece of evidence for this: Derrida directs questions to me and therefore he must assume that I am willing to understand them. Certainly this is completely unrelated to Kant's 'good will', but it does have a good deal to do with the difference between dialectic and sophistics." Gadamer's comments help us elaborate on the abstraction of the Enlightenment separation of knowledge and hopes and fears, addressed in part 2, as though the latter were not also positive features of the process of understanding.

3 Prior to recording, all were informed that they were encouraged to speak freely, that they would not be identified with particular quotations, that they could modify, withdraw, or otherwise elaborate on what they said or had said, that this was to be treated as more of a dialogue or conversation than an interview, that responses were encouraged to my questions and translations of what they said, that they were free to ask me questions, and so on. It is thus more accurate to call these situations "research conversations" (I offered versions of what they were saying to see if what was being said was fully understood) than interviews. While all were asked similar types of questions, the "research conversation" was unstructured, and the direction was particular to each conversation. The co-conversationalists were invited to respond to the claim and asked if they supported it, why, and so on. These transcribed conversations are rich with material about urban life, rural life, suburban life, parenting, modern times, questions of value, the extended family, the significance of place, the importance of mobility, the influence of technology and consumerism on parenting, and the difference between the contemporary era and the recent past, between entertaining oneself and being entertained, between the us and Canada, and so on. Given the purpose of the project, the focus of this chapter will be on the responses relating to parenting in a more rural setting, set against the background of my own participation in the same setting and the impressions that emerged from that participation. In the next chapter responses relating to the broader cultural issue of the relation between place and consumerism are examined.

4 "With this we come to a comprehensive concept that lies at the basis of all constitution of 'texts' and simultaneously makes clear the embeddedness of the 'text' in the hermeneutical context: every return to the 'text' – whether it contains a printed text or merely the repetition of what is expressed in conversation – refers to that which was originally announced or pronounced and that should be maintained as constituting a meaningful identity ... Here the task of the writer corresponds to that of the reader, addressee, interpreter; that is, to achieve such an

understanding and to let the printed text speak once again. To this extent, reading and understanding mean that what is announced is led back to its original authenticity" (Gadamer 1989, 35).

5 "Census reports make a dichotomous distinction between rural and urban. In Canada, for example, communities with a population size of less than 1000 people are classified as rural and those with a population of 1000 or more are designated as urban. Such a dichotomy between rural and urban based on a cut-off point of population size is obviously arbitrary. The arbitrariness of census definitions is further emphasized by the fact that they vary from one county to another. In the United States, for example, the cut-off point is 2500; in Greece, 10,000; and in some Scandinavian countries it is as low as 200. In India, on the other hand, a community will have to have a population of at least 5000 and a density of 1000 people per square mile before it will be designated as urban" (Dasgupta 1988, 3).

6 This emphasis on the positive expresses a particularly modern life-world orientation which, in a practical way, connects with the subjectism theoretically described in the last chapter. If "the world is regarded as basically measured by man ... whose task it is to master the world" (Palmer 1969, 144), then the above descriptions of Prairie Edge make sense. That is, the town is evaluated in terms of the benefits it offers to the individual – it is not an end in itself, which requires of the individual a move outside of self to the other (the town).

7 "For most Canadians now live in big cities, not small cities or towns, but places like Toronto, Vancouver and Calgary – far flung city states held together by telephones, satellite dishes and airplanes." Echoing a theme raised by Sim, this columnist goes on to say: "We don't see or hear much about how small cities and towns across the country have become homogenized dumping grounds for all those California-style houses, developments that make oodles of money for people who live somewhere else, but destroy any sense of pride in home-grown goods and services. The resentment that flows from not being listened to, from not seeing yourself reflected in the mainstream media, from being considered outside the mainstream, flows deep in places like this" ("Rural Albertans Feel Alienated," *Edmonton Journal* 29 April 1992, A15).

8 For example, "the local institutions had not been overlooked in the wave of affluence that seemed to envelop Agraville. There were fine new churches. Some of the few he recognised had been taken over by unfamiliar sects with modest names like True Believer or Select Disciples of Christ ... The schools had swollen out of all recognition. They were fed by the yellow buses which scoured the countryside for recruits to mix (sometimes uneasily) with the children from the enlarged population of the town.

"What surprised him most was the influx of civil servants. The municipal offices were greatly expanded, as was the regional hospital that had been little more than a clinic fifty years ago. Fifty years ago one 'agr. rep.' of the department of Agriculture had a small office over a grocery store. Now there were teachers, janitors, bus drivers, doctors, nurses, orderlies, policemen, firemen, and highway maintenance crews. Little wonder people complained about being overgoverned and over-taxed. Still, many citizens were busy as volunteers at the fire hall, in the churches, and service clubs" (Sim 1988, 65).

9 Sim (69–73) recommends that these people be called the "new ruralites" to emphasize their interest "in adapting to a new environ-ment" (69), in the way new arrivals to Canada are called New Canadi-ans. In this study, I continue to use the term "ex-urbanite" in order to emphasize the different experience (socialization) these people bring to their understanding of their new situation.

10 On the surface, the conclusions of this study suggest that the city is valued more for consumer reasons while the town is valued for more "traditional" reasons. As I will show, that difference is more apparent than real.

11 "Our economic system, schools, religious organizations, mass media, peer groups, and many other institutions and pressure groups impinge on a child's world; most often these influences are positive ones and helpful to the parent in the task of socializing children. But often these influences can be negative and counter to the direction parents are working toward so diligently" (Le Masters and De Frain 1989, 2).

12 This finding also relates to one in the statistical survey research of *Fear of Crime and Residential Location* (Michael S. Belyea and Matthew T. Zin-graff in *Rural Sociology* 53 (4) 1988, 473–86). They found (484) a greater fear of crime in the very rural areas and in urban areas, and a lesser fear of crime in small town populations.

13 At the least, in regard to the experience of raising children in Prairie Edge, these parents dispute the claim by Charles Long (*Life after the City* 1989, 108–10) that there is no safe place. While all might acknowl-edge, in modern fashion, that "worries come with the kids, not the location" (Long 1989, 109), these parents find that the town location lessens their worries.

CHAPTER EIGHT

1 "Whereas the Enlightenment needed to theorize a way of escaping from the prejudice which it found preceded it, Foucault's account of practices implicate the theorist inextricably – such a theorist realizes that he himself is produced by what he is studying ... he can never get

outside of it. Dreyfus and Rabinow underline the way Foucault's position differs significantly from the Enlightenment: the foothold we have is 'no longer one which is universal, guaranteed, verified, or grounded'" (Turner 1989, 17–18). See also ch. 2, n. 9.

2 See the debate between Habermas and Gadamer (Mueller-Vollmer, ed. 1989) for an elaboration of this issue.

CHAPTER NINE

1 *"Profusion* is evidently the most striking descriptive feature" of this postmodern age (Baudrillard 1994, 363).

2 Peter Gzowski's popular CBC Radio program, *Morningside*, featured an interview (July 1990) with three "urban refugees," who quit their "prestigious" and high-paying careers *in order to leave the city and live in the country.* The tone of the interview was of people who had the courage to "live the dream," who gave time to themselves and their personal fulfilment as against time given for the necessity of professional activity. In a similar article in *Mademoiselle* (April 1992), a reporter says that the "urban tide has turned, and it now seems like no one can escape their concrete jungle fast enough" (88). All of these are popular expressions, according to Jameson, of the phenomenon of the interrelation between postmodernism and consumer society.

3 See the readings in part 6 of *The Polity Reader in Social Theory* (Giddens *et al.* 1994).

4 While for my co-conversationalists there is an association between hometown and rural life (because this town is their place of birth and education), a city can as easily be experienced in a hometown fashion (McGahan 1982). The hometowners of this study should be seen as referencing not the rural *per se* but rather an attachment to the intersection of community and place. The term "ex-urbanite" no longer refers merely to people who have moved from the city but, more importantly, to a temptation (which exists by virtue of the postmodern capacity to be mobile) to develop a purely instrumental relation to place.

5 Clark (1978), in his study of people in northeastern New Brunswick, states that: "What was generally obtained, however, was what might be described as a state of social anomie. Most of the residents appeared to have little feeling about their social obligations, what they owed to their local community or to the society at large. For these people, the struggle for existence was too grim to give strength to a social consciousness." I am not disputing this claim. Rather, I am using it as a foil to highlight the choice my respondents (whose social and economic circumstances are very different) understood themselves to be making.

6 This, as Garfinkel (1967) has shown, is a limited and narrow conception of rationality.

7 Of course, and it should be obvious at this stage of the narrative, I am not doing description here. Prairie Edge, a settlement less than one hundred years old, does not literally correspond to a *gemeinschaft* social organization of old European rural life such as Tonnies had in mind. Like most towns in western Canada, it is neither ethnically nor religiously homogeneous and as a society is not held together by a common understanding expressed in folk ways. Using the conventional scientific sociological perspective, Prairie Edge, like most of rural life in contemporary Canada (Dasgupta 1988), will appear as a society organized on the basis of organic rather than mechanical solidarity.

8 In this way they are unlike Long or the people interviewed on CBC because they are not choosing the country for "lifestyle" reasons. The latter is a more recent 1990s phenomenon connected with the primacy given to personal fulfilment. In Berger's language, personal fulfilment rather than careers is the basic organizing principle for biographical projects. From within the self-understanding of these "lifestyle" individuals, this kind of orientation is assumed to represent an advance in personal liberation. Whether this advance actually promotes and strengthens consumer society or challenges it is a question that remains to be examined.

9 "The separating of time and space and their formation into standardized, 'empty' dimensions cut through the connections between social activity and its 'embedding' in the particularities of contexts of presence ... This phenomenon serves to open up manifold possibilities of change by breaking free of local habits and practices" (Giddens 1990, 20).

10 As Mark Hutter (1988, 120) suggests, an understanding of the uses of technology should be part of research on family. Telephones, planes, electronic mail, cars, etc. make physical dispersion and a form of regular contact possible. Dispersion no longer necessarily involves lack of extended kin contact.

11 "The decline of universalizing criteria, however, Baumann argues, is not inherently crippling. Postmodernity means coming to terms with ambivalence, with the ambiguity of meanings and with the indeterminacy of the future" (Giddens *et al.* 1994, 350).

12 "As long as modern powers clung resolutely to their intention of constructing a better, reason-guided, and thus ultimately universal order, intellectuals had little difficulty in articulating their own claim to the crucial role in the process: universality was their domain and field of expertise ... As long as modern powers insisted on the elimination of ambivalence as the measure of social improvement, intellectuals could

consider their own work – the promotion of a universally valid rationality – as a major vehicle and driving force of progress" (Baumann
1994, 352).

13 Long's book *Life after the City* is written unabashedly from the perspective of the consumer.

14 Charles Foran (1995, 72) provides a nice, lived-experience description
of the suburb he grew up in: "After all, suburbs like Willowdale didn't
promote belonging; they promoted living – prosperous, anonymous living. So long as a sense of history or belonging didn't interfere, didn't
complicate matters, it was okay. Just keep the nostalgia indoors. To
yourself."

CHAPTER TEN

1 Though religion and the economy have no logical connection, Weber
showed how the Protestant ethic and the spirit of capitalism were
sociologically connected.

2 "Consequently, human life is *eo ipso* dialectical. It is one and many at
the same time. At every moment it is itself and, exactly for that reason,
separated from itself, just as the 'what-it-is' (*ti estin*) of every existent
thing ultimately exists in such a way that it is in all that participates in
it (*to metechon*)" (Gadamer 1986, 122).

3 To answer this I return (in solid hermeneutic fashion) to his text but
now in order to recover the question that lies behind it. See Bonner
1994 for an explication and application of this method.

4 This does not mean that this cannot occur in the city – it only means
that in the city the relevant community has to be small.

5 To use the terminology of Mead, the "me" that the small town as a
generalized other nurtures is a "me" that orients to being held accountable for one's actions. Over time this ability to so orient becomes part
of the self of the actor, part of the "me" which the 'I' can reflect on
and provoke. Using more everyday terminology, this ability can
become part of the character of the person.

6 "Bentham laid down the principle that power should be visible and
unverifiable. Visible: the inmate will constantly have before his eyes
the tall outline of the central tower from which he is spied upon.
Unverifiable: the inmate must never know whether he is being looked
at at any one moment; but he must be sure that he may always be so"
(Foucault 1977, 201).

EPILOGUE

1 *The Edmonton Journal*, Friday, 20 January 1995, B2:

Boy, 13, charged in shooting
    Ian Williams
    Journal Crime Writer

A game of King of the Hill turned frightening for some 10-year-olds
in [Prairie Edge] this week when a 13-year-old boy brought out a
rifle and fired two shots.

    "All indications are that this was done to scare the kids away,"
said [Praire Edge] city police Sgt. Damian Herle.

    One shot was fired into the air and the other towards kids cower-
ing behind a pile of snow being used to play the game. The second
shot from the .22-calibre rifle pierced a garbage can.

    "It's very fortunate the children didn't get hurt," Herle said.

    The incident began after Tuesday as a group of kids were playing
on a snow pile in the city ...

    Some children began teasing the 13-year-old.

    The boy went inside his home and came back out to his backyard
with the rifle. Herle said the teen fired one shot into the air, then
went back inside to get another round of ammunition.

    When he came back, he pointed the weapon at a garbage can near
the snow pile and fired.

    None of the kids told their parents. School officials phoned police
after word began circulating in the school.

    The 13-year-old has been charged with numerous weapons
offences including dangerous use of a firearm and pointing a firearm.

Details of this story differ from the one I received. Only one source,
the police, is used. Two years later my son still disagrees with some of
the story's details and its focus. I note the emphasis on the shooting
and the way the story of the shooting took two tellings (a summary at
the beginning and a play-by-play which follows). The point of view of
the story is objective and detached as against my own lived experience
description.

2 "For the record" (as my youngest might say), it was reported in the
local weeklies in the following ways. There was no writer/reporter
byline attached to either story.

    In the *Prairie Edge Advocate*, 24 January 1995, 2, this small story was
ironically overshadowed by the larger story with the headlines: "Local
gun owners urged to voice their concerns; [Prairie Edge] youth facing
firearms charges":

On January 18, Police received a report of a firearms incident that
occurred the day before. Investigation revealed that a group of

young boys, 10 to 13 years of age, were playing on a snow pile
when one of the boys became upset, went into his residence
and brought out a rifle. The boy shot one round in the air and
discharged a second round into a garbage can near the snow pile
where the other boys were hiding. Fortunately no one was injured.
Police have seized a .22 cal. rifle and a 13-year-old (who cannot be
identified) is facing several firearms charges.

On January 13, Police were called to investigate two house break-
ins. One occurred in Victoria Park and the other in the Enevold
Drive area. Property stolen includes numerous jewellery items, a
VCR and cash. The break-ins occurred between 6:00 and 10:00 p.m.
Any person with information is asked to call the Police Service or
Crime Stoppers at 1–800–922-TIPS.

In the *Prairie Edge Patriot*, 25 January 1995, A5, the story was above a
large advertisement that said in large, bold letters,

Hey Kids!
Enter Our Valentine's Contest
& You Could WIN a Trip For
4 to West Edmonton Mall
Amusement Centre and Waterpark.

Teen charged with firearm offences
A [Prairie Edge] teen will appear in Young Offender Court on Feb.
2 following a Tuesday, Jan. 17 shooting incident where two .22-cali-
bre shots were fired. Investigations by the [Prairie Edge] Police Service revealed that a group of young boys, between the ages of 10
and 13 years of age, were playing a game of "King of the Hill" on a
snow pile when one of the boys became upset.

The teen went into his residence and brought out a rifle. According to [PE]PS officials, "The boy shot one round in the air and dis-
char[g]ed a second round into a garbage can near the snow pile
where the other boys were hiding. Fortunately no one was injured."

Police have seized the .22-calibre rifle and athe [sic] 13-year-old
teen is facing several firearms charges, including dangerous use of a
firearm and pointing a firearm.

The local police learned about the incident the day after when
school officials phoned. The officials relayed the details Jan. 18 that
had been circulating in the school.

The name of the youth cannot be published due to provisions of
the Young Offenders' Act.

Bibliography

Arendt, Hannah. 1958. *The Human Condition*. Chicago: University of Chicago Press.

– 1963. *On Revolution*. Middlesex: Penguin Books.

– 1968. *Between Past and Future: Eight Exercises in Political Thought*. Middlesex: Penguin Books.

Arensberg, Conrad and Solon Kimball. 1968. *Family and Community in Ireland*. 2nd ed. Cambridge, MA: Harvard University Press.

Aries, Phillippe. 1962. *Centuries of Childhood: A Social History of Family Life*. Trans. by Robert Baldich. New York: Knopf.

Aristotle. 1958. *The Politics of Aristotle*. Trans. by Ernest Barker. Oxford: Oxford University Press.

Baudrillard, Jean. 1994. "The Consumer Society." In Giddens, A., D. Held, D. Hubert, D. Seymour, and J. Thompson, eds. *The Polity Reader in Social Theory*. Cambridge: Polity Press.

Baumann, Zygmunt. 1994. "Modernity and Ambivalence." In Giddens, A., D. Held, D. Hubert, D. Seymour, and J. Thompson, eds. *The Polity Reader in Social Theory*. Cambridge: Polity Press.

Belyea, Michael S. and Matthew T. Zingraff. 1988. "Fear of Crime and Residential Location." *Rural Sociology* 53, no. 4:473–86.

Berger, Peter L. 1963. *Invitation to Sociology: A Humanistic Perspective*. New York: Anchor.

Berger, Peter L., Brigitte Berger, and Hansfried Kellner. 1973. *The Homeless Mind: Modernization and Consciousness*. New York: Vintage.

Berger, Peter L. and Hansfried Kellner. 1964. "Marriage and the Construction of Reality." *Diogenes* 46:1–25.

Blum, Alan F. 1971. "Theorizing." In Jack Douglas, ed. *Understanding Everyday Life: Toward the Reconstruction of Sociological Knowledge*. London: Routledge and Kegan Paul.

Blum, Alan F. and Peter McHugh. 1978. "The Risk of Theorizing and the Problem of the Good of Place: A Reformulation of Canadian Nationalism." *Canadian Journal of Sociology* 3, no. 3:321–47.

– 1984. *Self-Reflection in the Arts and Sciences*. New Jersey: Humanities Press.

Blumer, Herbert. 1969. *Symbolic Interactionism: Perspective and Method*. Englewood Cliff, NJ: Prentice Hall.

Bonner, Kieran M. 1990. "Motivation and the Desire to Learn: A Phenomenological Examination of the Teacher-Student Relation in the Context of a Liberal Arts Philosophy." *Dianoia* 1, no. 1:18–38.

– 1994. "Hermeneutics and Symbolic Interactionism: The Problem of Solipsism." *Human Studies* 17:225–49.

– 1997. *Power and Parenting: a Hermeneutic of the Human Condition*. Hampshire: Macmillan Press.

Bryson, Connie. 1990 (Jan./Feb.) "[Prairie Edge]: A City That Retains Its Small-Town Charm." *WestWorld* 16, no. 1:17–23.

Clark, S.D. 1978. *The New Urban Poor*. Toronto: McGraw-Hill Ryerson.

Clifford, James. 1988. *The Predicament of Culture: Twentieth Century Ethnography, Literature and Art*. Cambridge, MA: Harvard University Press.

Collins, Randall. 1982. *Sociological Insight: An Introduction to Nonobvious Sociology*. Oxford: Oxford University Press.

Dallmayr, Fred. 1988. "Praxis and Reflection." In Max Van Manen, ed. *Self Reflection in the Human Sciences* Edmonton: Lifeworld Editions.

Dallmayr, Fred R. and Thomas A. McCarthy, eds. 1977. *Understanding and Social Inquiry*. Notre Dame: University of Notre Dame Press.

Dasgupta, Satadal. 1988. *Rural Canada: Structure and Change*. Queenston, ON: Edwin Mellen Press.

Davies, Patricia. 1990 (June). "Concrete Angels." *Toronto: A Globe and Mail Magazine* 5, no. 3: 22–27, 48–51.

De Vries, Peter and Georgina McNab-De Vries. 1991. "Ethnography in Rural Cape Breton: Coping with Postmodernism." *Canadian Review of Sociology and Anthropology* 28, no. 4:483–501.

Douglas, Jack D., ed. 1971. *Understanding Everyday Life: Toward the Reconstruction of Sociological Knowledge*. London: Routledge and Kegan Paul.

Dreyfus, Hubert L. and Paul Rabinow. 1982. *Michel Foucault: Beyond Structuralism and Hermeneutics*. Sussex: Harvester Press.

Eichler, Maigrit. 1983. *Families in Canada Today: Recent Changes and the Policy Consequences*. Toronto: Gage.

Elliot, Henry C. 1974. "Similarities and Differences between Science and Common Sense." In Roy Turner, ed. *Ethnomethodology*. Middlesex: Penguin Education.

Fay, Brian. 1975. *Social Theory and Political Practice*. London: George Allen & Unwin.

Foran, Charles. 1995. *The Last House in Ulster: A Family in Belfast.* Toronto: HarperCollins.

Foucault, Michel. 1977. *Discipline and Punish: The Birth of the Prison.* New York: Pantheon.

Gadamer, Hans-Georg. 1975. *Truth and Method.* London: Sheed and Ward.

– 1986. *On the Idea of the Good in Platonic-Aristotelian Philosophy.* Trans. by P.C. Smith. New Haven: Yale University Press.

– 1989. "Rhetoric, Hermeneutics, and the Critique of Ideology." In Kurt Mueller-Vollmer, ed. *The Hermeneutics Reader.* New York: Continuum.

– 1989. "Reply to Jacques Derrida." In Diane P. Michelfelder and Richard E. Palmer, eds. *Dialogue and Deconstruction: The Gadamer-Derrida Encounter.* Albany: State University of New York Press.

Gans, H.J. 1968. "Urbanism and Suburbanism As Ways of Life." In R.E. Pahl, ed. *Readings in Urban Sociology.* London: Pergamon Press.

Garfinkel, Harold. 1967. *Studies in Ethnomethodology.* Cambridge: Polity Press.

Geertz, Clifford. 1973. *The Interpretation of Cultures.* New York: Basic Books.

Giddens, Anthony, ed. 1972. *Emile Durkheim: Selected Writings.* Cambridge: Cambridge University Press.

– 1991. *The Consequences of Modernity.* Stanford: Stanford University Press.

– 1991. *Introduction to Sociology.* New York: Norton.

Giddens, A., D. Held., D. Hubert, D. Seymour, and J. Thompson, eds. 1994. *The Polity Reader in Social Theory.* Cambridge: Polity Press.

GiddensCanada. 1991. Canadian Supplement for *Introduction to Sociology.* New York: Norton.

Goldenberg, Sheldon. 1992. *Thinking Methodologically.* New York: HarperCollins.

Grant, George. 1965. *Lament for a Nation: The Defeat of Canadian Nationalism.* Toronto: McClelland & Stewart.

– 1969. *Technology and Empire: Perspectives on North America.* Toronto: House of Anansi.

Habermas, Jurgen. 1988. *On the Logic of the Social Sciences.* Cambridge: Polity Press.

Hale, Sylvia. 1990. *Controversies in Sociology: A Canadian Introduction.* Toronto: Copp Clark Pitman.

Hansen, P. and A. Muszynski. 1990. "Crisis in Rural Life and Crisis in Thinking: Directions for Critical Research." *Canadian Review of Sociology and Anthropology* 27, no. 1:1–22.

Hareven, Tamara. 1975. "Family Time and Industrial Time: Family and Work in a Planned Corporation Town, 1900–1924." *Journal of Urban History* 1:65–89.

Hauser, P.M. 1965. "Observations on the Urban-Folk and Urban-Rural Dichotomies As Forms of Western Ethnocentrism." In P.M. Hauser and L. Schnore, *The Study of Urbanization.* London: John Wiley & Sons.

Heidegger, Martin. 1967. *Being and Time*. Oxford: Basil Blackwell.

– 1971. *Poetry, Language, Thought*. New York: Harper Colophon.

– 1977. *The Question Concerning Technology and Other Essays*. New York: Harper Torchbooks.

Helge, Doris. 1990. *A National Study Regarding At Risk Students*. Bellingham: National Rural Development Institute.

Henderson, A.M. and Talcott Parsons, eds. 1947. *Max Weber: The Theory of Social and Economic Organization*. New York: Oxford University Press.

Humphrys, A. 1965. "The Family in Ireland." In *Comparative Family Systems*, M. Nimhoff, ed. Boston: Houghton Mifflin.

Hutter, Mark, 1988. *The Changing Family: Comparative Perspectives*. New York: Macmillan.

Jameson, Frederic. 1983. "Postmodernism and Consumer Society." In H. Foster, ed. *The Anti-Aesthetic: Essays on Postmodern Culture*. Port Townsend, WA: Bay Press.

Lasch, Christopher. 1979. *Haven in a Heartless World: The Family Besieged*. New York: Basic Books.

LeMasters, E.E. 1957. "Parenthood As Crisis." *Marriage and Family Living* 19:352–55.

LeMasters, E.E. and John DeFrain. 1989. *Parents in Contemporary America: A Sympathetic View*. Belmont, CA: Wadsworth.

Lentin, Ronit. 1993. "Feminist Research Methodologies – A Separate Paradigm? Notes for a Debate." *Irish Journal of Sociology* 3:119–38.

Liebersohn, Harry. 1988. *Fate and Utopia in German Sociology, 1870–1923*. Cambridge, MA: MIT Press.

Littlejohn, Stephen. 1989. *Theories of Human Communication*. Belmont, CA: Wadsworth.

Litwak, E. 1960. "Geographic Mobility and Extended Family Cohesion." *American Sociological Review* 25:385–94.

Long, Charles. 1989. *Life after the City*. Camden East, ON: Camden House.

Loomis, Charles P. 1960. "Introduction: Tonnies and His Relation to Sociology." In *Community and Society*. East Lansing: Michigan State University Press 1–11.

Luhmann, Niklas. 1988. "Tautology and Paradox in the Self-Descriptions of Modern Society." In *Sociological Theory* 6:26–37.

McGahan, P. 1982. *Urban Sociology in Canada*. Toronto: Butterworths.

Mandell, Nancy. 1987. *The Family*. In Michael Rosenberg et al., eds. *An Introduction to Canadian Sociology*. Toronto: Methuen.

Martindale, Don and Gertrude Neuwirth. 1962. "Prefatory Remarks: The Theory of the City." In Max Weber, *The City*. New York: Collier 9–70.

Marx, Karl and F. Engels. (1848) 1965. *Manifesto of the Communist Party*. Peking: Foreign Languages Press.

– (1847) 1970. *The German Ideology*. New York: International Publishers.

- 1978. "Theses on Feuerbach." In Robert C. Tucker, ed. *The Marx-Engels Reader*. New York: Norton.

McDaniels, Susan. 1990. *Families Today: Change, Diversity and Challenge*. Edmonton: University of Alberta. Population Reprints 103.

McHugh, Peter. 1971. "On the Failure of Positivism." In Jack Douglas, ed. *Understanding Everyday Life: Toward the Reconstruction of Sociological Knowledge*. London: Routledge and Kegan Paul.

McHugh, Peter., S. Raffel, D. Foss, and A. Blum. 1974. *On the Beginning of Social Inquiry*. London: Routledge and Kegan Paul.

Mead, George Herbert. 1934. *Mind, Self and Society*. Chicago: University of Chicago Press.

Meyrowitz, Joshua. 1985. *No Sense of Place: The Impact of Electronic Media on Social Behavior*. New York: Oxford University Press.

Minar, David W. and Scott Greer. 1969. *The Concept of Community: Readings with Interpretations*. London: Butterworths.

Mueller-Vollmer, Kurt, ed. 1989. *The Hermeneutics Reader*. New York: Continuum.

Norris, Douglas A. and Kulbir Johal. 1992. "Social Indicators from the General Social Survey: Some Rural-Urban Differences." In Ray D. Bollman, ed. *Rural and Small Town Canada*. Toronto: Thompson Educational Publishing.

Pahl, Ray E. 1968. "The Rural-Urban Continuum." In R.E. Pahl, ed. *Readings in Urban Sociology*. London: Pergamon Press.

- 1969. *Whose City? and Further Essays on Urban Society*. Middlesex: Penguin.

Palmer, Richard. 1969. *Hermeneutics*. Evanston, IL: Northwestern University Press.

Redfield, Robert. 1947. "The Folk Society." *American Journal of Sociology* 52:293–308.

Reinharz, S. 1983. "Experiential Analysis: A Contribution to Feminist Research." In G. Bowles and R.D. Kelin, eds. *Theories of Women's Studies*. London: Routledge and Kegan Paul.

Rossi, Alice. 1968. "Transition to Parenthood." *Journal of Marriage and the Family* 30:26–39.

Schutz, Alfred. 1962 (1972 edition). *The Problem of Social Reality*. Collected papers 1. The Hague: Martins Nijhoff.

- 1967. *The Phenomenology of the Social World*. Trans. by G. Walsh and F. Lehnert. Evanston, IL: Northwestern University Press.

- 1977. "Concept and Theory Formation in the Social Sciences." In F. Dallmayer and J. McCarthy, eds. *Understanding and Social Inquiry*. Notre Dame: Notre Dame Press 225–39.

Schwartzman, Michael. 1990. *The Anxious Parent: Freeing Yourself from the Fears and Stresses of Parenting*. New York: Simon & Schuster.

Scott, Joan W. 1990. "Deconstructing Equality-Versus-Difference: Or, the Uses of Poststructuralist Theory for Feminism." In M. Hirsch & E.F. Keller, eds. *Conflicts in Feminism*. New York: Routledge.

Sennett, Richard, ed. 1969. *Classic Essays on the Culture of Cities*. New York: Appleton-Century-Crofts.

Sharrock, Wes and Bob Anderson. 1986. *The Ethnomethodologists*. New York: Tavistock.

Shorter, Edward. 1975. *The Making of the Modern Family*. New York: Basic Books.

Sim, R. Alex. 1988. *Land and Community: Crisis in Canada's Countryside*. Guelph: University of Guelph.

Simmel, Georg. 1971. "The Problem of Sociology." In *Georg Simmel: On Individuality and Social Forms*. Chicago: University of Chicago Press.

– 1971. "The Metropolis and Mental Life." In *Georg Simmel: On Individuality and Social Forms*. Chicago: University of Chicago Press.

Skolnick, Arlene S. 1987. *The Intimate Environment: Exploring Marriage and the Family*. 4th ed. Toronto: Little, Brown.

Smith, Dorothy. 1987. *The Everyday World As Problematic: A Feminist Sociology*. Boston: Northeastern University Press.

Stanley, Liz, ed. 1990. *Feminist Praxis: Research, Theory and Epistemology in Feminist Sociology*. London: Routledge.

Stein, Maurice. 1967. "The Eclipse of Community." In B. Rosenberg, ed. *Analysis of Contemporary Society*: vol. 2. New York: Thomas Crowell. 96–154.

Sussman, Marion. 1959. "The Isolated Nuclear Family 1959: Fact or Fiction?" *Social Problems* 6:333–40.

Taylor, Charles. 1977. "Interpretation and the Sciences of Man." In F. Dallmayr and T. McCarthy, eds. *Understanding and Social Inquiry*. Notre Dame: Notre Dame Press 101–31.

Tonnies, Ferdinand. 1960. *Tonnies: Community and Society (Gemeinschaft und Gesellschaft)*. East Lansing: Michigan State University Press.

– 1980. "Gemeinschaft und Gesellschaft" in Coser, Lewis A., ed. *The Pleasures of Sociology*. Scarborough: New American Library 169–71.

Tovey, Hillary. 1992. "Rural Sociology in Ireland." *Irish Journal of Sociology* 2:96–121.

Tucker, Robert C., ed. 1978. *The Marx-Engels Reader*, 2nd ed. New York: Norton.

Turner, Roy, ed. 1974. *Ethnomethodology*. Middlesex: Penguin.

Turner, Roy. 1989. "The Politics of the Field." In J. Gubrium and D. Silverman, eds. *The Politics of Field Research: Sociology beyond Enlightenment*. London: Sage.

Van Manen, Max. 1990. *Researching Lived Experience: Human Science for an Action-Sensitive Pedagogy*. London, ON: Althouse Press.

Wallace, Ruth A. and Alison Wolf. 1991. *Contemporary Sociological Theory: Continuing the Classical Tradition*. Englewood Cliffs, NJ: Prentice Hall.

Weber, Max. 1946. "Capitalism and Rural Society in Germany." In Gerth and Mills, eds. *Max Weber: Essays in Sociology*. New York: Oxford University Press.

– 1946. "Science As a Vocation." In Gerth and Mills, eds. *Max Weber: Essays in Sociology.* New York: Oxford University Press.

– 1947. *The Theory of Social and Economic Organization.* Trans. A.M. Henderson and Talcott Parsons. New York: Free Press.

– 1958. *The City.* Trans. and ed. by Don Martindale and Gertrude Neuwirth. New York: Collier.

– 1958. *The Protestant Ethic and the Spirit of Capitalism.* New York: Charles Scribner's.

Westhues, Kenneth. 1982. *First Sociology.* New York: McGraw-Hill.

White, Burton. 1975. *The First Three Years of Life.* New York: Avon.

Williams, Raymond. 1973. *The Country and the City.* Oxford: Oxford University Press.

Winch, Peter. 1977. "The Idea of a Social Science." In F. Dallmayr and T. McCarthy, eds. *Understanding and Social Inquiry.* London: University of Notre Dame Press. 142–58.

– 1977. "Understanding a Primitive Society." In F. Dallmayr and T. McCarthy, eds. *Understanding and Social Inquiry.* Notre Dame: University of Notre Dame Press 159–88.

Wirth, Louis. 1938. "Urbanism as a Way of Life." *American Journal of Sociology* 44, no. 1:1–24.

– 1969. "Rural-Urban Differences." In Sennett, ed. *Classic Essays on the Culture of Cities* 165–9.

John Yerxa Research Inc. 1992 (March). *Images and Issues 1992: Assessing the Quality of Life in Urban and Rural Communities.* Edmonton.

Young, M. and P. Wilmott. 1963. *Family and Kinship in East London.* London: Routledge and Kegan Paul.

Zimmerman, Don. H. and Melvin Pollner. 1971. "The Everyday World As a Phenomenon." In Jack Douglas, ed. *Understanding Everyday Life: Toward the Reconstruction of Sociological Knowledge.* London: Routledge & Kegan Paul.

Index

analysis/analytic theory. *See* dialectical analysis

aporia 89

Arendt, Hannah: between past and future 159; courage 194; destructiveness of consumerism 173; freedom 212n2; mass society 217n6; *polis* 185, 186, 190; responsibility 198, 199, 200; web of relations 133, 193; world of alienation 90–1

Aries, Phillippe 122

Aristotle 178; city size 185, 186; ethics 197

Bacon, F. 88

Baudrillard, Jean: consumer desire 165; postmodernism 224n1. *See also* consumerism; postmodernism

Baumann, Zygmunt: consumer freedom 173; modern enlightenment 167; modernity 225n12; postmodern ambivalence 165; postmodern society 169, 176, 177. *See also* consumerism; postmodernism

Berger: art of mistrust 83, 84; ecstasy 169

Berger *et al.* 79; ethical analysis of 155, 169–73; homelessness 155; legitimation of consumerism 169–72; modern consciousness 60, 134; phenomenology 218n11; plurality of life-world 63–4, 75; social life-world 60–3; urbanization of consciousness 37, 63–4. *See also* consumerism; life-world; phenomenology; radical interpretive sociology *Bildung* (self cultivation) 89, 148, 185, 197. *See also* Gadamer; radical interpretive sociology

Blum 79, 149

Blum & McHugh 17, 49, 79; dialectical analysis 213n4; language 66; need for discourse 145–6; principle 148, 149; technological thinking 177. *See also* dialectical analysis; McHugh *et al.*

Blumer, Herbert 49, 79, 95. *See also* symbolic interactionism

Bonner, Kieran: modern parenting 102, 121, 137; parental anxiety 110;

parent-child principle 166; practical wisdom 128, 192; solipsism 54

Britain, urban-rural distinction in 53–4. *See also* Pahl

Camrose ix, 220n1. *See also* Prairie Edge

Canada: cities 50; new countryside 111–17; urbanization 212n1; Western 110. *See also* new countryside; Prairie Edge; Sim

capitalism: Marx 15–18; Tonnies 21; Weber 31–2

Chicago 40, 214n1

Chicago School of Sociology 39–48, 50

Clark, S.D. 50, 157, 224n5

Clifford, James 13–14; critique of social science 143; engaging otherness 47; ethnography 47, 119; modernist discourse 25, 47. *See also* modernism; postmodernism

community: extended family 22, 42, 150, 156–9, 162. *See also* gemeinschaft; rural

conceptualizing rurality 8, 10; dichotomy 48; life-world analysis

industrial revolution 13,
211–12n1
Ireland 4, 115
irony 46, 48

Jameson, Frederic 140,
153, 154; the suburb,
174

knowledge by discovery
71–6 passim, 83–98
passim; basic premise
77; epistemological
limits 79–81; epistemol-
ogy 71, 74, 77, 83–85;
as interpretation 81. *See
also* knowledge cre-
ation; modern mistrust;
radical interpretive
sociology
knowledge creation 8, 71–
6; dialectic 94–8; good-
will 97–8; hopes and
fears 88–90; radical
interpretive perspective
148; scientific mistrust
83–93 passim; testing
for truth 78. *See also*
knowledge by discov-
ery; oriented research;
radical interpretive
sociology

Lasch, Christopher 216n5
Lentin, Ronit 143, 216n2
Levine, Saul 86
Liebersohn, Harry:
Simmel 27–8; Tonnies
20, 23–4, 213n7; Weber
34
life-world: Husserl 58, 61;
parental 64–5, 66, 75,
102, 136–9; plurality of
63–6, 72, 75; pre-given
experience 58; reality
definition 61–2; of sci-
ence 91–4, 95; social 60–
3. *See also* Berger *et al.*;
phenomenology; radical
interpretive sociology
Littlejohn, Stephen 71, 72,
81

lived experience 99. *See
also* life-world;
phenomenology
Long, Charles 112; end of
rural isolation 153;
place as unnecessary
164; rural neighbour-
hood 129; small town
behaviour 181–2, 193;
world mobility 154. *See
also* consumerism

McGahan, Peter 50
McHugh, Peter 79, 80,
establishing truth 80
McHugh *et al.* 83. *See also*
Blum & McHugh; dia-
lectical analysis
Marx, Karl: capitalism 15;
critique of positivism
16–17; dialectic 19,
213n6; false conscious-
ness 18; feudalism 15–
18; rural idiocy 5, 15,
18; slothful indolence
212n3; *Theses on Feur-
bach* 19
mass communication 52
Mead, George H. 95,
226n5
methodology: survey 16–
17. *See also* knowledge
by discovery; oriented
research; radical inter-
pretive sociology;
science
Meyrowitz, Joshua 52
Michalko, Rodney 72,
211n1
modern consciousness 14,
25, 134, 199; analysis of
139–40; engaging other
13–15, 18–19, 24–6, 34–
6, 57; organization of
knowledge 60–6
passim; questioning
limits 14, 18; Redfield
46–7; Simmel 27; trans-
formation 46, 59–65
passim, 199. *See also*
Berger *et al.*; life-world;
phenomenology;

radical interpretive
sociology
modern family 51,
218n14. *See also*
modern parenting;
parental life-world
modern parenting:
burden 137–8; responsi-
bility 120–3; standards
124. *See also* commu-
nity; family; parental
life-world; rural
modern mistrust 74, 83, 84,
87. *See also* knowledge
by discovery; science
modernism 13. *See also*
modern consciousness
modernity: dark side 21;
self destruction 34–6.
See also modern con-
sciousness; subjectism

new countryside 111–14,
117, 176, 177, 194,
222n8, 223n9, 225n7
Nietzsche 20, 83
North America 31–2, 37–
8. *See also* Chicago; Chicago School; modern
consciousness

oriented research 14, 36,
39, 58, 66, 140–1, 148–9,
176–8, 197–200. *See also*
conceptualizing rural-
ity; radical interpretive
sociology
other: disappearance of
35, 44, 47–8, 55–8; to
modernity 34–6, 38, 44–
8, 173; as obstacle 18;
rural as 13–15, 38. *See
also gemeinschaft*;
modern consciousness

Pahl, Ray 5; city as
choice 53–4, 126, 154;
urban-rural continuum
110, 125–7; urban-rural
difference 49, 53–4
paideia 148–50, 185, 197.
See also Bildung